RACISM ON THE VIC

While there are many studies of nineteenth-century race theories and scientific racism, the attitudes and stereotypes expressed in popular culture have rarely been examined, and then only for the latter half of the century. Theatre then was mass entertainment and these forgotten plays, hastily written, surviving only as handwritten manuscripts or cheap pamphlets, are a rich seam for the cultural historian. Mining them to discover how 'race' was viewed and how the stereotype of the black developed and degraded sheds a fascinating light on the development of racism in English culture. In the process, this book helps to explain how a certain flexibility in attitudes towards skin colour, observable at the end of the eighteenth century, changed into the hardened jingoism of the late nineteenth. Concentrating on the period 1830 to 1860, its detailed excavation of some seventy plays makes it invaluable to the theatre historian and black studies scholar.

HAZEL WATERS is co-editor of the journal *Race & Class*, and has had many articles published in the area of racism and theatre. This is her first book.

RACISM ON THE VICTORIAN STAGE

Representation of Slavery and the Black Character

HAZEL WATERS

CAMBRIDGE
UNIVERSITY PRESS

CAMBRIDGE UNIVERSITY PRESS
Cambridge, New York, Melbourne, Madrid, Cape Town, Singapore, São Paulo, Delhi

Cambridge University Press
The Edinburgh Building, Cambridge CB2 8RU, UK

Published in the United States of America by Cambridge University Press, New York

www.cambridge.org
Information on this title: www.cambridge.org/9780521107556

First published 2007
This digitally printed version 2009

A catalogue record for this publication is available from the British Library

ISBN 978-0-521-86262-2 hardback
ISBN 978-0-521-110755-6 paperback

Contents

Illustrations

Acknowledgements

This book has been a long time in the making, and the thanks I owe to friends, colleagues, scholars and fellow students are many and various. What I owe to my truest friend and comrade, A. Sivanandan, Director of the Institute of Race Relations, is incalculable, not only for his inspiration and encouragement over many years but also for his tireless generosity of spirit. It has been both privilege and fulfilment to work at the IRR as Siva's colleague and co-editor of *Race & Class* for almost four decades; writing this book would not have been possible without him. My friends and colleagues – really dearest family – at the IRR – Jenny Bourne, Liz Fekete, Harmit Athwal and Arun Kundnani – have all helped and supported me more than I can say, with ideas, criticisms and suggestions, and readings and rereadings of parts of the manuscript, as well as with taking on extra work themselves in order to free my time. Thank you.

And I owe a debt of gratitude to Michael Slater, Emeritus Professor and Fellow of Birkbeck College, who first got me hooked on Victorian theatre, and guided and directed my research with the most skilful of hands. This book has been greatly enriched by his enthusiasm and encyclopaedic knowledge. Professor Nicola Bown, also of Birkbeck, gave me invaluable advice and comments, for which I heartily thank her. And I must also mention my fellow students from the Victorian studies MA course at Birkbeck, who developed the same passion for Victorian theatre – especially Anna Brown, Terri Natale, Sally Sanderson and Rachel Summerson.

To Jan Carew, Guyanese historian and writer, and Emeritus Professor of Northwestern University, I owe great thanks, not only for his encouragement but for generous gifts of material not available in Britain. As I do to Bernth Lindfors, Emeritus Professor of the University of Texas, Austin, who has given freely of his knowledge, expertise and most recent research, as well as documents not otherwise available to me. The bulk of my research has been carried out in the British Library and the University of London Library; to their staffs, always helpful despite the increasing pressure on their services, my sincere gratitude. Thanks, too, to Professor Cedric Robinson, University of California at Santa Barbara, whose work is truly exemplary; Professor Avery Gordon, UCSB; Professor Barbara Harlow, University of Texas, Austin; Professor Neil Lazarus, University of Warwick; Marika Sherwood; and my friend and former colleague, Tessa Hosking.

My husband, John Drinkwater, has not only helped in ways too numerous to mention, but has borne the brunt of my obsession with this research over many years, keeping it and me going. It could never have been completed otherwise. But, despite the fact that, in many ways, this book has been a collective enterprise, all its errors are mine alone.

Introduction

On 1 February 1749, two young African men, a prince and his companion, attended Covent Garden to see a performance of Thomas Southerne's *Oroonoko*, whose protagonist is an African prince tricked into slavery by a ship's captain. What is remarkable is that they had themselves been tricked and sold into slavery by a ship's captain while on their way to England for education. Such abductions were not unknown, but their plight had caused a furore; a ransom had been paid for them by the British government and they had been presented to the king himself. Their appearance at the theatre and the sensation this caused among the audience, who greeted them with a burst of applause, was a rare and instantaneous fusion of life and art. For the audience, it combined the theatrical experience of Southerne's highly popular play with the theatrical spectacle of the two real-life abductees, 'doubl[ing] the tears which were shed for *Oroonoko* and *Imoinda*'. For the young men, the pathos of this theatrical reflection of their own experience was almost too much – one had to leave before the play's end; one remained, weeping the whole time.[1] It is an episode which evokes all those ramifications (and occasional contradictions) of Britain's involvement with slavery and slavetrading on which its international commerce and prosperity was built; a trade which, at the time of the young men's capture, was reaching unprecedented proportions. The cultural context within which slavery was opposed or accepted, justified or reconciled (with varying degrees of success) with the prevailing ideas of the age, was one that was, at bottom, largely defined by what could be described as an early form of globalisation – if not in the totalising modern sense of the term, at least in the sense of the economic subordination of the Americas, the Caribbean and parts of Africa to European powers, particularly Britain.[2]

While this particular episode is a heightened instance of the relationships (and disjunctions) between art and reality, it nonetheless points to some of the ways in which the development of dramatic performance and theatrical fashion drew on and re-presented underlying material realities. Unlike other cultural forms, theatrical performance was accessible to lettered and unlettered alike; the stage was able both to reflect and inflect prevailing cultural assumptions in a continuous, semi-subterranean process of change and development. It was a process that, eventually, led to the enslaved African prince Oroonoko being pushed off the English stage by another, but far more degraded, figure: the American slave grotesque, Jim Crow. Just as economic history demonstrates the increasing complexity of Britain's dependence on the nexus of slavery, commerce and international trade in slave-produced commodities, so any exploration of its cultural history will also spread out beyond its own seas. And, in many ways, it will follow those trade winds that first carried it to America, Africa, the Caribbean. For even the history that produced and then discarded Oroonoko is only part of a larger, more complex history of the development of the black stereotype during the nineteenth century. It was a stereotype that crossed continents; it was the obverse of the international black-led struggle against the continuation of slavery in North America after it had largely been abolished elsewhere.

The underlying purpose of this book is to chart some of that process of development during a period of rapid and formative social change; to trace how racial assumptions in Britain evolved from a certain flexibility at the end of the eighteenth century to a greater rigidity, elaboration and entrenchment by the second half of the nineteenth. This, in turn, paved the way for the more highly developed racial consciousness of the classic period of imperialism. My primary concern is with the early Victorian period up until the late 1850s, but it is not possible to understand this without locating it in a much earlier historical context; for example, the thread of Southerne's *Oroonoko*, first staged in 1695, can be traced through almost the subsequent century and a half. Although much work has been done on investigating and analysing the development and propagation of scientific racism towards the end of the nineteenth century, much less has been done on how racial attitudes were more widely popularised, especially during its first half.[3] While in contemporary society pseudo-scientific, semi-racist ideas can filter down from intellectual or political elites to become, in simplified form, general currency through the agency of the tabloid press and the mass media, transmission of such ideas before the advent of universal education and mass literacy was more indirect and less pervasive.[4]

The theatre, however, was one venue open to large, cross-class sectors of the population. Jim Davis and Victor Emeljanow have analysed the mixed nature of the nineteenth-century theatregoing public, showing it as one of

1 The Victorian audience as seen by Phiz 'Pantomime night', *Illustrated London News* (8 January 1848), courtesy of Senate House Library, University of London

the most attractive features of the cultural life of the period.[5] Moreover, both the opportunism with which the theatre, always greedy for new matter, seized its raw materials and the haste with which it breathed them into dramatic life render the underlying attitudes and images conveyed that much more transparent; they are only scantily disguised. The theatre, then, provides an unparalleled archive, primarily through the agency of the Lord Chamberlain (in his capacity as dramatic licenser and censor), of the surviving materials of popular culture; an archive that runs unbroken throughout the period.[6] There is an overwhelming volume of source material, both printed and manuscript, only a selection of which (though I hope a substantial and representative one) is analysed here.

The popular theatre of the nineteenth century, whose remit embraced, however fancifully, the lives and concerns of the humble as well as the great, depended on stereotype. It depended on the instant recognisability of the scheming villain, the wicked landlord, the brave hero, the doughty heroine, the innocent child, the good old man, the loving aged mother. And black-skinned characters featured in it to an unexpected degree, from minor walk-on parts to major roles. But to what effect were the recognisability and dramatic impact of black-skinned characters put? How did the dramatic functions they fulfilled reinforce, extend or possibly challenge accepted 'common sense' racial assumptions? At the start of the period under discussion, the black character evoked fear or pathos. Often a figure of vengeance, he became less terrifying as the threat of rebellion that he posed receded, though as he did so, the figure of the mulatto female avenger briefly appeared in the mid-nineteenth century – and exposed another way in which racial theorising crossed the Atlantic. There was also a tradition of the comical black servant who, ultimately, became the progenitor of the most degraded black image. For it was the stereotypes spawned by 'nigger minstrel' comedy that came to dominate, even in vehicles – like the *Uncle Tom* plays – that might, at first sight, seem antithetical to them.

This book attempts to map out a terrain that has, hitherto, remained largely untrodden. Even less has it been explored to show not just this stereotypical feature or that, existing as it were discretely, but the connecting links between one stage and the next; the ongoing change and degradation of the image of the black character. Because it traces, as closely as possible, a process which happened over time, this study is largely chronological; but because it attempts to examine the history of an idea, as filtered through popular culture, it is also thematic and analytical.

My approach is primarily empirical, based on extensive readings of largely forgotten plays to discover how black-skinned characters (initially Africans, latterly African Caribbeans and African Americans) were represented; what kinds of functions they fulfilled in the drama; what their roles were; the type of language they used; the sort of language that was used of them; what was depicted of their relationships with other characters; in short, what the plays in which they figured might indicate about how blacks were perceived culturally. Because this material is so unknown today, I have used extensive quotations from it to illustrate my argument. And, where possible, I have also attempted to contextualise the readings of the plays with reference to contemporary reviews and comment, to gain, if only crudely and obliquely, some conception of how these images might have been received. As much of the dramatic material on which the research is based was performed at the minor theatres, comparatively little of it appears to have been extensively reviewed, but so pervasive, if largely overlooked, is the black presence on the English stage that every chapter contains leads to related areas that could fruitfully have been investigated, but which would have bulked this book out to even more inordinate length.

While the basic subject matter of *Racism on the Victorian Stage* is the theatrical discourse on race of the first half of the nineteenth century, it is based on an understanding of racism that sees this discourse as fashioned and altered by material social, economic and political circumstances. Racism is a phenomenon that, as A. Sivanandan has so forcefully shown, 'does not stay still; it changes shape, size, contours, purpose, function – with changes in the economy, the social structure, the system and . . . the challenges, the resistances to that system'.[7] This is as true for the nineteenth century, a period of fundamental social and political upheaval, as it is for today.

What became obvious was that slavery was the major material and structural influence on the ways that blacks were depicted. It was slavery, both its imposition and the decades-long struggle against it, that shaped the image of the black as presented for popular consumption. Slavery was an oft-repeated theme of nineteenth-century commentary and a frequent, almost constant, refrain in plays and entertainments of all descriptions. Such allusions could range from the almost reflexive yoking of Englishness, liberty and slavery in numerous nautical melodramas, to slavery's incorporation as a major dramatic theme. This is the case, for example, with the abolitionist dramas of the late eighteenth century, such subsequent works as George Colman's *The Africans* (1809), Thomas Morton's *The Slave*

(1816), Douglas Jerrold's *Descart, the French Buccaneer* (1828), or, later still, the *Uncle Tom* plays of the 1850s.

No amount of such cultural mediation, however, could alleviate the brutalities of the slave system for those who were its victims or fully expose its true nature to those in whose name it was carried on, though it may well have served both to keep the issue in the public consciousness and to pacify that consciousness. Slavery's destruction was a work of untiring persistence at a multitude of levels, from the ladies' committees for abolition to the impassioned, valiant resistance of the enslaved themselves. 'I would rather die upon yonder gallows than live in slavery'[8] were the last words of Samuel Sharpe, condemned to death in May 1832 for his central role in the major slave rebellion that erupted in Jamaica from 1831 to 1832. In London, one week later, a parliamentary select committee was appointed to 'consider . . . Measures . . . expedient to adopt for the purpose of effecting the extinction of slavery throughout the British Dominions'.[9] Slavery was no longer officially tenable.

Sharpe does not figure directly in my story here, but the actions that he, and thousands like him, took in their battles for freedom form an oblique and, even today, largely hidden context against which that story has to be set. Theirs was an experience of capture, enslavement and resistance that, initially, was sentimentalised and, ultimately, subjected to the grossest contempt. To understand the ways in which this was carried out, it is necessary to begin much earlier than the nineteenth-century heyday of popular theatre. For those representations of the black figure cannot be understood without some analysis of eighteenth-century drama. And it is not possible to look at that without casting backwards to two of the seminal texts of black dramatic representation, Shakespeare's *Othello* and Southerne's *Oroonoko*. They, in turn, demand a brief contextual resumé, which is where this book will begin, for the historical memory which is retained in this most evanescent and changeable of genres is phenomenally long.

CHAPTER I

From vengeance to sentiment

From Oroonoko to Gambia, from Zanga to Hassan, from Karfa to Couri, from Muley to Black Sam, through all the manifestations of Pompey and Quashee, the black figure on the early nineteenth-century English stage embodied the processes of a racism continually reinventing itself culturally. Theatre then was much like television now. Before mass education and mass literacy, and in a period of explosive urban and industrial growth, it was *the* popular medium, drawing its audiences from all but the very poorest, with many going night after night. Bills were long, lasting from around six until midnight or maybe later, and varied, changing every few days. The appetite for new material was insatiable, much of it cobbled together from a variety of elements. There were old favourites and pastiches of them, stuff pirated from rival theatres, versions of French plays, reports of British victories past and present, circus, spectacle and pantomime, dumbshow, performing elephants, lions, dogs ... And in all this melee, the black character (inevitably a white actor in heavy makeup) fawned or thundered, was, by turns, terrible, contemptible, grotesque. In this he expressed not just that well-known psychological projection, the 'Other', but an ingrained, dynamic relationship to the development of racism in the nineteenth century.

While the raw material for these representations came from the accretion of folkloric prejudices built up over centuries, the crucible in which the elements were initially combined was largely fashioned from much earlier literary sources. Traces of these continued to inhere in nineteenth-century dramatic entertainment long after their initial expression. The earliest dramatic representations of the black character tended to focus on the figure of the evil Moor, a stereotype reversed by *Othello* but largely validated by *Titus Andronicus*, though the *direct* influence of both these plays on the future development of the black image was, on the whole, slight. More important was Thomas Southerne's *Oroonoko* (1695) which continued to be performed, in bowdlerised versions, up to and including

7

the first quarter of the nineteenth century, and was also widely used as a source for subsequent representations.

Some of the earliest representations of the black – apart from blackfaced devils in the mystery plays – are to be found in late sixteenth- and seventeenth-century masques and Guild pageants featuring 'Moors', whether as happy, carefree slaves or brilliant, gaudy exotics. In their stage presence during this period, in plays such as George Peele's *The Battle of Alcazar* (1589), Thomas Dekker's *Lust's Dominion* (1600), William Rowley's *All's Lost by Lust* (1619) and Aphra Behn's *Abdelazer* (1677), they were given over almost wholly to monstrous evil and driven by overwhelming lust.[1] Lust was not only a mortal sin in itself but also a threat to the foundations of Christian civilised society. Outside the moral framework altogether, these black figures are linked explicitly to the devil, their black skins standing in for their evil natures. Of these purely evil creatures, the most complex is Aaron, in Shakespeare's *Titus Andronicus* (1594). But this character, too, was rendered even more one-dimensionally evil in Edward Ravenscroft's 1686 reworking of the play, which took away Aaron's love for his child and his reflections on the nature of blackness, to render him a greater monster. The evil Moor, in addition to his other sins against God, is almost always a murderer of the most shocking sort. Muly Mahamet (*The Battle of Alcazar*) commits parricide and fratricide; Eleazar (*Lust's Dominion*) commits regicide; to say that Aaron (*Titus Andronicus*) encompasses the murder of the emperor's brother Bassanius, two of Titus's sons and two of his paramour Tamora's, gives only a pale impression of his capacity for evil. (That the figure of Aaron was drastically reworked in the mid-nineteenth century by the black tragedian Ira Aldridge adds yet another layer of complexity to the multifarious ways in which the black character was developed.)

Othello should also be considered here, for he is both of his era and outside it, and his shadow stretches far over the coming centuries. '[O]f all the plays in English dramatic history, no other play until the twentieth century offered a black hero of Othello's stature'.[2] Certainly many of the elements of the stereotype are there, but configured in a way that is the antithesis of the stereotype. The grossness of lechery springs from Iago's lips, not from Othello's dignified avowals of love; a princely warrior, his service is to the state, not to its destruction; he is not the conventional Moorish villain but the villain's dupe. It is not until the very last that

Othello, outmanoeuvred by the machinations of Iago, falls into the dominant stereotype of the murderous black, tormented by sexual insecurity into the evil act of killing Desdemona. Barthelemy, in a highly persuasive discussion of the play, locates it in the theatre of its time to argue that despite 'his best efforts to the contrary, Othello cannot escape the role fated to Moors on the stage, and as he moves to free himself of the confines of the role, he moves inexorably closer to it . . . Iago wishes to ensnare Othello in the confines of the stereotype that Othello struggles so desperately to escape.'[3]

Elsewhere he comments that '[i]n spite of the remarkable endurance of *Othello*, its ability to influence positively the portrayal of Africans on the stage is . . . almost negligible',[4] a statement which this study bears out. Nonetheless, the towering stature of the play, the continued frequency of its performance throughout the seventeenth, eighteenth and nineteenth centuries, meant that it was a rich if generalised source of themes and ideas for later dramatic portrayals, a standard and, perhaps as frequently, a target.

But, Othello apart, the generality of those sixteenth- and seventeenth-century representations, with their emphatic portrayals of the villainous and terrifying Moor, can be seen as deriving from the ever present fear of Moorish rule over Europe. For the Moors were a power to be reckoned with, their empire stretching, at its height, from China to India, into the Middle East, across much of Africa and north 'from Portugal's Atlantic coast, through the Iberian peninsula, over the Pyrenees, into France's Rhone Valley and . . . along the Biscay coast'.[5]

Moorish sovereignty over Spain – which had brought art and science, learning and libraries, as well as Islam – was not brought to its end until 1492, with the fall of Granada and the mass expulsions that eventually followed. But, before that, the long and bloody struggle of Christendom against 'Mohammedanism' had already set a cultural context for the perception of 'Moors' (the definition of who counted as a Moor was extremely flexible). Not surprisingly, the stage Moor was the dark embodiment of every anti-Christian quality that could be imagined.

However, there is another significance to 1492 which also bears directly on this narrative. For it was the Columbian voyages from that year on that inaugurated Europe's involvement in postmedieval chattel slavery and led to the full-blown horrors of the Atlantic slave trade and industrial-scale slave production. Slave-grown sugar from the West Indies was first shipped to Spain in 1515; 'three years later . . . [came] the first cargo of captives from Africa to be shipped [directly] to the West Indies'.[6] By the eighteenth and nineteenth centuries, this trade had become so enormous and significant that the overriding factor which defined the context within which the black stage character operated was not his adherence to another god or gods but his (sometimes her) status, actual or potential, as a slave.

The disjunction between the earlier and later representations stems, in my view, not solely from the obvious differences in historical period, but from the different nature of the challenge which the black posed to white society. This was no longer derived from the threat of conquest but from the integration of slavery into the economic foundations of society and the reflection of cultural values that it threw up. Black-skinned slaves were the engine of the economic development of European slavetrading and slave-owning societies,[7] yet glaringly gave the lie to those societies' professed Christian belief systems and to the concept of a common humanity in which those beliefs were held to be rooted.

In Christ all men are free, and to Christ all men are to be brought. But slaves were commodities, bought and sold, their value to be extracted at the lowest cost and for the greatest profit. Yet were they not also – somewhere – made in God's image? The ongoing attempt to reconcile these two irreconcilables lies at the heart of much of the creation of racial stereotypes. One could, of course, do as the early Spanish conquistadors did to the American Indians – read out a proclamation in Spanish, calling on them to accept the true God and, when they did not, declare them heathens, *sub-homines*, whom it was the moral duty of their conquerors to enslave and set to work. (The moral duty of doing God's work and making His creation even more bounteous was, too, of great assistance in justifying the seizure and exploitation of the lands in which the *sub-homines* dwelt.) Or one could claim scriptural authority for the enslavement of dark-skinned peoples on the grounds that they were cursed as the descendants of Ham and doomed to be the servants of servants. And was not slavery – at least the enslavement of captives in war – justified by ancient authority, from Aristotle onwards? Another way of resolving the contradiction was to emphasise the rightness of submission to earthly authority. All human-kind are slaves to sin in the eyes of God; only his service is perfect freedom: it is the afterlife, not the earthly one, that matters. In any case, were Africans not better off as slaves under European direction than left in their original benighted state? Furthermore, the profitability of slave labour was its own justification – that it was of such utility proved its rationality. But, whatever the particular current of thought, always funda-mental to blacks' servile status was the perception of their innate inferi-ority, its patterning continually reworked according to contemporary notions.[8]

It is the continuing reinterpretation of slavery that shapes the image of the black presented in popular culture. Elements drawn from the characterisation of the fearsome Moor did indeed persist in the dramatic representation of the black figure up to the early years of the nineteenth century. The love of evil for its own sake, the 'hot blood' and concupiscence of the black male (and, on occasion, the sexual appetite of the black female character) can still be traced, but the figure that emerges bears, on the whole, little correspondence to those earlier terrifying sixteenth- and seventeenth-century caricatures. It is generally weaker and more contemptible. By the eighteenth and nineteenth centuries, the explanatory context for the black dramatic character is, overwhelmingly, slavery. White creations, they have, with only rare exceptions, little independent imaginative life. Their role is justificatory of black subordination, even when accusatory of slavery itself. In the pattern of their development, they refract, albeit obliquely, the socio-economic and colonial interests of a Britain that was emerging as a world power, as well as the debate around the humanity, or otherwise, of the black.

OROONOKO – THE SOURCE

From this perspective, one of the most important literary sources of black representation – more important as direct source material than *Othello* because it was more imitable and more overtly relevant to issues of slavery and colonialism – was Aphra Behn's novel *Oroonoko* (1688).[9] While *Othello* supplied motives of sexual jealousy and sexual relations between black and white, Behn supplied themes of African nobility and revolt. Both, in different ways, stressed revenge as a motif. Behn was also the author of a fairly typical 'evil Moor' drama, *Abdelazer* (1677), which owes something of a debt to *Titus Andronicus* via *Lust's Dominion*, and in which Abdelazer subverts the social order through his debauchery of the Spanish queen. He is ultimately destroyed through his lust for her.[10] But although this may have influenced Edward Young's later *The Revenge* (1721), it had nothing like the pervasive influence that *Oroonoko* was to have. The one looked back, the other was used to anticipate the themes that would preoccupy a later age. Whereas Abdelazer was the old stereotype, the product of a semi-feudal era in which Christendom was the dominant force, Oroonoko was the product of a new age, marked by an emergent capitalist world order whose driving force was slavery.

While Behn's *Oroonoko* was the source, it is the playwright Southerne's enormously influential dramatisation of it (also entitled *Oroonoko*), first

performed in Drury Lane in November 1695, that later dramatic developments have to be set against, since the themes identified by Southerne
were readily adapted, transformed, disfigured and reconfigured by later
writers.[11] His reshaping of *Oroonoko* remains the closest to the original,
but there are some significant derogations from the novel.

Southerne's plot revolves around the enslavement of a West African
prince of great dignity and nobility, Oroonoko, and his doomed love for
his wife Imoinda. Set, like Behn's novel, in Surinam,[12] the main action of
the tragedy (there is also a parallel comic plot which actually opens the
play) commences with the unloading of the new cargo of slaves, including
Oroonoko, and their distribution by lot. Oroonoko, who had been tricked
into captivity by the slavetrader Captain Driver, is to be the property of the
Lord Governor (who never appears in the play) and is taken on his behalf
by the 'liberal' slaveowner, Blanford. It is to Blanford that Oroonoko
recounts his story. As in Behn, he has been separated from his beloved
Imoinda by his father, the king, who desired her for himself and, on being
thwarted by Oroonoko, sent her into slavery. Imoinda, renamed Clemene,
is already in Surinam, also a slave of the Lord Governor under Blanford's
care, and desired as a mistress by the Lieutenant Governor, the acting head
of the colony.

Oroonoko, entrusted with a sword by Blanford, succeeds in foiling an
attack on the plantation by the indigenous Indians, in the course of which
he and Imoinda are reunited (the Indians were attempting to carry her off).
Allowed by Blanford to live together as man and wife, they are, for a time,
happy. Blanford has even allowed Oroonoko a servant, in the form of
his old friend and loyal henchman, Aboan, also a slave. Urged by Aboan
to lead a revolt, Oroonoko initially refuses but, on discovering that his
unborn child will also be condemned to slavery and that Imoinda is likely
to be taken for the new Governor's sexual use, consents. The revolt is
betrayed. All except Aboan, Oroonoko and Imoinda capitulate; they are
then tricked into yielding, but not before Oroonoko has killed the ship's
captain who sold him into slavery in the first place. Loaded with chains and
stretched out on the ground, in a manner reminiscent of the actuality of
slavery, Oroonoko is released by Blanford and another of the more liberal
planters, Stanmore, who both agree to bring Imoinda to him. Imoinda,
meanwhile, foils an attempted rape on her by the Lieutenant Governor,
steals his sword and escapes. Warned by the tortured and dying Aboan that
similar torture and brutality await him, Oroonoko resolves, with Imoinda,
their joint suicide. This is accomplished, but not before Oroonoko has
killed the author of his tragedy, the Lieutenant Governor.

In this, at least, his revenge is more successful than the utter waste and futility depicted by Behn. In the novel, having killed Imoinda as a prelude to killing the acting Governor and then killing himself, Oroonoko is so desolate with grief that he stays mourning by the corpse until its decomposing smell leads a search party to him. His end – dismemberment while still alive, the burning of parts of his body and the distribution of the rest among the plantations to serve as a warning to others – is both more resonant of the harshness of slavery and more completely dehumanising than any fate that Southerne's Oroonoko suffers. This is a significant softening of the implications of Behn's tale, as is the fact that, in the novel, Trefry (Southerne's Blanford) is the one who desires Imoinda, though he does not attempt to force her; in the play, no such association is made. Blanford's feelings, as well as his actions, are beyond reproach.

The play was an immediate success: Southerne was considered a master of pathos and sentiment, and the tenderness of the doomed love between Oroonoko and Imoinda was judged to appeal particularly to women – 'the Favourite of the Ladies' was one contemporary comment on the play.[13] D. E. Baker, in the 1782 edition of *Biographia Dramatica*, called it 'one of the best Tragedies in the English language' and the 'most finished, and the most pathetic of his plays'.[14] The 1812 edition of *Biographia Dramatica* summed it up for a later generation as continuing 'to give pleasure in the tragic parts of it to every sensible and feeling auditor; the love of Oroonoko and Imoinda being, perhaps, the tenderest and at the same time the most manly, noble, and unpolluted that we find in any of our dramatic pieces'.[15] It remained popular throughout the eighteenth century and was regularly performed at the two London patent theatres licensed to perform legitimate drama. When Drury Lane staged *Oroonoko*, Covent Garden would, apparently, respond with *Othello*, and vice versa. R. L. Root notes that *The London Stage* lists 315 performances up to the close of the eighteenth century.[16] *Oroonoko* continued to be staged well into the nineteenth, though in bowdlerised forms that, when subjected to fairly close textual analysis, reveal a degradation and coarsening in the way that the black character is presented. Thus it is possible to chart obliquely something of the ongoing changes in the way blacks were perceived.

What Southerne takes from Behn is the tragic nobility of the hero Oroonoko and his love for Imoinda. Tellingly, Southerne has changed Imoinda from Behn's exotically described African princess to a white woman, the daughter of a European at Oroonoko's father's court (a 'Mistake', according to one contemporary[17]). In this there is an echo of *Othello*, though not in the actual relations between Imoinda and Oroonoko, while Imoinda's willing and active suicide both recalls and contrasts with the death of Desdemona. The change from black to white adds to the dramatic tension. It renders Imoinda a more acceptable object of love in the eyes of a white audience than a black woman would have been, and brings the pathos of the lovers' plight closer to their sympathies. And it casts Oroonoko, a prince, in a more vulnerable position before her, as well as emphasising his exceptional status. Moreover, it would have added credibility to the Lieutenant Governor's initial reluctance to force her consent, despite his ardent passion for her. Black women were only very rarely seen as objects worthy of love on the English stage, and even more rarely beloved by black men. But, also, that Southerne can present white Imoinda and black Oroonoko as equally bound to each other and equally committed to dying together if they cannot live in freedom would indicate that, at this period, skin colour alone did not determine identity or status. It reflects a certain flexibility of attitude towards racial difference that subsequently ossified into hardened contempt. As Roxann Wheeler has shown of the eighteenth century, skin colour, in the sense of a rigid binary of black and white, was often less preeminent as an issue of difference than Christianity or 'civilisation'.[18] Both 'Christianity' and 'civilisation' resonate throughout *Oroonoko*.

It is worth remembering, too, that, in the early days of the trade, small numbers of Europeans were also sold into slavery or 'barbadoe'd'[19] so the pejorative associations of slavery, though largely linked with blacks, were not, initially, exclusive to them. But Southerne does not use Imoinda's colour to raise the question of the enslavement of whites, though this became a theme in later dramas. And, indeed, the casual passing reference in the play to the colony's white slaves would indicate that this was relatively unproblematic. What discussion there is of slavery's cruelty relates to Aboan; of its indignity and morally humiliating nature, to Oroonoko. Imoinda's status as a *white* slave is unremarked. It is her beauty and role as Oroonoko's wife that are insisted on; enslavement is essentially the context in which she, like Oroonoko, operates and has to make choices. As in Behn's novel, the distinction is clearly made between the natural nobility of Oroonoko and the generality of slaves. To Aboan he is 'A prince, born for the good of other men/Whose god-like office is to draw the sword/Against oppression and set free mankind'.[20] In the words of the 'liberal' slaveholder Blanford, 'Most of 'em [African slaves] know no better; they were born so and only change their masters. But a prince born only to command, betrayed and sold! My heart drops blood for him.'[21]

The desire for revenge, given great weight in Behn, is in Southerne also. However, the drama's complexity and emphasis on the depth and nobility of Oroonoko's love for Imoinda mean that it is less foregrounded than it later became when Young's *The Revenge* (see below) was added to the list of dramatic sources. In Behn's novel it is Oroonoko's desire to live with Imoinda in a freedom that is continually promised and continually denied that motivates his revenge. Freedom is the issue, and Imoinda's death the sacrifice to that revenge. At this point, one of the major themes linked inextricably to the black presence on the stage emerges. Obsessive revenge is the prime motivation for a whole galaxy of black characters, from the tragic to the grotesque. What also becomes clear as the figure of the noble slave mutates in the drama, from Southerne's *Oroonoko* onwards, is that the shocking savagery of the plantocracy as a group, its unvarnished betrayal of truth and justice, which are presented as a matter of fact in Behn's novel, are, with few exceptions, elided. Only a residue remains of what, in Behn, had been the indictment of a class – condemnation henceforward is directed only at the odd slavetrader or single bad slaveowner. The charges Behn makes against a Christian hypocrisy which allows Oroonoko to be lied to, tricked and betrayed still linger, sometimes quite powerfully so, but the portrait of the plantocracy as a 'degenerate race, who have no one humane virtue left, to distinguish 'em from the vilest creatures'[22] is rarely to be found, except at the height of abolitionist fervour. Thus Southerne's drama gives more scope for decisive action and more prominence to the liberal elements of the planter class (Blanford, Stanmore) than does Behn, whose Trefry (the Blanford character) is ultimately unable to protect Oroonoko in any meaningful way.

Written at a period of massive commercial growth, when 'King Sugar' had begun to generate undreamed-of profits and when English merchants had begun to take over the commanding heights of the slave trade from the Dutch, the play does not so much examine slavery as use it as a dramatic context for exploring more refined concerns of feeling and sensibility – questions of nobility and revenge, of pathos and doomed love, of honour and Christian value. According to R. Jordan and H. Love, at the time of its writing Southerne was seeking patronage from one of the wealthiest of plantation owners, Christopher Codrington.[23] The play is careful not to condemn outright the buying and selling of slaves *per se*; indeed, no less than the main protagonist himself justifies the legitimacy of this commerce, to the discomfort of more than one subsequent commentator:

> *Oroonoko*: If we are slaves, they did not make us slaves,
> But bought us in an honest way of trade
> As we have done before 'em, bought and sold
> Many a wretch and never thought it wrong.
> They paid our price for us and we are now
> Their property.[24]

It is left to Aboan to voice the most compelling plea against slavery, as he urges an Oroonoko unconscious of the slaves' 'heavy grievances' and 'weary drudgeries' to lead them in revolt against 'the bloody cruelties' executed 'on every slight offense'.[25]

When the revolt fails, it is not, as in Behn's original, both the Aboan figure (Tuscan) and Oroonoko who are bloodily tortured, but Aboan alone – distancing the violence of slavery from the central protagonist. Throughout the play the dignity, honour and honesty of Oroonoko, the loyalty of Aboan and the love and strength of Imoinda are contrasted with a range of other values, in particular the cynical treachery of the slavetrader, Captain Driver, the self-seeking lust and betrayal of the Lieutenant Governor and the mercenary cruelty of the slaveowners who, however, fill little more than a choric role in the play. Blanford alone gives some substance to Christian values: 'for his sake', declares Oroonoko, 'I'll think it possible/A Christian may yet be an honest man'.[26] It is worthy of note that Imoinda's father, who died for Oroonoko, intercepting a poisoned dart aimed at him, had 'changed his gods for ours'.[27] Oroonoko, superior in so many ways to his situation, turns a mirror on to 'civilised' Christian society's view of itself, and the reflection does not flatter.

> *Oroonoko*: I am unfortunate, but not ashamed
> Of being so. No, let the guilty blush,
> The white man that betrayed me. Honest black
> Disdains to change its colour.[28]

Yet enslavement need not necessarily be abusive. 'We are not monsters all,' says Blanford as Oroonoko experiences his first despair at his captivity, promising that he shall 'find nothing of [the] wretchedness', the '[h]ard fare and whips and chains' he apprehends.[29] The emphasis throughout is on the contrast between the mighty and impassioned love of Oroonoko for Imoinda and the toils within which he is caught.

Indeed, that context of enslavement can be seen both as a foil to Oroonoko's natural nobility and a stratagem that allows the evocation of extremes of pathos and sentiment. He has the dignity and bearing of the tragic hero, and the impassioned, succinct and moving blank verse of his diction gives him more dramatic potential and presence than almost all his successors. Ultimately, however, the scope for his character and its expression in action remain limited – for although this is not a play about slavery, slavery provides a context of such absolute control that no protagonist could overcome it. Oroonoko's conflict is not internal, as with the greatest figures of tragedy, eliciting our deepest human sympathies and involvement. It is not his own weakness that finally destroys him, but the sheer weight of external circumstances. Othello could not have existed as a slave.

Running in tandem with the tragic action is a comic plot, in which two sisters (one disguised as a man) have come to Surinam to look for husbands – the theme of buying, selling and tricking into a good bargain in marriage resonating with the buying, selling and trickery involved in slavetrading. But in the comic plot, the gloves are off and there is no glossing over of the hard, commercial nature of the enterprise, or of the necessity for it. Thus the comparisons implied between the sisters' situation and slavery are more hard-hitting than most discourse on it in the main plot. Take, for example, the comment by Welldon (Charlotte in disguise) on a woman's search for a husband. It is an ugly business transaction in which the woman is the commodity: 'They say there is a vast stock of beauty in the nation, but a great part of it lies in unprofitable hands; therefore, for the good of the public they would have a draft made once a quarter, send the decaying beauties for breeders into the country to make room for new faces to appear.'[30]

A breeder was the term for a female slave who was used solely to replenish slave stock and whose children were taken away from her as soon as they were old enough to be put to labour. The comic plot involves much sexual innuendo between a wealthy, slaveowning widow and Welldon, culminating in Welldon's organising a surrogate partner for the widow's bed. The bartering for marriage makes no concessions to sentiment, for Charlotte is deemed to have made a good marriage by taking on the wealthy widow's 'boobily son', even though he soon tires of her and begs for release.

Increasingly, the comic plot came to be seen as immoral and out of keeping with the noble and pathetic sentiment of the rest of the play, and the acting version of Southerne's drama was rewritten in 1759 by Dr Hawkesworth, 'of the sect of presbyterians' to remove it.[31] The removal, though regarded as a necessary cleansing of 'the Augean stable', was not entirely successful. In the judgement of the authors of the 1812 *Biographia*

Dramatica: 'there seems somewhat more wanting than such a mutilation, to render this play what one would wish it to be . . . the little further extent that [Dr. Hawkesworth] has given to the characters of Aboan and Hotman [the slave who betrays the rebellion] seems not sufficient to fill up the hiatus which [the] . . . omissions have occasioned.'[32]

The critic John Genest, writing of Hawkesworth's version (played at Drury Lane in December 1759 with Garrick in the lead) called it 'a very bad alteration of Southerne's play . . . [Hawkesworth] has omitted all the comic scenes except part of the first act – to supply the deficiency he has added some few insipid scenes of his own'.[33] Nonetheless, it was the bowdlerised form of Southerne's play that came down to later generations. What Southerne bequeathed to subsequent dramatists were the themes of black dignity, nobility and revenge; of captivity, freedom and slavery. These raw materials, combined in a variety of ways (with less and less emphasis on the positive elements of the image) formed the stuff of a range of later dramas, from the lofty to the scurrilous.

Despite the fact that slavery *per se* was not the subject of the play, later generations assumed it was. Hence, as views on slavery began to polarise and the movement to abolish the trade got under way in the 1780s, the play was increasingly criticised for not making an explicit condemnation of the institution. Hawkesworth's version, it is true, had already focused the play more directly on slavery, both by the omission of the comic plot and by amplifying, in the first scene, the dialogue of the slaveowners, about whose callousness and coarseness we are left in no doubt.[34] One who saw the drama as a potential enlister of recruits to the anti-slavery cause was John Ferriar. In the preface to his own rewrite, he explained, 'When the attempt to abolish the African slave trade commenced in *Manchester*, some active friends of the cause imagined, that by assembling a few of the principal topics, in a dramatic form, an impression might be made, on persons negligent of simple reasoning.'[35] (Manchester, despite the dependence of much of its industry on supplies of slave-grown cotton, emerged as a major centre of abolitionism; in December 1787, shortly before the publication of Ferriar's play, some 20 per cent of the city's adult male population signed the first petition demanding abolition.)[36] Ferriar went on:

Although the incidents appeared even to invite sentiments adverse to slavery, yet Southern [*sic*], not contented with refusing them, delivered by the medium of his Hero, a grovelling apology for slave-holders . . . and an illiberal contempt of the unhappy Negroes is so entwined with the fabric of the Piece, that it was impossible to separate it, without making large encroachments on the Author's design.[37]

It is hard not to agree with Ferriar when he pours scorn on the impracticability of the slaves' plan for revolt, on 'the absurdity, of this familiar talk, of *planting a colony*, under the eyes of a force superior in arms and discipline ... the leader of an insurrection, avowing that he trusts to *some accident* for the execution of his purposes'.[38] But the staging of an organised revolt was not Southerne's dramatic purpose: his emphasis was on the tragedy of Oroonoko's and Imoinda's love, with slavery as that love's overarching context and determining element. Whether Ferriar's version was ever performed or not, it reads rather like a tract. The first scene, for example, leads straight into a discussion between Blandford (*sic*) and the Lieutenant Governor on the wrongs of slavetrading. 'You know', declares Blandford, 'the waste of blood with which our annual recruits of these wretches are purchased. You know that by supporting the demand for them, you encourage the worst villainies that the heart of man can devise, and can you call this series of violence, treachery and murder by the exalted name of Commerce.' For the Lieutenant Governor, 'our sugar canes sweeten all these bitter recollections', though he goes on to regret paying 'fifty or sixty pounds' every time a ship comes in 'for a fellow who perhaps hangs or starves himself in the course of the first month'.[39] As well as being somewhat wooden, the play's attack on slavery may perhaps have been too committed. For example, in Liverpool, the leading slavetrade port in the country and the most assiduous in petitioning *against* abolition, *Oroonoko* and its variants were said to be prohibited as 'reflecting too much on the conduct of those Liverpool merchants engaged in the Slave Trade'.[40] But then, in the actor G. F. Cooke's memorable phrase, '*There is not a brick in your d – town, but what is cemented by the blood of a negro!*'[41]

Other direct rewrites of *Oroonoko* included one by Francis Gentleman, played in Edinburgh with some success in 1760, and one anonymous, never acted version, whose alterations were, according to J. W. Dodds, 'unbelievably bad'.[42] *Oroonoko*'s influence can also be seen in Thomas Bellamy's *The Benevolent Planters*, acted at the Theatre Royal Haymarket in 1789.[43] This most undramatic of dramas – it is really more like a pageant – is interesting only for the larding of sentiment with which it confuses the issue it purports to address. The prologue, 'spoken by Mr Kemble in the character of an African sailor', calls on 'mighty Kannoah', god of the 'sable race' to 'Prosper the great design – thy children free/From the oppressor's hand, and give them liberty' but, then again, under the mild rule of 'The Benevolent Planters', 'SLAVERY IS BUT A NAME'.[44] Genest found it 'a poor thing, but the moral to be inculcated is excellent'.[45] The benevolent planters of the title say things like 'may heaven increase the brothers of humanity'; their main concern is the wellbeing of their slaves, 'the jetty tribe', from whom, however, 'reasonable obedience is what we expect'.[46] The planters are organising an archery contest for their slaves. At this, one of the twelve male slaves, after competing, is to be allowed to choose his beloved from among the twelve female slaves and lead her to liberty. There is a noble male African slave, Oran, who has been converted to Christianity but is separated from his beloved Selima and in despair for her, while the beautiful Selima, also an African slave, is in equal despair at her separation from her beloved Oran. As the planters tell us virtually at the outset that they plan to reunite the two, even that morsel of dramatic potential is lost. And since one of each pair of the other contestants also seems to lead off his beloved (fortunately, no two choose the same partner), it comes across rather like one of those well-meant children's games where everybody wins and no one loses. John Philip Kemble, a noted Oroonoko and a powerful Zanga in *The Revenge*, played Oran, and Mrs Kemble, Selima. When the two are finally reunited, Oran gives expression to his refined sensibility: 'Lost in admiration, gratitude, and love, Oran has no words, but can only in silence own the hand of Heaven; while to his beating heart he clasps its restored treasure.[47]

Now liberated as, presumably, the overall victor, he begs to abase himself: 'O my masters! for such, though free, suffer me still to call you; let my restored partner and myself bend to such exalted worth.' The whole concluded with an appeal to 'Afric's sable sons' to rejoice in 'honour of this happy day', sung to the tune of 'Rule Britannia'.[48]

So impossibly pure and full of religiosity has the Oroonoko figure become that he has, in this instance at least, left notions of revenge far behind. But if, for some, the revenge motif did not fit easily into the image of the noble enslaved African, it had nevertheless continued to figure in dramas featuring black characters. Of these, one of the most notable and influential was Young's *The Revenge*.

Young's protagonist, Zanga, looked backwards to the stereotype of the evil Moor of the sixteenth and seventeenth centuries and also forwards as a potent source of imagery, however degraded from the original, for the plays of the late eighteenth and early nineteenth centuries.[49] If Oroonoko can be seen as the noble African whose values transcend those of his 'masters', for whom honour is paramount and for whom revenge is basically a reversal of injustice, then Zanga, a Moorish prince who invokes the 'holy prophet' to see him 'torture/This Christian dog',[50] is undoubtedly among the most inventively vicious of his kind. For him, honour demands revenge carried to its extreme. *The Revenge* was considered to have been derived in part from Behn's *Abdelazer* – but while the protagonists of both are towering figures, expressing overwhelming hatred and an excess of thwarted passion, Zanga is not motivated by lust as was Abdelazer.

'VENGEANCE IS STILL ALIVE . . .'

Zanga, majestic, demonic, implacable, is the impassioned, imaginative heart of Young's play. The love-lorn jealous posturing that he foments in his hated conqueror, master and 'friend', the Spanish prince Alonzo, is, by contrast, tedious and time-consuming, absurd even within the world of this highly stylised artificial drama. Despite Mrs Inchbald's judgement that the play was 'but seldom brought upon the stage',[51] the records appear to show that it was fairly frequently performed during the eighteenth and early nineteenth centuries. In Inchbald's view, all the interest of the play focused on Zanga, whose 'high-sounding vengeance . . . charms every heart' and in whose portrayal Young was deemed to rival Shakespeare. '[T]he actor who performs Zanga must be [the play's] sole support. – This character is of such magnitude, and so unprotected by those who surround him, that few performers will undertake to represent it . . . Mr Kemble stands foremost.'[52] It was 'equal, if not superior to anything in our language', according to Dr Johnson.[53]

In the case of Zanga, the theme of black revenge becomes all-consuming. Othello turned Iago, he has a direct and powerfully expressed motive for his hatred. Not only was he conquered and captured, he was turned by his conqueror into a personal body servant:

> *Zanga*: I then was young; he plac'd me near his person
> And thought me not dishonoured by his service.
> One day . . .
> For something, or for nothing, in his pride,
> He struck me – while I tell it do I live? –
> He smote me on the cheek. I did not stab him;
> For that were poor revenge. E'er since, his folly
> Has striven to bury it beneath a heap
> Of kindnesses, and thinks it is forgot.
> Insolent thought! and like a second blow![54]

There is an awareness here of the degradation not so much of conquest as of the enforced submissiveness derived from Zanga's circumscribed status, which, significantly, Alonzo completely fails to realise. It is, in its way, a telling exposition of the master-slave relationship, its insight striking the modern reader all the more forcefully, given the assumptions of the time

that 'slaves' would be 'grateful' for considerate treatment; that these inferior beings were transparent to their 'masters', their motivations as easily
read as those of children. Is not this part of what makes Bellamy's *The
Benevolent Planters* so unpalatable?

Alonzo, the 'conqueror of Afric', is finally utterly subdued by Zanga's
machinations. Zanga, whose revenge encompasses not only inducing
Alonzo to murder his greatest friend Don Carlos (after making Carlos
suffer agonies by relinquishing Leonora, the beloved of them both, to
Alonzo), aims also at inducing Alonzo to murder Leonora, out of jealousy.
Alonzo, brought to the fever pitch of suspicion against Leonora – who kills
herself rather than be so accused – then attempts his own death, Zanga thus
ingeniously killing three birds with one stone. Further torment awaits:

Alonzo: O Zanga!
Zanga: Do not tremble so; but speak.
Alonzo: I dare not.
Zanga: You will drown me with your tears.
Alonzo: Have I not cause?
Zanga: As yet you have no cause.
Alonzo: Dost thou too rave?
Zanga: Your anguish is to come;
         You much have been abus'd.
Alonzo: Abus'd! By whom?
Zanga: To know, were little comfort.
Alonzo: O, 'twere much!
Zanga: Indeed?
Alonzo: By Heaven: – O give him to my fury!
Zanga: Born for your use, I live but to oblige you: –
         Know, then, 'twas I.
Alonzo: Am I awake?
Zanga: For ever.[55]

It is hard here not to feel more thrilled by Zanga's terse, ironic mastery
than appalled by his villainy. His last-minute, brief remorse once Alonzo is
dead carries little conviction and the play returns to the utterly mundane
with the Spanish King Alvarez's concluding homily on the '[d]readful
effects of jealousy', his warning lest 'each man finds a Zanga in his
heart'.[56] It could also be argued that, to a modern reader, this exposes
Zanga as he truly is, the sinister racialised projection of a white psyche that
has been indelibly marked by its complicity in practising, and hence
justifying, chattel slavery. What prevents the warning that Zanga poses
about the dangers of slavery from coming too close to home, is the distancing
in time and space of the action, the absurd ease with which all fall into

Zanga's trap and, most importantly, the fact of Zanga's original status. Like his predecessor Oroonoko, like Oroonoko's descendant Gambia in Thomas Morton's *The Slave* (1816), Zanga is of royal blood; it is his lineage as much as his racial/cultural origin that impels him to revenge. Class, it would seem, can offset colour, rendering such a protagonist worthy of respect as well as fear.

But it was not only through the figures of Oroonoko and Zanga that the theatrical debate on slavery and blackness was conducted. The latter half of the eighteenth century, and in particular the last quarter, saw the production of a number of dramas which dealt with the issue in different, and not completely reductive, ways. It was a time of revolutionary ferment (most obviously in France and the American colonies), in ideas and in conceptions of liberty and the natural rights of man. Dr Johnson, for whom no man was 'by nature the property of another' once notoriously toasted 'the next insurrection of the Negroes in the West Indies'.[57] Tom Paine, who is said to have been the inspiration for the founding of the American Anti-Slavery Society, helped to draft the first abolition Act in Pennsylvania, 1780.[58] The American colonies had been lost after a bitter struggle – one side-effect of which was that numerous former slaves who had been promised freedom in return for fighting for the British made their way to England, often penniless and destitute, adding their numbers to a black population which, in London, numbered at the time some 5,000 to 7,000.[59] It was a period of increasing slave rebellions (British expeditionary forces were tied down for several years in the Caribbean), culminating in the establishment of the first black republic in Haiti at the dawn of the new century. There was intense debate in England over slavery, in particular the slave trade, even as that trade was growing to 'extraordinary dimensions'.[60] Ottobah Cugoano and Olaudah Equiano, former slaves both campaigning with the 'Sons of Africa' for slavery's end, published their narratives. Thomas Clarkson had begun to travel the country tirelessly in the cause of abolition; books and pamphlets rolled off the presses; mass petitions circulated up and down the land. And did the air of England automatically confer freedom on those with slave status? Lord Mansfield's judgement on the Somerset case (1772), instigated by that indefatigable friend of liberty, Granville Sharpe, was by no means unequivocal on the issue of the personal liberties of the 'slave' as opposed to his owner's property rights in him; nonetheless, it was understood as such both by the London blacks present in Westminster Hall that day and by the supporters of slavery.[61] The belief in England as the home of an inalienable liberty for all – in contrast to those upstart Republicans in America – quickly became established as definitive.

It furnished, or rather refurbished, a national image which was to resonate through the drama long after.

Among the plays which touched on slavery were Isaac Bickerstaffe's *The Padlock* (1768), Henry Bate's *The Blackamoor Wash'd White* (1776), George Colman's *Inkle and Yarico* (1787), William Macready's *The Irishman in London; or the Happy African* (1792), Matthew 'Monk' Lewis's *The Castle Spectre* (1797), Frederick Reynolds's *Laugh When You Can* (1798) and John Fawcett's 'serio-pantomime', *Obi* (1800). Both *The Castle Spectre* and *Obi* retain the focus on the figure of the avenging black. The remainder, classified as comedies, follow two different paths of development; one which can be traced, albeit circuitously, further into the future and one which more or less ends in the early years of the nineteenth century.

The Castle Spectre, with its powerful use of gothic spectacle – haunting music, castle dungeons, ghosts, secret passages – the appeal and range of its emotionalism, its use of shock and surprise and its sensationalist language was an immediate success with the public.[62] While Oroonoko reflected a belief in the dignity of man and the value of liberty and Zanga reflected the terrors of an unbridled excess of cruelty – the underside to the super-rationalism of Enlightenment values – Lewis, through the medium of the gothic, united the two. Osmond, the powerful and emotionally tortured villain of *The Castle Spectre*, has caught his niece Angela in his toils and is holding her captive. Unbeknown to her, Osmond already holds her father and her brother in his dungeons. He intends to coerce Angela into giving herself to him. Angela, brought up in secret by a farmer and his wife, is loved by the noble Percy, who has wooed and won her in the guise of an ordinary peasant. Four black slaves do Osmond's every bidding. Lewis himself makes the comparison between Hassan, the foremost of them, who 'has lost everything, even hope' and whose hatred is directed 'at large against mankind' and Young's Zanga 'whose hatred is confined to one object'. However, Lewis's subsequent comment that Zanga's revenge is 'no sooner accomplished than [repented]' overestimates the quality of Zanga's repentance and downplays the sheer power of his hatred.[63]

That most rational and discriminating of critics, Genest, was highly disparaging of the wild medley of the gothic: 'the great run which this piece had, is a striking proof that success is a very uncertain criterion of merit – the plot is rendered contemptible by the introduction of the Ghost … where a Friar was concerned, Lewis' mind was strangely warped. The introduction of the black slaves seems to be an anachronism.'[64] Lewis himself was insouciant: 'I by no means repent the introduction of my

Africans ... and could I have produced the same effect by making my heroine blue, blue I should have made her.'[65]

The point is that, in a highly charged fantasy world like that of *The Castle Spectre* with its emotional appeal to subconscious fears and beliefs, the blackness of the slaves, which has also been for centuries the blackness of the devil, is a dramatic heightening of Osmond's own villainy. Nor is this all, for Osmond's capacity for wickedness is amplified by that most implacable of motivations, the revenge of the subordinated who have no other way of achieving self-affirmation. Hassan's revenge on white society for his enslavement and the destruction in his world of all natural ties is to be achieved through aiding and abetting Osmond to do as much evil as possible. The impact of *The Castle Spectre* was evidenced not only in popular enthusiasm (its initial run was forty-seven nights, at a time when anything between two and six was the norm) but in the attacks made on it for 'extremely licentious' language and 'violently democratic' sentiments, charges against which Lewis defended himself when he issued the printed version of his play.[66] The censor also cut some of the speeches attacking slavery, though not this crucial declamation from Hassan:

Oh, Saib! my heart once was gentle, once was good! But sorrows have broken it . . . I have been dragged from my native land, from a wife who was every thing to me, to whom I was every thing! Twenty years have elapsed since these Christians tore me away; they trampled upon my heart, mocked my despair, and, when in frantic terms I raved of Samba, laughed, and wondered how a negro's soul could feel! . . . In that moment, when the last point of Africa faded from my view, when as I stood on the vessel's deck, I felt that all I loved was to me lost for ever, in that bitter moment did I banish humanity from my breast. I tore from my arm the bracelet of Samba's hair; I gave to the sea the precious token, and while the high waves swift bore it from me, vowed, aloud, endless hatred to mankind.[67]

Such a speech adds a powerful dramatic charge to Osmond's evildoing, which is thus intensified not only by its own resources of lust and cruelty but by the perversion of what was once truly noble – Hassan's love of wife and home. Yet Hassan is also viewed through the lens of racist belief as other than human, as the bestial black, and that association also amplifies Osmond's villainy. Osmond's lust for evil is both fearful and compelling; it repels and fascinates; it is not distanced from the emotions as would be the case with a more cerebral dramatic approach. Similarly, the evil that has been done to Hassan and the evil that he will do combine to render him a figure of terror. It is not hard to see the fear that Hassan evokes as similar in essence to that evoked by Zanga – a compensatory mechanism for the profound suppression of inclinations towards natural justice that was necessary if slavery were to be maintained. Driven, because of his race, from the family of man, Hassan and his like return as the stuff of nightmare. Echoes of this speech sounded, though with increasing faintness, through the drama long into the next century. That they became fainter is due to the ways in which the black figure was gradually divested of his fearsomeness.

Three-finger'd Jack, the central protagonist of *Obi*, a 'serio-pantomime' by the popular actor Fawcett, is, too, given over wholly to destructiveness.[68] The pantomime was based on Benjamin Moseley's *A Treatise on Sugar*,[69] with its account of a real slave escapee and rebel, Jack Mansong, who carried out raids in Jamaica for some two years before his capture.[70] Although there is no overt suggestion in the pantomime of his motivation, for all is in dumbshow apart from the songs, yet the unfolding of events implies his unrelenting hostility to white domination. In one sense, vengeance is here the white prerogative, the riposte to black revolt. Jack is a lawless terror, existing outside the beneficent world of the plantation, dwelling in a cave and heading a band of robbers who live in superstitious dread of him and his grotesque-looking mother, an Obeah woman. Obeah, a '"Creolised" Caribbean religion with indigenous African roots', involved incantations, ritual practices and the use of charms.[71] A retention of African beliefs and practices in the new and hostile environment of the slave plantation, it played a significant organisational and ideological role in slave revolts, in particular a major revolt in Jamaica in 1760, and was consequently feared and suspected by the planter class.[72] Jack's cave is hung with bones, rags, teeth, animal skins, and so on. It is not difficult to see in this an echo of the Maroon communities of Jamaica – escapees from the plantations who established their own independent communities; with whom the British authorities had been forced to sign a peace treaty in 1739; and who had gone to war against the British in 1795–6. In the play, in 1800 still close to the event, Jack's evil needs no further explanation – that he is outside colonial, plantation control is enough.

For the plantation slaves, however, life is sweet. They 'love massa, when he good':

> No lay stick on negro's back –
> We love much kouskous he gives for food,
> And save us from Three-finger'd Jack.[73]

Jack the rebel, with his continuation of African cultural practices and traditional religion, is their only fear; when they hear of him they tremble and run:

> Kolli, kolli, kolli, we swear all –
> We kill him when we come near him –
> But no swear loud, for when we bawl,
> Three-finger'd Jack he hear us.[74]

These may have been among the first stage slaves to celebrate their bondage so enthusiastically, but they were by no means the last. However, they receive their reward, for Jack is finally hunted down and killed by two of them, Quashee and Sam, in return for the promise of freedom. Jack has committed the unforgivable crime of kidnapping the owner's daughter, Rosa, after he has already shot, wounded and captured Rosa's husband-to-be. At the last, 'Quashee crosses his forehead, and tells him [Jack] he has been christened. Jack is daunted and lets his gun fall.'[75] Thus Christianity defeats black magic. The scene ends with Jack, already faint with loss of blood, about to be decapitated by Sam and Quashee as the curtain descends. All has been made secure – the Obeah woman and the band of robbers have been captured and rounded up. The message, of hierarchy and colonial control, of black inferiority and white tutelage (Christianity makes an almost-man of Quashee) is utterly transparent, reinforced by every detail of the on-stage disposition of characters and chorus, song and dance. All culminates in a 'grand march and procession'. Here is just a brief extract from more than a page of direction:

> Six Soldiers, in pairs
> Four Boys of Chorus, in pairs, with Triangles
> Four Men of Chorus, in pairs, with Streamers,
> The Ladies of Chorus, with green leaves.
> Four Men of Chorus, in pairs, with Illuminated Lanterns on Poles.
> Six Dancing Negresses, with Bells.
> Two Slaves, bearing Jack's Head and Hand.
> Two Slaves.
> Eight Boys, with Lanterns, *viz.* – Four on each side of the
> Two men bearing Head and Hand.
> The Planter.
> The Captain.   Rosa.[76]

In the overseer's concluding words:

> Here we see villainy brought by law to short duration
> And may all traitors fall by British proclamation.[77]

It should be noted that villainy as transgressive and threatening as Jack's demands not only death, but, in a throwback to Behn's *Oroonoko*, publicly displayed mutilation, publicly celebrated. *Obi* continued to be regularly revived in the first quarter of the nineteenth century and the role of Jack was played on a number of occasions by 'O' Smith. A popular actor, particularly in the large minor theatres such as the Surrey and the Coburg with their predominantly local and lower-class audiences,[78] he earned this sobriquet from his portrayal.[79] The power implied by an outlaw status that needed such extreme measures to control it must have been emphasised when played by an actor of Smith's commanding physique and 'deep sepulchral voice'.[80]

'ME WISH TO DE LORD ME WAS DEAD'

However, the vengeful or implacably hostile black was by no means the only black dramatic figure whose roots were put down in the eighteenth century. There was also the comic black servant. He and she were to descend ultimately into even greater stereotypical degradation than their revengeful counterparts, who were, at least, deemed worthy of inspiring fear.

If the lineage of the black avenger can be traced back to Oroonoko and Zanga, then the line of the comic, irrepressible and bolshy black servant or slave can be traced back to Mungo in Bickerstaffe's *The Padlock*, first performed at Drury Lane on 3 October 1768, with Charles Dibdin as Mungo.[81] Written by Bickerstaffe at the suggestion of John Moody, an actor who had lived in Barbados, it was a popular success and 'Mungo here, Mungo there, Mungo everywhere' became, for a time, a catchphrase.[82]

The plot, adapted from Cervantes, revolves around the desire of a wealthy and ageing planter, Don Diego, to marry a young, beautiful and poor woman, Leonora. She is to be kept in his house under the guardianship of a duenna for three months, to test her virtue and suitability for the marriage and, at the end of the period, to be returned unspotted to her parents or to be made the wife of Diego. Her only outings have been to early morning Mass, where she has been observed, and loved, by the young Leander – whose source of information on the young woman has been Mungo, Diego's black house-slave, with whom Leander has scraped an acquaintance. As might be expected, Don Diego has to go away, leaving Ursula the duenna and Mungo in charge – all to be padlocked in the house as a precaution against 'mischief': 'a woman's not having it in her power to deceive you is the best security for her fidelity'.[83] Diego's plans are foiled by a combination of Ursula, Mungo and Leander. Diego, returning unexpectedly, finally repents of his cruelty, for 'sixteen and sixty agree ill together', and unites Leonora and Leander.[84]

Mungo, who is instrumental in bringing the lovers together, is vocal about his the wrongs done to him as a slave and uncowed by his status:

Diego: There's a pistreen for you; now tell me, do you know of any ill going on in my house?
Mungo: Ah, Massa, a damn deal.
Diego: How! that I am a stranger to?
Mungo: No, Massa, you lick me every day with your rattan; I'm sure, Massa, that's enough mischief for a poor Neger man.[85]

Mungo's song follows:

> Dear heart what a terrible life am I led!
> A dog has a better, that's shelter'd and fed:
> Night and day 'tis de same,
> My pain is dere game:
> Me wish to de Lord me was dead.[86]

Subsequently, when Diego has returned to the house and is trying to discover the high jinks going on, the drunken Mungo damns his master to his face, to which the shocked Diego responds:

Diego: Monster, I'll make an example of you.
Mungo: What you call me names for, you old dog?
Diego: Does the villain dare to lift his hand against me?
Mungo: Will you fight?
Diego: He's mad.
Mungo: Dere's one in de house you little tink. Gad he do you business.
Diego: Go, lye down in your stye and sleep.
Mungo: Sleep! sleep you self; you drunk – ha! ha! ha! Look, a padlock: you put a padlock on a dore again, will you?[87]

The Padlock is refreshingly and boisterously disrespectful of authority – Bickerstaffe himself was something of an outsider, probably a homosexual, who was forced to flee the country after having been accused of soliciting a soldier for sex.[88] But although Wylie Sypher has called Bickerstaffe 'probably the first [dramatist] to bring upon the stage the realistic Negro who became a minor comic figure', this is probably something of an exaggeration, suggesting a more nuanced character than that actually portrayed.[89] Nonetheless, Mungo does display a vigour in the way he protests against his lot and the home truths he tells his master that is denied to his successors, who are more thinly drawn. Take Cubba, for example, in

Macready's slight but popular two-act farce, *The Irishman in London; or, the Happy African.*[90] This, as much an opportunity for Jack 'Irish' Johnston to shine as the garrulous servant Murtoch Delaney as anything else, revolves around a miserly father seeking to marry his daughter, Caroline, to an Irish gentleman (Colloony) with large estates. Naturally, she loves another, who is denied access to her and whose ingenious manservant manages to bring Caroline and her lover together. Caroline also has a female friend and companion, Louisa. All of the action and humour is carried forward by the servants – the 'Happy African' of the title is Cubba, Caroline's maidservant who, like others to come, is motivated only by love of her mistress and will follow her anywhere: 'Me leave my country and friend for sake of my Missa – Missa be everyting to poor Cubba.'[91]

Cubba knows her place in the order of things for, although 'Good black face be happier den bad white', she knows how unworthy she is to love Delaney.[92] This sudden passion is completely unprepared for in the action and presumably was inserted purely for the comedy inherent in these stock figures expressing notions of romance:

Murtoch: ... There, honey, my eyes are shut – go on ...
Cubba: Me love you a dearly – but me no want you love me – dat be very
            wrong – Your face white, me poor negro – me only tell you make me
            easy, den me pray for you be happy.
Murtoch: I knew it – I knew it – Black, brown, green, or yellow, I bother them
            all ... I wish she was not sooty.[93]

But while both these themes – love of the master and the comical nature of romance in relation to blacks – were to surface again and again in nineteenth-century plays, they are still not subjected here to the viciousness of expression that was to come. In the same way, the dialect in which both Mungo and Cubba speak, while a clear marker of their status and meant to be comical in its own right, is not as strained and forced as such servant/slave dialect would later become. There is, indeed, a very sharp distinction between those black characters who speak some kind of dialect and those who do not. The latter, those to be feared or respected in some way, reflect, in this, some trace of the values of universalism that shaped them. Thus, while they lack what soon became a form of speech that indicated their degraded status, they also fail to convey any sense of cultural difference. Universalism both gives and withholds.

An oblique comment on the black servant figure is Henry Bate's *The Blackamoor Wash'd White* (1776), though this is of more interest for what it prefigured than for its influence at the time.[94] It was met with a riot on performance (not apparently in reaction to the play itself, but in response to comments made in Bate's newspaper, the *Morning Post*).[95] The basic situation is bizarre in the extreme. An irascible old squire, Sir Oliver, highly mistrustful of both his wife and his daughter, decides to sack all his servants (whom he believes to be in league with the intrigues of the two women) and replace them with 'a suite of blacks'. The daughter's ardent lover, Frederick, then assumes a blackface disguise in order to gain employment with Sir Oliver, under the name of Amoroso. As Frederick/Amoroso is, like every other black character on the stage, a white actor in black makeup, he is indeed indistinguishable from every other black slave or servant we have seen. He, too, speaks in the same dialect, calling himself 'poor Blacky-man', using 'no' for 'not', 'me' for 'I', etc. However, as we are aware of the doubletake – we know that he is a white man playing a white man playing a black, and not just a white man playing a black – he is allowed a much more pointed sense of irony and wit than if he really were meant to be just a black servant. For example, caught by Sir Oliver playing and singing to his daughter, 'Amoroso' explains his song thus:

Frederick: Vy dere was in my Country, Massa, an Old Jealous Gyptian man ver cross and rich – he had ver fine cherry tree – fine fruit . . . White and Red dat he watch himself day and night and never sleep.
Sir Oliver: He was in the right of it . . . why I myself am afraid of thieves, every day of my life . . .
Frederick: So a young Teaf, watch old Cross, when he sleep one day in de shade – quite tire – and sun hot – and he go softly tip-a-toe – creep up a tree – pluck a fruit – sweet and good – O it make my lip water! . . .
Sir Oliver: And so robb'd him of all his cherries?
Frederick: All indeed Massa . . .
Sir Oliver: . . . let me see the young rascal that can catch me off my guard.
Frederick: No Massa – you long head – no Cheat a you – no! no![96]

As well as the extended joke being played on Sir Oliver, which is repeated in different ways throughout the play, it is worth noting how effective, through its rhythmical simplicity, the story of the cherry thief is: and, more importantly, that no black servant could actually play such a trick against his master or gain the upper hand to the extent that Frederick/Amoroso does. And he certainly would not be allowed to get away with the kind of sexual undertone to his dialogue that is present in the cherry thief story.

The only one who comes close to Frederick/Amoroso in ingenuity, though he is not presented as a comic figure in himself, and all his exploits are in the service of his master, is Sambo in Reynolds's 'indifferent comedy', *Laugh When You Can*.[97] Sambo, who is highly resourceful, manages to keep his master (Delville) from a liaison with a married woman (Mrs Mortimer); helps to save Mrs Mortimer's marriage when her husband finds out what is in the offing; averts a duel between Delville and Mortimer; and prevents Delville from being arrested for debt, through his knowledge of the correct wording of an arrest warrant. 'Trust him! Ay with my life!' is Mrs Mortimer's assessment – and that is before he has displayed any of the enterprise he goes on to show.[98] Sambo is the archetype of the noble black. Brought to England at the age of six and 'trained up 'midst all the follies and dissipation of London, though his head has been enlightened, his heart remains uncorrupted',[99] he is the moral arbiter of the play, as in this exchange with the maid Dorothy when she attempts to bribe him on behalf of her mistress, Miss Gloomly.

Dor: ... (*Showing a purse full of sovereigns.*) Here, take them; and now, Sambo – (*Forces it into his hand.*)

Sam: (*Throwing the purse down.*) S'life! does she think I'll betray my master?

Dor: Heyday! – Why not, sir? – When was your master so liberal? Did he ever make you a present of anything so valuable?

Sam: I don't know: he made me a present of myself; and, poor as you may think the gift, I'll not sell it for all the gold in the universe!

Dor: Not sell it! ... no, Mr Negro – let me remind you, that people of your complexion are often bought and sold.

Sam: And so are people of yours. Black men are not the only men that are bought and sold: everybody has their price, particularly chambermaids – they are always knocked down to the best bidder.[100]

Unlike the comic servants, Sambo does not speak in any form of dialect and is as eloquent, as the above extract shows, as any other character in the play. In this, unlikely as it sounds, he is more of the lineage of Oroonoko, or even Hassan, than of Mungo or Amoroso. His was not a line of development that was followed to any great extent and he is, in fact, a figure drawn straight from the literature of the abolitionist movement, which is discussed in more detail below.

SLAVERY AND SENTIMENT

There was also a third approach exemplified in the drama, which followed the line neither of the noble, sometimes vengeful, African nor of the comic servant, but partook of both and which, for want of a better term, I shall call the figure of sentiment.

The eighteenth-century abolitionist vision of the black slave was, as Adam Lively has shown in *Masks*, compounded of pity and sentiment and developed through a moral sensibility which was as much emotional as philosophical.[101] The radical breakthrough in the conceptualisation of humanity's place in the world that was the Enlightenment meshed with a new emphasis on the cultivation of feeling and sensibility; on fostering an empathetic and imaginative response to suffering, and on each individual's moral duty to alleviate it. In England this was indebted in its turn to the rapid growth of 'vital religion' and the burgeoning Evangelical movement. Notions of personal sin, personal responsibility and personal redemption – for God's 'amazing grace' was there for all – not only fuelled the movement to redress the evils of slavery, but also helped to shape some of the ways in which the slave was seen, as an innocent, suffering, sometimes noble, sometimes passive victim.[102] As David Brion Davis has argued, 'if there was a note of artificial sentimentality to the pining, agonizing slaves who became stock characters in the literature of the late eighteenth century, they gave a directness and emotional intensity to rational arguments that had long been ignored.'[103]

The Benevolent Planters is perhaps the play that lays on most thickly this refined sensibility to the plight of the black slave (even as it hedges its bets on slavery itself), and without any leavening of humour. But the most important play which tapped this vein, though in its vigour and liveliness it was by no means confined to it, was Colman's comic opera, *Inkle and Yarico*, first performed in London on 4 August 1787. An immediate success, it continued to be performed throughout the nineteenth century. Inchbald was quite clear about its import and neatly ties up the popularity of the drama with its inherent appeal to the foremost proponents of that moral sensibility which sought the abolition of slavery:

This is a drama, which might remove from Mr Wilberforce his aversion to theatrical exhibitions, and convince him, that the teaching of moral duty is not confined to particular spots of ground; for, in those places, of all others, the doctrine is most effectually inculcated, where exhortation is the most required – the resorts of the gay, the idle, and the dissipated . . . [*Inkle and Yarico*] was popular before the subject of the abolition of the slave trade was popular . . . It was the bright forerunner of alleviation to the hardships of slavery.[104]

Inkle and Yarico is much more fun than this might suggest. Colman took his story from a tale in one of the earlier accounts of the West Indies, Richard Ligon's *A True and Exact History of the Island of Barbadoes*, subsequently retold by Richard Steele in the *Spectator*. Like the Oroonoko story, this is one of the founding legends of anti-slavery.[105]

In the original Yarico is an enslaved Indian woman who falls in love at first sight with an English sailor when he and his mates are under attack from her (still free) countrymen and hides him in a cave until they can both escape by ship to Barbados – where he sells her. Sypher sees Steele's retelling of the story as 'directed against hard bargains ... Inkle is a youthful Gradgrind; the artless Indian maid eclipses the calculating European ... Steele creates ... the female to Mrs Behn's Oroonoko'.[106]

To the basic situation of the abandonment of the calculating Inkle (who has been brought up always to weigh and measure cost and benefit) in an American jungle inhabited, it would seem, by Africans as well as Indians,[107] and his rescue by the beautiful Princess Yarico, Colman has added a lively extra dimension through the provision of Inkle with an outspoken and comical manservant, Trudge, and an Indian 'chum-chum', Wowski, for him. Inkle is supposed to be on his way to Barbados to contract an arranged marriage with the Governor's daughter (who is already in love with a dashing young captain). No mere anti-slavery text, the opera dashes on with great fun, good humour and some wit. There is a suggestion of real tenderness when Inkle first spies Yarico asleep in her charming (and slightly gothic) cave:

Inkle: By heaven! A woman!
Trudge: ... Faith, it is a woman. Fast asleep too.
Inkle: And beautiful as an angel!
Trudge: And, egad, there seems to be a nice little plump bit in the corner! Only she's an angel of a rather darker sort.
Inkle: Hush! Keep back! She wakes![108]

Despite Trudge's apparently greater coarseness of approach (as befits a lower-class character, the lover he is provided with is both darker-skinned and much less naturally refined than Yarico), he is far more constant than Inkle in his recognition of the underlying equality between black and white, and the primacy of human values in relations between people. On arrival in Barbados, Inkle, despite his (temporarily genuine) protestations of undying faithfulness to Yarico, is soon overtaken by the commercial instincts ingrained in him over a lifetime. He seeks to sell her in order to free himself to marry the Governor's daughter. Trudge is genuinely shocked:

Inkle: ... When she has read this paper, seem to make light of it, tell her it is a thing of course, done purely for her good. I here inform her that I must part with her. D'ye understand your lesson?
Trudge: Pa – part with Ma – madame Ya – ric – o!

Inkle: Why does the blockhead stammer? I have my reasons ... And let me tell you, sir, if your rare bargain [Wowski] were gone too, 'twould be the better ...

Trudge: I'm sorry for it, sir; I have lived with you a long while. I've half a year's wages, too, due the 25th ulto. for scribbling your hair and dressing your parchments. But take my scribbling, take my frizzing, take my wages, and I and Wows will take ourselves off together. She saved my life, and rot me, sir, if anything but death shall part us.[109]

Trudge has already had to stand up for his 'black fair' on arrival in Barbados, both to the maid Patty (who is disgusted by 'hottypots' and at the thought that anyone could kiss a 'black-a-moor'[110]) and to a planter who has tried to buy her. Trudge expresses, indeed, an honest, unrefined but genuinely moral sensibility. It is he who makes the comparisons between Wowski's untutored, natural veracity and the Christian values of hypocrisy and greed. Given this, Lively's judgement of the play as making only 'one or two bland passing gestures to anti-slavery' and as the 'most striking instance' of a work 'designed – with, one may conjecture, varying degrees of cynicism – to appeal to or exploit a popular interest' is unfairly dismissive.[111] A modern production of *Inkle and Yarico* honestly played, with the original songs and music, showed beyond doubt that the anti-slavery message comes strongly over. There is real distaste for Inkle's plan to sell Yarico – and corresponding delight when, in this ultimately benevolent world, he experiences the rapid transformation (as rapid as his earlier love) that makes him renounce his commercial instincts.[112] And even in the study, the nuances of the following exchange between Trudge and the planter come across. Trudge has to struggle a little with himself before he can repudiate the scorn of the society he knows:

Plant: Hey-day, the booby's in love with her! Why, sure, friend, you wouldn't live here with a black?

Trudge: Plague on't, there it is! I shall be laughed out of my honesty, here ... I may feel a little queer, perhaps, at showing her face, but damme if I ever do anything to make me ashamed of showing my own.

Plant: Why, I tell you, her very complexion –

Trudge: Rot her complexion! I'll tell you what, Mr Fair Trader, if your head and heart were to change places, I've a notion you'd be as black in the face as an ink bottle.[113]

Sir Christopher, the Governor, sums up the morality that informs the play – the same morality that informed the anti-slavery movement: 'the feeling heart never knows greater pride than when it's employed in giving succour to the unfortunate'.[114] Yarico, 'a sweet unsophisticated she-savage',[115] with her beauty, her more refined diction and her loving tenderness and loyalty to Inkle, and Wowski, with her rough and tumble air, her simplicity and her comical/savage take on the white Christian world, may well be stock characters, though curiously mingled of 'Indian' and 'black'. But they owe, also, much more to humanity than many that came after them.

CHAPTER 2

The beginning of the end for the black avenger

Enjoyable and successful as *Inkle and Yarico* (1787) was, and despite its sustained popularity, it did not usher in a more nuanced approach to the image of the black character presented for popular consumption; rather, there was a deterioration, though this is not immediately apparent. As the nineteenth century opened, the same basic dramatic fare that had been available for the past fifty years and more still continued to be played, masking a process of change that can be seen only in retrospect. What gradually becomes clear is that the type of drama derived from abolitionist sentiment, such as George Colman's *The Africans* (1809), declines and the classic expression of black nobility in *Oroonoko* degrades, evidenced in the 1806 published version of the play (reprinted in 1834), its 1817 revival and Thomas Morton's 1816 reworking of it as *The Slave*. There is a corresponding decline in the forcefulness of the figure of the black avenger, evidenced in Douglas Jerrold's *Descart, the French Buccaneer* (1828) and C. P. Thompson's *Jack Robinson and his Monkey* (1829), coupled with an increasingly emphatic national self-congratulation over Britain's role in the abolition of the slave trade, as in Morton's *The Slave* and J. T. Haines's *My Poll and my Partner Joe* (1835).

The long and bitter years of war with Napoleonic France, only finally concluded by 1815, and carried out against a domestic background of burgeoning industrial and economic change, engendered an emphasis on the peculiarly *English* nature of liberty as the birthright of all classes of its people, to be sharply distinguished from foreign republican and Jacobin notions, that sounded throughout much of popular drama. That, in fact, the political pendulum had swung sharply to the side of repression at the end of the eighteenth century, does not seem to have dented this, though, in any case, the Lord Chamberlain, in the person of Examiner of Plays would, as far as his writ ran, have excised anything untoward. However, it may have added to the fervour with which English liberty was celebrated that the climate of repression began to ease from the first decades of the nineteenth century, cautiously, sporadically and intermittently. And liberty was always invoked whenever slavery was.

Most of the plays I have discussed so far were performed at the patent houses of Covent Garden and Drury Lane, permitted by royal authority to perform legitimate (basically spoken) drama under a monopoly system that went back to the reign of Charles II.[1] They were joined, in the summer, by the Haymarket. (Outside London, magistrates were empowered to license local theatres.) But the early years of the nineteenth century were marked by massive population growth, especially in the major cities, with, for example, London's 1 million people (1801) almost doubling by 1831, so that numbers of new so-called minor theatres sprang up. Cheap, accessible and popular, they evaded the monopoly stranglehold of the patent theatres by concentrating initially on pantomime, music and dumbshow or a hybrid form known as 'burletta', which incorporated some dialogue. These were mostly located in the expanding lower-class districts: the Surrey and the Coburg (later Victoria, today's Old Vic) south of the Thames, for example, and, subsequently, the Pavilion, the Grecian and, later, the Britannia in the east of London. While performances of *Oroonoko* (1695), *The Revenge* (1721), *The Castle Spectre* (1797), *Inkle and Yarico*, *Laugh When You Can* (1798) and *Obi* (1800) continued at the patent houses,[2] some plays, such as *Obi* and *The Castle Spectre*, less purely dependent on the spoken word alone, successfully escaped into the minors.

Frequently as all these were played, however, a change in the way the black figure was represented was beginning, slowly, to emerge. The abolitionist movement had helped to sharpen both pro- and anti-slavery views; the slave rebellions that culminated in the St Domingue revolution and led to the establishment of the black-led Haitian republic not only inspired Wordsworth's magnificent ode in praise of Toussaint L'Ouverture, but also fuelled the rise of systematic racial theorising aimed at justifying black slavery. As Robin Blackburn observes, 'The new racism drew on age-old prejudices, but was far more purposive and polemical than the ethnic conceits that abound in the literature of earlier times . . . It was held that blacks must be kept in bondage since they were childlike, lazy and dangerous. Racist doctrines were calculated to justify functioning slave systems.'[3]

This is not to say that popular drama simply transmitted, say, the historian Edward Long's sexual horror of black people or his belief that they were equivalent to apes, somewhere in the great chain of being between man and the lower creation; Lord Kames's argument that they were virtually a separate species; or Hume's conviction that, as such, they were 'naturally inferior to the whites'.[4] Yet echoes of these beliefs, particularly Long's febrile imaginings, began to sound with increasing frequency as the nineteenth century wore on.

But if, of all the dramas considered so far, *Obi*, with its transparent pro-slavery theme of hierarchy and control, was to be the harbinger of future themes and images, there was still, in the first decade or so of the century, mileage left in the anti-slavery 'message'.

THE LAST OF SENTIMENT

In 1807, after years of parliamentary attempts, the abolition of the slave trade was finally enacted (it had very nearly been passed in the 1790s, until the tide temporarily turned against it in the clampdown of the final years of the century). Colman, whose *Inkle and Yarico* had couched anti-slavery sentiments in comedy and romance, brought out his own drama, *The Africans; or, War, Love and Duty* at the Haymarket (of which he was manager) on 29 July 1809, no doubt partly in response.[5] It is somewhat unusual in that Colman, who is following a French original, *Selico*, itself part of the literature of French anti-slavery, has located his drama wholly within an African context – quite precisely in the 'town of Fatteconda ... situate between the rivers Senegal and Gambia'.[6] It is, moreover, a context which – in sharp contrast to the Indian/African crossover in *Inkle and Yarico* – distinguishes between the Foulahs, followers of Islam, and the warlike marauding Mandingoes, presumably animists (their king, Demba, swears 'by the serpent that's my deity').[7]

The story opens with the projected marriage of Selico, who lives with his mother and two brothers (Madiboo and Torribal), to Berissa, the daughter of the Islamic 'priest' Farulho. However, the subsequent wedding feast is interrupted by a threatened incursion from a Mandingo raiding party. Selico is persuaded that his duty lies in protecting his mother, to whom he returns after an emotional farewell to Berissa, who, with her father, retreats for safety to 'the house of prayer'.[8] Meanwhile, the Mandingo warriors enter 'yelling and brandishing fire-brands – they tear down the [wedding] tent ... when it is demolished, the town of Fatteconda is seen in flames'.[9] Selico, on his return to the town, finds it empty, in ruins, and with evidence of the savage murders of Farulho and Berissa. By this time, almost all Fatteconda's inhabitants have been seized to be sold into slavery, but Selico is reunited with his two brothers who, with their mother, are now almost starving. Devastated by the loss of Berissa, he plans to sell himself as a slave to provide for his mother. He is unsuccessful, however, for he is considered too light-skinned to be truly hardy – a reflection of the belief that the dark-skinned African is the closest to the brute and so most fitted for the brutish work of slavery. Indeed, in the West Indian colonies it was 'regarded as improper ... to work mulattoes in the fields'; their admixture of 'white' blood rendering them less fit for drudgery.[10] Although there is no suggestion that Selico is of mixed race, that he is light-skinned, as the actual Fulani in fact are, here dilutes the perception of his 'Africanness', making his nobility and thoughtfulness more credible to an audience. It is one measure of the distance that has been travelled since a black-skinned Oroonoko could be equated with such qualities.

Foiled at selling himself into slavery, Selico hatches an even more desperate scheme. The Mandingo King Demba's favourite female captive has been abducted, and Demba has offered a reward of 400 gold pieces for the abductor's capture. By assuming responsibility (falsely) for the abduction, Selico hopes to win the reward money for his brothers. However, the female captive, condemned with Selico to torture and execution, is revealed to be Berissa, recaptured – and the man who actually attempted to release her from Demba's hold, her father, the priest Farulho. So moved by the tale of Selico's sacrifice and Berissa's purity is the bloodthirsty Demba – 'some have said 'tis my nature/To be too lavish in decrees of death'[11] – that he not only pardons all concerned, but also makes a present to Selico and Berissa of two thousand crowns, thus demonstrating that '[a]ll Africans have hearts'.[12]

What is particularly noteworthy about the play is the elevation of its subject matter. All the African characters speak in blank verse; the Foulahs are given to lengthy passages of reflection on nature, love, familial ties, duty – especially to the parent – and sacrifice. The Mandingoes, of whom we see much less, stress war, pride and their own harsh justice. In all of this the play is cast very much in the mould of noble sentiment and sensibility, typical of much anti-slavery literature. There is also a third, largely comical and, in parts, highly unlikely white element in the mix – the good-hearted cockney Henry Augustus Mug and a group of English slavetraders. Mug, who had fallen foul of raiding parties on his journey through Africa, has been enslaved – for his own protection – by Farulho as part of his household. As soon as it is safe for him, Mug is to be released to travel home. In a reprise of the Trudge and Wowski relationship, he has fallen in love with Sutta (an echo of sooty?), also one of Farulho's black slaves. Captured by the Mandingoes in the same raid that destroys Fatteconda, he has been pressed into King Demba's service, by virtue of his quick wits and ability to read and write, as secretary-cum-adviser.

There is a quite deliberate moral hierarchy operating, with the Foulahs' adherence to Islam rendered indistinguishable from the highest Christian imperatives. But more than this, the Foulahs' lighter skins (they are the 'prettiest of the negroes' and 'lighter by ten shades' than their black neighbours[13]) are equated with higher levels of civilisation and moral values. Such values are evidently not totally incompatible with ownership of slaves, as long as that ownership is enlightened. The bloodthirsty, darker-skinned Mandingoes, in contrast to the Foulahs, live by warfare aimed at supplying their fellows as slaves to the more ruthless European traders. 'When Afric conquerors tread the field,/Slaves are the harvest battles yield.'[14] Even the Mandingoes, though, recognise certain human values and live by a code of honour, as witness the final liberation of Selico, Berissa and Farulho.

Class also obtrudes – Sutta, Mug's 'dingy Venus, of the dumpling sort', is the only character to speak in the usual black dialect.[15] But she is allowed, albeit briefly, to challenge the prevailing valorisation of white-skinned attractiveness over black-skinned ugliness:

Mug: ... But, ah, Sutta! Should you ever go with me to Snow-Hill, what pretty things I would turn for you!
Sutta: Wish you turn ugly thing for me, now.
Mug: How?
Sutta: Turn your face t'other way, massa Mug; – 'cause when you look me full, it make me jump.
Mug: Jump! What for?
Sutta: Skin like tooth – white all over.
Mug: ... So, you object to my complexion? (*Sutta nods*) And my features, too, perhaps.
Sutta: No; pity you not black – for your features look like negro man, very.[16]

It is as if, with these characters, Colman casts off the ponderous, aspirational nature of his main theme to play with ideas of equality between black and white. Is Mug, who looks 'like negro man very', being downgraded to the blacks' status, or is the 'negro man very' being raised to the level of Mug's lower-class whiteness?

But it is with the European merchants who come to purchase slaves that the most heartfelt – as opposed to high-flown – condemnation of the slave trade emerges. Fetterwell, 'long known as a merchant in the slave trade', is introducing his fellows to Mug, Demba's 'secretary at war'. In this lies a harsher echo of the critique of mercantile values expressed in *Inkle and Yarico*.

Fet: ... Here's Mr Flayall, bound to Barbadoes – Mr Grim, going to Jamaica – young Mr Marrowbone, once a carcass butcher in Clare-Market, but an estate dropping to him in the West India Islands, he now barters for blacks, instead of bargaining for bullocks, – Captain Abraham Adamant, who lost his left leg when the inhuman negroes chucked him down the hatchway, for only stowing fifteen in a hammock, in hot weather.[17]

The language here has a force and liveliness that it all too often lacks in the verse passages, as has the dialogue between Mug and the traders when he twits one of them with the thought of what would happen if he were put up for sale. Mug returns us firmly to mainstream, self-congratulatory, abolitionist sentiment, however, in the following exchange:

Fet: We must make short work of this [the sale], as this will be our last venture; for, when I left London, a bill was passing that will kick our business to the devil.

Mug: I am very glad to hear it. The work begins in the natural quarter, and the stream of freedom flows from the very fountain head of true natural liberty.[18]

The play appears – perhaps somewhat surprisingly, given the extent to which the action is padded out with long blank verse speeches ('this Jumble', John Genest termed it[19]) – to have become quite popular. It was played thirty-one times throughout the summer of 1808;[20] Genest records its being revived in 1819, 1822, 1823 and 1824, and it was reprinted in Cumberland's *British Theatre*. Much of its initial popularity was no doubt owing to the comic talents of John Liston, who represented Mug 'with all his broad-faced humour and grotesque gravity'[21] and the performance as Selico of Charles Young, who was deemed 'mainly instrumental to the final success of the piece'.[22] First responses were mixed. *The Times* found that the first two acts were well received, but 'what must be called the plot, being then clearly developed, the third act went off very heavily, and with considerable disapprobation'.[23] The *Literary Panorama* was utterly scathing:

We should not have believed Mr C. had been the author of it, considering the name he has already acquired; unless he had written it for a wager . . . We are truly concerned to witness such a degradation in literature; nor could the dull exhibition of the slave trade, or all the clap-traps about its abolition; nor the black and white jokes; nor the bandy-legged, bow-legged sarcasms of Mr. Madiboo [a brother of Selico], excite any other sentiments in our mind than disgust.[24]

But these 'clap-traps', whose point was emphasised by Mug as quoted above, were perhaps what kept it in the repertoire. They fitted in well with a growing spirit of national self-satisfaction over the issue of the slave trade that was later to surface in such diverse vehicles as *The Slave* and *My Poll and my Partner Joe*. D. G., in his preface to the Cumberland edition of *The Africans*, seems to have thought on these lines: 'This play was received with very great applause – and deservedly; for Mr. Colman again put his axe to the root of the Upas Tree of Slavery; which, to the honour of British humanity, is now grubbed up and laid prostrate for ever!'[25]

A SEA CHANGE

In many ways, *The Africans* marked the tail-end of the eighteenth-century portrayals of the black, with its unusually consistent emphasis on (light-skinned) black nobility, (dark- and light-skinned) honour, and Christian values (albeit under a thin disguise of Islam). However, as in the ever popular *Inkle and Yarico*, Colman eschewed the figure of the black avenger. But that figure still continued to tread the boards – of the plays discussed so far, *The Revenge* and *The Castle Spectre* appear to have been performed most frequently in the early years of the nineteenth century. *Oroonoko*, performed at Covent Garden in 1806, was apparently not seen again on the London stage until Edmund Kean's electrifying revival of it at Drury Lane in 1817, evocatively and revealingly reviewed by William Hazlitt, who considered it 'one of his best parts'.[26]

Hazlitt found the 'pathos' of Kean's performance intensely moving. In the 'first meeting between [Oroonoko] and Imoinda . . . the transition to tenderness and love . . . was even finer than the expression of breathless eagerness and surprise'.[27] His initial response expresses the fiercely exotic conception of the black that harks back to an earlier period, to the image of the African current in the eighteenth century: 'In a word, Mr. Kean gave to the part that glowing and impetuous, and at the same time deep and full expression, which belongs to the character of that burning zone, which ripens the souls of men, as well as the fruits of the earth.'[28] He goes on:

at the suggestion of the thought, that . . . Imoinda will become the mother, and himself, a prince and a hero, the father of a race of slaves, he starts and the manner in which he utters the ejaculation 'Hah!' at the world of thought which is thus shewn to him, like a precipice at his feet, resembles the first sound that breaks from a thunder-cloud, or the hollow roar of a wild beast, roused from its lair by hunger and the scent of blood. It is a pity that the catastrophe does not answer to the grandeur of the menace; and that this gallant vindicator of himself and his countrymen fails in his enterprise, through the treachery and cowardice of those whom he attempts to set free, but 'who were by nature slaves!' The story of this *servile war* is not without a parallel elsewhere . . . only changing *black* into *white* . . . The political allusions throughout, that is, the appeals to common justice and humanity, against the most intolerable cruelty and wrong, are so strong and palpable, that we wonder the piece is not prohibited.[29]

So far, so powerful. Yet, stirred as he is by the emotional and political impact of the play, Hazlitt goes on to express, nonetheless, a certain distaste for its actual matter. His tone changes abruptly when he moves from consideration of Oroonoko and Imoinda to the context of the slaves' revolt: 'The negroes in it (we could wish them out of it, but then there would be no play) are very *ugly customers* upon the stage. One blackamoor in a picture is an ornament, but a whole cargo of them is more than enough. This play puts us out of conceit with both colours, theirs and our own; the sooty slave's and his cold, sleek, smooth-faced master's.'[30]

Hazlitt, then, encapsulates in the space of this one review both the appeal to the tender-hearted sensibility that anti-slavery literature depended upon and the visceral disgust for the fact of blackness, except as an exotic adjunct.[31] What can account for this disjunction? As represented on stage, the slaves would have appeared in traditional stark black makeup, probably wearing black gloves and stockings – here, before the eyes, affronting the senses, are en masse those figures by now linked irredeemably with inferior and servile status. But I would speculate that Kean, as Oroonoko, would have used the 'tawny' makeup that he used for Othello. Thus he would not have represented the black-skinned African as graphically as his supporting cast; that, combined, of course, with his exceptional status as protagonist in the drama, would have sufficiently distinguished him from his fellows to elicit a markedly different response. That Hazlitt is so irked by a numerous black presence, given his praise of the play, is, I think, revealing. The use of the word 'cargo' by such a master of language to signify that presence cannot be accidental. It is also a demonstration that the understood artificiality and convention of a theatrical representation may nonetheless evoke in the spectator a direct correlation with present social realities. Both reflect on to, and inform, each other. Of course, audiences are sophisticated enough to realise that what they are witnessing is not a straightforward transliteration of experience, but an ideal shaping of it, expressed via the medium of dramatic stereotype; yet it would surely be wrong to suggest that such stereotypes do not influence the perception of social reality. Hazlitt's 'cargo' was perhaps ironical, but it is a significant irony that demonstrates how the concept of black humanity has been increasingly circumscribed, linked primarily to ideas of buying and selling property.

M⁺ KEAN as OTHELLO.

2 **Edmund Kean as Othello** courtesy of V&A Images/Theatre Museum

And to answer Hazlitt's question about why the play was not banned for its revolutionary implications, it did not need to be prohibited because it already accommodated such circumscription. The version of *Oroonoko* that Hazlitt saw was 'in all probability not Southerne's play, but Dr. Hawkesworth's version of it'.[32] This, as well as omitting the subplot, also instigated other changes which ultimately detracted, if not from the nobility of the hero, from his intelligence and from the humanity of his fellow slaves.

Some of these changes are revealed by a close comparison of Southerne's original with the later published versions. For example, Mrs Inchbald's edition of 1806 is all but identical to that published in *The Acting Drama* (1834), which purports to have been revised by John Philip Kemble himself. Both omit not only the subplot, but also a number of Oroonoko's speeches.[33] They place more emphasis on slavery and the revolt – but, at the same time, the slaves are shown to be more easily tricked and betrayed. Aboan, Oroonoko's loyal follower and the man who persuades him to lead a revolt, is, in Southerne's original, shown to be suspicious of the intemperate Hottman, the slave who, despite his wild speeches urging revolt, betrays Oroonoko to the authorities in exchange for his own freedom. Indeed, in Southerne, after Oroonoko has enticed Hottman into revealing the cowardice underlying his boasts, Aboan wants to kill him to prevent the possibility of betrayal – which Oroonoko will not allow: 'We'll not set out in blood.'[34] In the later versions Aboan's suspicion is transformed into a quick and eager acceptance of all Hottman's wild promises; Hottman is never sounded out by Oroonoko and so the slaves are rendered easy and stupid prey to their enemies.

Similarly, Oroonoko's explicit condemnations of Christianity as practised by its professors, already less frequent in Southerne's play than in Behn's original, are further watered down. Thus, in Southerne's original, Oroonoko's condemnation of his cowardly fellow slaves:

Oroonoko: To think I could design to make those free,
          Who were by nature slaves; wretches design'd
          To be their masters' dogs, and lick their feet.[35]

is balanced by his continuation:

          Whip, whip 'em to the knowledge of your gods,
          Your Christian gods, who suffer you to be
          Unjust, dishonest, cowardly, and base,
          And give 'em your excuse for being so.[36]

In the 1834 version this latter passage is omitted. Similarly, much of the interchange between Oroonoko and Imoinda in Act 5, scene 5, when they are resolving on their joint suicide, has been cut, making Imoinda more passive and Oroonoko less tender. The process of reducing the drama's complexity and the amount of agency and universal human quality allowed to Oroonoko is well under way.

THE GAMBIA TWIST

This reduction of the complexity allowed to the black figure can be evidenced in a number of ways. There is both the degradation of the avenging figure, whose most powerful avatar is Zanga, and the degradation (through bombast and absurdity) of black nobility, whose incarnation is Oroonoko. Both themes come together in Thomas Morton's popular rewriting of *Oroonoko*, entitled *The Slave, or the Mother and her Child* (also subtitled *The Revolt of Surinam* – a more accurate indication of its concerns, for mother and child play little part in the action, except as objects of desire).[37] Morton, only one of whose plays survives today in a modern edition, was a highly successful and popular dramatist, writing mostly for Covent Garden where, in 1828, he became reader of plays.[38] *The Slave* was first performed at Covent Garden in November 1816, with the young William Macready in the leading role of Gambia; doing 'it ample justice . . . his deep sonorous voice gave full effect to the animated sentiments and wild eloquence of the generous slave'.[39]

Described by Genest as 'the most successful play which came out in 1816–17',[40] a success which he deemed 'greater . . . than it deserved . . . the grand part of Gambia . . . is unnatural to the last degree',[41] the play continued to be performed well into the 1850s – and was again revived at the Grecian, in east London, as late as 1865.[42] A dreary subplot mimics Southerne's, though without its wit or purpose; two cousins attempt to wheedle an ugly old aunt (Miss Von Frump) out of her money by promises of marriage.

The play, set in a Surinam that is under British control, opens in the midst of a revolt[43] whose chief purpose appears to be for the slaves 'To burn, insult, and massacre even their own countrymen'.[44] Morton, having thus economically established the greater guilt of the victims of slavery, carries this theme through in the character of Gambia, a man of superhuman strength and fidelity, who, in his own words, 'Nature has kindly fitted . . . to [his] fate'.[45] Slavery is denounced, but in a way that takes any discomfort out of the denunciation:

Gov: No misery to endure?
Gam: Misery! Sir, I am a slave: – In that all human wretchedness is comprehended
. . .
Gov: Your story –
Gam: Is soon told. In Africa I was a slave.
Gov: A slave?
Gam: The vilest – the slave of fierce ambition; revell'd in luxuries purchased by blood; stimulated by Europe's baubles; hunted my fellow men – But the hunter was taken in the toils! just, full retribution, even to the uttermost pang, is now my doom; that freedom I denied to others, is now far from my hopes as hell from heaven . . . That innocent man I sold to slavery – he has pardon'd me. Can I forgive myself?[46]

Oroonoko's involvement in the slave trade, which serves to mark him out from his fellows as of royal lineage, here becomes a crime far greater than that of any of the colonial agents involved.

Gambia's motivation, like that of other black figures, is vengeance ('to his nation, revenge is virtue'[47]), though not for his enslavement. Here Morton has recast the Oroonoko/Imoinda theme, turning its intensity to absurdity. Gambia is desperately and hopelessly in love with the beautiful, light-skinned Zelinda, also a slave. She is, for him, 'the only sweet that's mingled in my cup of bitterness ... thou art my sun, I live but in thy light'.[48]

Gambia's animus is directed at Captain Clifton, Zelinda's white would-be husband and the father of her child. Clifton is anxious to obtain her freedom and marry her. Zelinda had once saved Clifton's life (how, we are not told), but perhaps this helps to account, at least partially, for the white officer's devotion to the female slave. Gambia also once saved the child from certain death. On learning that Zelinda remains devoted to Clifton, Gambia swears revenge, for 'Europe's cold sons may sink into nerveless apathy; but Afric's fiery children know no sleep of passion ... what remains to fill this bosom but revenge, precious, sweet revenge! Let your proud son of freedom tremble at the vengeance of a slave.'[49]

Trusted by the Governor to fight with the colonists against the resurgent slave rebellion, Gambia takes his revenge in an unusual way when the following encounter takes place. Clifton, who has just parted from Zelinda, is ambushed by 'rebel negroes'. Hearing Zelinda cry out, Gambia rushes in. Seeing his hated rival in the rebels' power, he exults, 'strike home – they bear him away – now I'm revenged!'

Zel: Oh! mercy! mercy!
Gam: That voice! ... It is that voice that never called in vain! Yes, proud Briton, thou shalt feel, and own my power! ...
Zel: Ah! Gambia rushes on him! – No, he battles on his side! – he preserves him!

Clifton is saved, and suitably grateful:

Clif: African! not for my life preserved, but in atonement for the wrongs I did your noble nature, behold me bend before thee.
Gam: Ah! my proud rival, have I brought you there? Why, this is noble vengeance.[50]

For this heroism, Gambia is rewarded, at Clifton's instigation, with his freedom: 'Liberty! give me the language of gods to tell that I am free! ... Generous Briton! prophetic be my tongue! when thro' thy country's zeal, the all-searching sun shall dart his rays in vain, to find a slave in Afric ... write but on my tomb, that Gambia died free!'[51]

Nor is this all. Clifton, who had earlier travelled to Europe to purchase Zelinda's freedom and been cheated of all his money at the gaming table by one Lindenburg, alias Chevalier Alkmar, is, through Lindenburg/Alkmar's machinations, thrown into a debtor's prison. (Lindenburg has turned up in the colony, having fled the scenes of his crimes in Europe.) To save Clifton, Gambia sells himself *back* into slavery to Lindenburg, who is also now Zelinda's master and has the usual evil designs on her. Not only does Gambia rescue Zelinda and her child after a desperate fight with Lindenburg; not only does he spare Lindenburg's life ('he was my foe, but he was prostrate',[52]), he is even instrumental in rehabilitating him. For, says Gambia, 'while struggling to remove the weapon that rankled in its wound, I saw, seared in your breast, the brand of – Thief'.[53]

Lind: ... Slave! I am in thy power – how wilt thou use it?
Gam: In saving, if I can, my master's life. By inflicting that wound, I preserved the innocent – by healing it, I may save the guilty ...

[The scar of the wound will destroy the mark of the thief.]

Lind: Name thy reward –
Gam: I never traffic with my humanity.[54]

There is only one prize commensurate with such nobility. Freedom alone is not enough:

Gam: England! shall I behold thee? Talk of fabled land, or magic power! But what land, that ever poet sung, or enchanter swayed, can equal that, which, when the Slave's foot touches, he becomes free! – his prisoned soul starts forth, his swelling nerves burst the chain that enthrall'd him, and, in his own strength he stands, as the rock he treads on, majestic and secure.[55]

This, then, is what Gambia's revenge ultimately amounts to. *The Slave* exemplifies how the awkwardness of issues like slavery, and the awareness of national complicity in them, can be not only contained but actually tailored and twisted into outright flattery of the audience. The greatest condemnation is reserved for those Africans who have indulged in supplying the slave trade; it is made quite clear that a state of unbridled liberty is considerably worse than existence under slavery. Slavery was still legal in the Caribbean and English possessions at the time that Morton wrote *The Slave* and any extra-legal measures to liberate Gambia and Zelinda are emphatically stated to be beyond the law, 'the iron law', in the Governor's phrase. What is stressed is that England alone is the home of justice and liberty. As D. G. (whose preface to *The Slave* in the Cumberland edition condemned the institution far more unequivocally than anything in Morton's play) put it, 'It is delightful when our amusements are thus rendered conducive to humanity.'[56]

'A BLOW, AND YET THE STRIKER LIVES!'

If *The Slave* was little more than a fervently patriotic adaptation of *Oroonoko*, produced at a time when there was still apprehension in Britain about the forces of revolution overseas, and involving the purposeful manipulation of a character who already fell into a fairly predictable pattern, then a reduction of a different sort afflicted the archetypal black revenge figure as he progressed, or, rather, regressed, through the century. While for Zanga the blow he had been struck was just one aspect of the whole psychological debasement of his enslavement, for subsequent black characters, the remembered grievance of the unmerited blow alone is sufficient motive for their villainy. Increasingly, such characters are now to be seen not only in the sporadic revivals of the old standards played at Covent Garden and Drury Lane, but also in newer fare in the minor theatres.

For Couri, the African leader thirty years a slave, who escaped back to his native land (Jerrold's *Descart, the French Buccaneer*, Coburg, 1828[57]), it is the blow from a master whom he had learnt to love for his kindness that finally tilts him over the edge and drives him to vengeance:

Couri: Time wore on; one day he rebuked – I answered him – he struck me. Yes! even now I tremble from the blow: I had been scourged, but I could smile and bleed, for I scorned the wretch that goaded me; but from one that I had succoured – loved! . . . From that hour I vowed revenge.[58]

It is worthy of note that, even for such a radically inclined writer as Jerrold, a slavemaster *can* be considered capable of winning a slave's genuine love, so deeply ingrained has become the notion of white beneficence and moral superiority. Yet Jerrold was writing at a time of political ferment, when the old social order had begun to crack and when movements both for parliamentary reform and for ending slavery were reaching a crescendo. So, in tones reminiscent of those of Hassan some thirty years earlier, Couri can voice his powerful anger at his enslavement:

Couri: Insult! grinding, degrading odium! 'Tis now thirty years since, entrapped from my country, my skin gave me to the white man for his drudge. – I will not now relate the scenes, the woes I have endured – how, companioned as beasts, I've seen my fellows toil, a merciless, jaundiced wretch stalking in proud authority o'er bleeding hearts.[59]

Couri is not the only black character in this brief melodrama – there is also his loyal lieutenant, Scultuo and the black traitor, Scalpa, both of whom play fairly minimal parts in the action. More leeway is given to

Chaco, black servant to the joking and quick-witted Luckless Tramp, one of the English party wrecked on Couri's shore. Chaco speaks in the usual black servant dialect and has saved Tramp from drowning; in a quid pro quo, Tramp saves him from being set on fire. That much is fairly familiar from innumerable plays featuring shipwreck on alien lands, though Tramp's repartee is funnier and more adroit than is often the case. But the main focus of interest is Couri. He already invites our sympathy, for, despite his hatred of whites, it is the shipwrecked English whom he assists and the marauding French pirates (aided by Scalpa, they have stolen his beloved daughter Imla) whom he has sworn to hunt down.

Couri is a somewhat tragic character whose revenge against his former master finally rebounds upon himself, for Imla is his former master's child, whom he stole and brought up as his own. That his revenge is of such a domestic nature reflects the fact that Jerrold is writing at what is almost the apogee of domestic melodrama. Couri's former master turns out to be none other than Descart, the French buccaneer who, at the last minute, when Imla's true identity is revealed, has to change sides to help the English rescue her from the pirates. Couri, though, despite his passionate invective, is a black who knows his place. He will have to be left behind when Imla is reunited with her own kind. When Bland, the English naval captain, asks Couri, '[W]hy not accompany us?,' he replies:

> *Couri*: What, I? Oh, I have seen the proud-built world – have felt its best refinement. I accompany! – What, the black man! – why even my Imla, my dearest, doating Imla, when civilised, might blush for the poor negro, her foster-father?[60]

A child of nature – an association with which is an enduring feature of the black stereotype – Couri can be truly free only in his own country: 'here are my woods – here roll the waves that bore my youthful limbs – here I am equal'.[61] So the dramatic resolution that is available to Yarico and Wowski can no longer even be considered for Couri – not just because he committed an initial wrong, for his subsequent actions more than atoned for that – but because the racial hierarchy is by the time of Jerrold's play that much more firmly entrenched. The very strength of Couri's attack on slavery is counterbalanced by his equally certain awareness and acceptance of that hierarchy, for 'we are poor unlettered wretches, nature's meanest, most imperfect offspring – inasmuch as we differ in complexion with her fairer, her more god-like children'.[62]

Yet Couri still has presence and dignity; his language has power. Not so the evil black sailor Muley in C. P. Thompson's potboiler *Jack Robinson and his Monkey*, a nautical melodrama first performed at the Surrey.[63] In yet another instance of the way that nineteenth-century popular drama retains historical traces of past centuries, the name Muley must surely be descended from George Peele's Muly Mahamet, the evil blackamoor in *The Battle of Alcazar* (1589).

For Muley, who mutinies against his captain, again it is the blow he has been struck that motivates his vengeance. But all the (uncomfortable) context of entrapment and slavery on which Jerrold so powerfully insists has vanished. Muley is just naturally wicked:

> *Muley*: I have received a blow – yes, a blow; and yet the striker lives. Now mark an African's revenge! [*The* Captain *is bound*] Lower the boat there quick; stow provisions lads – plenty mind; the compass and a chart. And you fair lady, shall share our perils, or our safety.[64]

Muley and the mutineers escape to a nearby island, leaving the captain lashed to his sinking vessel. It is left to the honest tar, Jack Robinson, shipwrecked on the island years earlier, to pay lip-service to the horrors of slavery. Finding Muley unconscious on the shore, he declares:

> *Jack*: Ah! a son of Afric's clime – perhaps he was a slave; if so, death was no punishment, but a blessing! Poor fellow! I will not mourn for you, for now no more you'll quail before a tyrant master's eye – no more your flesh will bleed beneath the torturing lash![65]

That such a sentiment is placed in the mouth of the iconic figure of the British sailor includes the audience in a comforting sense of moral superiority that overrides any uneasy awareness that Britain may still be complicit with such an institution. The sailor was *the* working-class dramatic hero, defender of England and of the oppressed. He was a figure that elements of the Thames-side Surrey's audience could be expected to identify with, even though in this instance Jack was not played by the great sailor hero and actor, T. P. Cooke. Certainly, the drunken, thieving and ungrateful Muley is himself far too degraded and simple-mindedly villainous a character to be allowed to express such sentiments. All he can compass is his desire for revenge:

> *Muley*: Oh genius of revenge fire my breast; a blow demands a life – Psha! Life for a blow is but puny vengeance! . . . More brandy Diego . . . Come, brandy! A blow! Oh, for that blow, a thousand living deaths shall torture him. Come, for revenge! Brandy! Brandy and revenge![66]

It is left to Jack Robinson's tame monkey, Mushapug (played by an actor) to fight Muley and rob him of his pistol – thus graphically and dramatically equating the African with the ape – albeit it is Jack who fires the final shot that kills Muley. The whole concludes with all on board a rescue ship shouting 'Victory! Victory! For England, O! for England' and the singing of 'Rule Britannia'.

'DANCE, YOU BLACK ANGELS!'

That spirit of national self-congratulation, though not always peddled as shamelessly as by Morton, or as grossly as by Thompson (a far lesser figure) is expressed over and over again in those dramas that celebrate Britain's nautical role. It is against this backdrop that the image of the black continued to be fashioned. The 'tar dramas' carried a whole freight of imagery and symbolism equating the 'trackless deep' with true liberty. It was, after all, control over the high seas that had enabled Britain most recently to thwart Napoleonic ambitions. Those years of war with France had inflected the very notion of liberty as in the English gift – and the English saw themselves as gifting that liberty to traded African slaves. When this powerful national idea was reinforced by the dramatic recon-struction of the genuinely valiant role of the navy in patrolling the high seas against the slave trade, it gave such dramas a powerful extra charge. That national, semi-mythic hero, the true tar, was directly involved in slave liberation.[67] And although the actual numbers of vessels seized and captives liberated were small in comparison with the size of the trade still being carried on, nonetheless, the myth and the reality reinforced each other. But the collision of myth and reality allowed some interesting contradictions and inconsistencies to surface.

Perhaps the classic example of this is the immensely popular *My Poll and my Partner Joe*, which was written when naval actions against the slave trade were at their height and in the immediate aftermath of the abolition of slavery *in toto* in 1833.[68] First performed at the Surrey in 1835, with T. P. Cooke as Harry Halyard, a Thames wherryman pressed into naval service, it was frequently revived up until the 1850s. Harry falls foul of Black Brandon (who is seeking to have the elderly waterman, Sculler, arrested for debt) by first fighting Brandon and then standing bail for Sculler. At Brandon's instigation, Harry is pressed into the navy. The harsh injustice of this is powerfully expressed by Harry:

Harry: Fiends incapable of pity first gave birth to the idea, and by fiends only is it advocated. What! force a man from his happy home, to defend a country whose laws deprive him of his liberty? But I must submit; yet, oh, proud

lordlings and rulers of the land! do ye think my arm will fall as heavily on
the foe as though I were a volunteer? No! – I shall strike for the hearts I
leave weeping for my absence, without one thought of the green hills or
the flowing rivers of a country that treats me as a slave![69]

This passionate and populist logic might seem, on the face of it, a barrier
to Harry's becoming (as he does, and as it is necessary for him to be) 'one of
the best seamen that ever trod a plank – one of the most fearless spirits that
ever handled a cutlass'.[70] The effect of this passage, with its evocation of
'green hills', 'flowing rivers' and 'happy home' is to appeal precisely to the
notion of a tranquil, timeless, rightly ordered England which, though
belied in the practices of its 'lordlings and rulers', is Harry's birthright
and is what he and others like him will fight to the death to defend.
England is the home, simultaneously; of slavery (instanced by the press-
gang) and of freedom. Harry's England is the England of the people, in
which injustice is seen for what it is, class-bound; yet there is also an
emotional and moral submission to that injustice, through the medium
of national identity and the ties of the family – 'the hearts I leave weeping' –
all compounded in the notion of duty. The duality of 'duty' is played upon.
In response to Harry's speech, Bowse, the press-gang officer, declares,
'Duty is duty, and must be done.' To which Joe, Harry's friend and
partner, replies, 'So says the thief when he serves the devil.'[71] But this
acerbic response is contained within a more acceptable notion of duty.
Harry vows to return an admiral, since go he must, and his mother, with all
the emotional authority that her status as the good old woman of melodrama gives her, replies 'stifling her sobs', 'You must, boy. I know you will
do your duty as a man; but for the sake of the young lass, and for the old
lass, too, don't be rash, my Harry: be a hero –.'[72]

The rightness of this submission is demonstrated through the rest of the
play. Harry does develop heroic status. When we next encounter him, on the
deck of the *Polyphemus*, he is about to be disciplined for being too recklessly
courageous in the nation's service and bringing about the capture of twenty-
six prisoners with their ammunition and supplies. Harry becomes the
archetypal liberator, fulfilling the navy's policing role against the slave
trade and his old enemy, Black Brandon. Brandon is a pirate slaver, his
ship *Black Bet* crammed with slaves, 'black cattle', chained to the floor and
guarded by an armed seaman carrying a whip. Brandon is as coarse and
brutal as his opponent is passionate and fine-spirited: 'Hark ye, ye nigger
animals, if I hear the least noise, or see the least sign of grumbling among ye,
I'll make sharks' meat of every devil of you . . .'[73] In a tableau which must

have called forth images of the abolitionist icon of 'Am I not a man and a
brother?', the enslaved Zinga enters from the hold '*heavily manacled – he
creeps close to* BRANDON, *and falls on his knees*' to beg the release of his wife,
Zamba.[74] Zamba has been imprisoned in Brandon's cabin, presumably for
Brandon's use and also to punish Zinga for an attempted escape.

Zinga repeats, like Hassan, the African's familiar and terrible litany of
seizure from his native land:

Zinga: Three years ago you tore me from my country, – from the presence of my
parents, and the arms of the maid, who is now my wife; regardless of my
shrieks and cries, you dragged me away to slavery; my heart was broken;
and, if I murmured, the lash was my only answer.[75]

In contrast to earlier plays which use this theme, Zinga is not motivated
by revenge. His moral superiority is absolute:

Zinga: Yet, master, I did not seek revenge . . . one night when you were sleeping,
my knife was at your throat; but I thought of the words the good white
man said to me at my own home, when he taught us his religion, and I
conquered the temptation.[76]

The submissive, pleading passivity which this picture of 'poor Zinga'
conjures up is only briefly disturbed when, after being struck by Brandon,
he staggers and '*making a weapon of his chain he rushes to strike*
BRANDON'. Zinga is, however, whipped back into submission '*till,
overcome by pain, he crouches piteously at the feet of* BRANDON, *who fells
him with a blow*'.[77]

To delay the pursuing *Polyphemus*, Brandon proposes dropping one of
the slaves over the side: 'if they shorten sail to pick him up, we gain time;
if they don't, the sharks will get him'. Such actions were by no means
unprecedented. Christopher Lloyd quotes an account of a French slaving
vessel in which the slaves and most of the crew went blind from ophthal-
mia; before reaching land, thirty-nine blind Africans were thrown overboard. It was said that the tracks of a slaver could be followed by pursuing
its trail of sharks.[78] Brandon fixes on Zinga's wife, Zamba, for the ploy.
But poor foolish Zinga believes that Brandon means to reunite him with
Zamba, the nature of the exchange and his reversion to speaking of himself
in the third person emphasising his childlike helplessness:

Enter SAILORS *with* ZAMBA, L. – *she rushes into the arms of* ZINGA.
Bran: Tear them asunder! (*the* SAILORS *separate them*)
Zinga: (*piteously*) No, no; you mistake: master captain has given me my dear wife,
my own Zamba; master will make Zinga happy.[79]

Zamba is tied into a hogshead and lowered over the ship's side – but is dramatically rescued by Harry, who leads a boarding party on to the *Black Bet* to liberate the slaves. Even as he is in the act of releasing them, Brandon, downed by Harry but not out, tries to shoot him in the back. Brandon is then shot dead by the comic figure Waxend, also one of Harry's Thames-side fellows, who had been kidnapped and forced to serve on the *Black Bet*. The cowardly but well-meaning Waxend frequently refers to himself as a 'white nigger', maintaining at a comic level the assertion of a link first stated by Harry between white class oppression and black slavery. Such a link, however, can only be of the most tangential kind, for it is necessary to the story of Harry Halyard, as to all the narratives of slave freedom, that England is synonymous with liberty, encapsulated in this climactic speech of Harry's:

> *Harry*: And, do you hear, boys? let the wounded be looked to – let the poor niggers go free upon deck. Dance, you black angels, no more captivity, the British flag flies over your head, and the very rustling of its folds knocks every fetter from the limbs of the poor slave.[80]

From cattle to angels in one act; this strong rhythmical language, with its opposition of flags and fetters, emotionally reiterates the essential Englishness of liberty. One of the ways in which the contrast between Harry and Brandon is reinforced is through the sharp distinction in their use of language. To Brandon, his captives are 'nigger animals', 'beasts', 'black bait', 'cattle'; Harry, on the other hand, speaks of 'angels' and 'ebony gentlemen', and, when he sees Zinga and Zamba reunited, he puts them on the same level as himself and his beloved:

> *Harry*: Lord love my eyes, the poor creeturs are lovyers [*sic*] – she's the Poll of his heart; tip us your black fin, my honest fellow; there's one at home I'd give the world to hug in my arms as you do your brown fair one here. – Here's a bit of her silky hair – it's my breast-plate in the day of battle, and my library of comfort in the dark hours of the night-watch.[81]

Yet this dramatic expression of genuine emotional equality is visually undercut for the audience by the fact that Zinga and Zamba both lie prostrate at Harry's feet in gratitude. They know their place, even if Harry is such a true Englishman that he refuses to see it.

It will be obvious from the passages quoted so far that, although Zinga's status is that of helpless victim and suppliant, dependent on his rescuer, he is, within that role, accorded a certain dignity. His language, apart from the referral to self in the third person when appealing to Brandon, is untainted by neologisms or attempts at 'black' speech – attempts which, within a year or so, were to reach unparalleled heights (or depths?) of absurdity. Indeed, Zinga is even allowed to play an active, though strictly subsidiary, part in enabling Harry's dashing capture of the slave fort and Brandon's 'pirate horde' (*sic*).[82]

So, by the first third of the nineteenth century, black nobility has passed through bombast and affectation ('fustian enriched with embroidery' was the judgement of one reviewer on *The Slave*)[83] to pleading, almost femi-nised dependency in Zinga – who is not even a conduit for exploring ideas of slavery, freedom and justice, for that now falls on Harry Halyard, the honest tar. On the other side of the coin, the threat posed by black vengeance on a slavetrading society has receded to the tamed and self-defeating rebelliousness of Couri or the stupid, drunken mutinousness of Muley. All are securely held within a fixed and increasingly dominant racial paradigm.

What headway could a young black American, determined to pursue his dream of an acting career, make against all this?

CHAPTER 3

Ira Aldridge and the battlefield of race

For all the hyperbole, the rhetoric about liberty and England did have a genuine basis. There was enduring class inequality, but it was a society in which domestic slavery was rarely practised.[1] In this, it contrasted enormously with America, where slavery was the norm in the southern states and, although officially ended in the North by 1830, had been replaced there by a whole raft of discriminatory measures aimed at ensuring black subordination.[2] It is no coincidence that such measures came to be known collectively as 'Jim Crow', for that eye-rolling, shoe-shuffling, fast-talking, singing and dancing white parody of black mores began its cultural take-over of American audiences at around the same time. It is the mid-1820s and the English campaign against slavery is once again on the ascendant even as, in America, endemic resistance to slavery is fermenting – most notably in the South in 1822 in a planned, widescale revolt under Denmark Vesey.

Although, at this period, there was a dramatic traffic between England and America, involving plays and star actors (Edmund Kean appeared in New York in 1820), for a black would-be actor, the scope to pursue a career in America was virtually nonexistent. Even the audiences were segregated, blacks being confined to the galleries of theatres like the large and popular Park theatre in New York with its rumbustious working-class audiences. The only known black venue in New York, the African theatre, which had been created by free blacks around 1820, was closed down a few years later after a white riot; it reappeared and was visited by the comedian and impersonator Charles Mathews in 1824, but its existence was fragile and uncertain and it did not survive long in the climate of hostility that surrounded it.[3] But one of those who may have appeared there and whose imagination was certainly fired by it[4] – and also perhaps by having seen Kean himself perform – was the young Ira Aldridge, the son of a black minister. Although destined for the ministry, Ira rejected this path to pursue a vocation as an actor. But only overseas was this even remotely possible. Hence, at the age of about eighteen, in 1824 or 1825, he came to England, never returning to his native land, though he went on to perform extensively across continental Europe. Aldridge's career spanned some forty or so years, from his first performance in England at the Royalty theatre to his last performance at the Theatre Royal Haymarket in 1865. He died of a lung complaint while on tour in Lodz, Poland, in 1867.[5]

That career was coterminous not only with the ferment over slavery and abolition but also with the further entrenchment of a racism that scored deep into English society. Any examination of how that racism developed, of the forms it assumed in popular culture, must also take into account how it was contested, where it was challenged. None issued that challenge at the cultural level more powerfully or consistently than Aldridge. But the evidence for this has to be pieced together from a variety of sources. As is so often the case with the written nineteenth-century record, its sheer volume, combined with its literacy and articulacy, while expressive of the assumptions of a professional elite, tends to mask the multiplicity and complexity of what lies beneath the surface; of reaction and response, of intention and purpose. What did it mean, for example, when the Irish tragedian Barry Sullivan was escorted by a torch-light procession through the streets of Dublin after success in England? Was it just a tribute to his stage skill, or did it resonate with that deeper, insistent claim to freedom from British rule?[6] Just as there is a barely detectable – but once found unmistakable – taint of subversive mockery of the English in so much of the material written by jobbing Irish play-wrights for the English stage, so there is, in the stuff of Aldridge's career, an increasingly overt claim for black liberty and equality. That claim high-lighted a deepening polarisation over questions of black capacity and threw into sharp relief the more degraded images of the black that were gaining currency.

The evidence for this claim lies, in part, in the types of roles that Aldridge played and that formed his basic repertoire over many years; parts that he honed and performed, night after night across the land. Many of them were derived from the vision of the noble, wronged and often vengeful black; other parts of his repertoire demonstrate an intention to push against the limitations of those familiar (and increasingly dated) black roles and included playing in whiteface.

Aldridge's early appearances on the English stage took place, then, against the backdrop of intense agitation over slavery, when it became clear that abolition of the trade had not led slavery itself to wither away.

The forerunner of the Anti-Slavery Society was formed in 1823; in 1825 it began publishing the *Anti-Slavery Reporter*. A network of local branches publicised the issue and organised petitions to Parliament; it was one of the earliest mass propagandising movements and inaugurated a new approach to effecting political change. At the same time, the pro-slavery interests also began to muster their propaganda, for the sugar industry was already showing signs of a decline in its profitability, which induced greater exploitation of slave labour, not less.[7] Hence it was timely that, in October 1825, Aldridge should appear at the Coburg as the lead in 'a grand West Indian Melodrama, called *The Revolt of Surinam, or A Slave's Revenge*.[8] The playbill itself makes much of the topical nature of its slavery theme (and links it once again to national pride in championing liberty):

This Piece exhibiting a most faithful Portrait of the horrors that arise out of that dreadful traffic, which it is the proudest boast of Britain to use her best efforts towards suppressing, must receive an immense portion of additional interest from being supported in its principal Character by a *Man of Colour*, and one of the very race whose wrongs it professes to record.[9]

The play was, in fact, an adaptation of *Oroonoko* – 'only the *razee* of Southern's tragedy'[10] – and, as such, already had a long history as a statement about slavery and race. It is impossible to discover what version Aldridge played, but presumably it would have been some variant of Dr Hawkesworth's 1759 rewrite. Despite the distortions thus visited on it, enough would have remained to make the play still controversial, at least with a black actor in the leading role. The 'bombast and affectation' detected in the play by *The Times*[11] would have been countered by the physical reality of a powerful young black actor, from a slave society, portraying an all-encompassing passion for his white wife and making a doomed bid for freedom and revenge. The subsequent reviews, all struck with the 'novelty' of Aldridge's appearance, attest to this, either by their ferocious lambasting of Aldridge's audacity in daring to appear at all, or by their praise for his performance.

The Times, with heavy-handed humour, was unqualifiedly racist in its assessment. Aldridge's appearance is first bracketed with that 'at the Surrey Theatre [of] a man who plays a monkey in the most natural manner possible'. He is then further put in his place by being described as 'what Mr. *Doubikins* calls "a *genuine nigger*"'. Doubikins was the name Charles Mathews had appropriated for the comic Yankee slaveowning character of his American 'At Home' performances, first given at the English Opera

House (later the Lyceum) in March 1824. These will be discussed in more detail subsequently, but it is worth pointing out that Mathews also parodied a black actor he had seen at New York's African theatre. This parody, which Mathews performed throughout his career, clung to Aldridge until Mathews died in 1835, though it is unlikely that Aldridge was in fact the occasion for it.[12]

The reviewer, having thus firmly located Aldridge in the racial hierarchy (his features 'although ... of the African character, are considerably humanized'), then goes on to discuss the performance:

His figure is unlucky for the stage; he is baker-knee'd and narrow chested; and owing to the shape of his lips, it is utterly impossible for him to pronounce English in such a manner as to satisfy even the unfastidious ears of the gallery ... The audience wondered and laughed at him all through the play until he stabbed his wife, and then they applauded him loudly; but it was not until he killed himself that their delight grew outrageous.[13]

Yet after such a build-up (whose racial prejudice is buttressed by its class prejudice), the worst that *The Times*'s reviewer can actually say of Aldridge's acting is that he is 'not ... worse than the ordinary run of such actors as are to be seen at the Coburg Theatre'. But as if regretting even such a grudging acknowledgement, the reviewer once again turns the attack on to Aldridge's skin colour. He is not black enough to fit the preconception. Perhaps he should be replaced by the 'blackamoor' who 'sweeps the crossings at the end of Fleet-market', for the 'gentlemen in the gallery ... looked for nothing lighter than a chimney-sweeper on May-day'. Moreover, sneered the reviewer, the 'black worsted stockings' of Aboan (Oroonoko's loyal friend and lieutenant) did not match Aldridge's own colour, which was 'but little darker than the dun cow'. The whole is finally skewered down with a reference to Day and Martin boot polish, ever the cliché, particularly for the black *slave*.

I have quoted this review at length because it is paradigmatic of the way in which, increasingly, blackness comes to be dealt with. There is the opening frame of reference to a theatrical novelty and, apposite to the black stereotype, the monkey; the opposition of what is African to what is recognisably human; the outright distortion of the physical description (needless to say, none of the many prints, drawings, portraits and later photographs of Aldridge point to the physical deformity alleged by *The Times*); the black crossing sweeper (who haunts theatrical criticism wherever black characters or storyline are involved, and who deserves his own footnote in history[14]), and the perennial, endlessly repeated Day and Martin joke.

Not all the reviews were so hostile. The popular, liberal paper the *Globe*, for example, declared the 'importation of Mr. Keene [Aldridge's original stage name] from the African Theatre . . . a lucky hit'. On the whole, the reviewer felt

his conception of the character was very judicious . . . Several of his touches in the last scene were impressive and . . . brought down spontaneous plaudits. His enunciation is distinct and sonorous, though his voice is deficient in modulation and flexibility; his features appear too hard and firm to admit of outwardly exhibiting the darker passions and most embittered sufferings of the heart. But he looks his character.[15]

Aldridge continued to play at the Coburg for the next few months, before taking up an engagement at the Theatre Royal, Brighton, in December. It was after a performance at the Coburg that he met his first wife, Margaret Gill, 'who appeared to have entertained something more than an admiration for the dark actor . . . She saw his "visage in his mind", and within a brief period from that accidental introduction entered into a matrimonial alliance with him.'[16]

It was, according to the black historian Edward Scobie, marriage with a white woman that engendered even greater hostility to Aldridge within the powerful West India and slavery interest, leading to his disappearance from the stage for about a year after his career had been fairly successfully launched.[17] The West India interest in the unreformed Commons ensured that, despite the comprehensive nature of the agitation against slavery, its repeal could not be passed without electoral reform.[18] The Society of West India Merchants and Planters was a highly active body which, through its literary committee, propagandised the pro-slavery case, funding publications and buying up and distributing favourable material gratis to booksellers.[19] Moreover, as its minutes show, '*The Times, The Chronicle, The British Press, The Herald, The Representative, The Courier, The Globe and Traveler, John Bull*, and *The English Gentleman* opened their columns to the committee in return for monetary consideration.'[20]

The existence of such an underlying current of opinion, stronger in London where the West India interest was most powerful and active, may perhaps explain the fact that, although Aldridge had undoubted and continuing success in the provinces, including Bath and Dublin, engagements on the London stage were few and far between – and then almost invariably at the minor theatres.

ALDRIDGE'S ROLES

It is significant that many of Aldridge's major roles were from plays that predated the nineteenth century. As such, almost all contain echoes of Enlightenment values: the dignity of man, the worth of freedom, the necessity of restraint. Or, as with *The Castle Spectre* (1797), they reflect that spectral Other of the Enlightenment – gothic excess. The black characters can symbolise both aspects of the culture that produced them. There is the tragic dignity of humanity robbed by slavery of its native and natural associations – wife, children, home and native land – which is stressed not only in *Oroonoko* and its variants but also in *The Revenge* (1721), *The Castle Spectre* and *The Slave* (1816), as well as the fear inspired by the desire for revenge for all this. The roles of Oroonoko, Gambia, Zanga and Hassan were all played by Aldridge throughout his career, and it could be argued that he did much to keep these plays in the repertoire. That these, along with Othello, were Aldridge's staple roles for more than thirty years indicates the corresponding failure of contemporary plays to take black characters seriously, except in one or two instances. In this Aldridge did have an effect on the nature of black representation, in that, if these plays did not extend the boundaries of the black stereotype, at least they retained some connection with the broader vision of the past.

His portrayal of Zanga, a prince turned by the experience of enslavement into a towering figure of vengeful cunning and cruelty, was frequently praised, even though the shortcomings of the drama itself were acknowledged. 'He made as much of *Zanga* as it is possible to do of so wordy, blustering and clumsy an Iago' stated the review in the radically inclined *Douglas Jerrold's Weekly Newspaper*, after a largely favourable assessment of Aldridge's qualities generally.[21] Or, as the *Era* put it, 'As Zanga he is exceedingly fine, looking the character of the Moor to perfection, and acting it with great power and correctness. For the tragedy itself we have little regard.'[22] And the *Morning Post* found it 'interesting to witness the acting of Mr. Ira Aldridge, a native of Africa, giving utterance to the wrongs of his race in his assumed character, and standing in an attitude of triumph over the body of one of its oppressors. England has, however, done its duty ... witness the millions paid for the manumission of the blacks.'[23]

Even the comic character of Mungo, in which Aldridge was judged to excel,[24] has an independence of spirit that was denied to later comic blacks. Much, too, was made in the reviews of his versatility in turning from the tragedy of *Othello* to the broad comedy of *The Padlock* (1789). Although such versatility was expected of the nineteenth-century actor, the frequency of comments on Aldridge's skill in this respect lead one to believe that it was exceptional.[25]

From the outset, Aldridge seems to have been concerned to push at the boundaries of the roles available to him. Thus, quite early in his career, he undertook white roles – an extremely bold approach that would excite comment even now. He played Rolla in *Pizarro* (1799) (a part which stressed the value of freedom), the Dutch sea captain Hatteraick in *Guy Mannering* (1816) and the title role in *Bertram* (1816).[26] He even added Shylock to his repertoire, for the sympathetic nature of which portrayal, he was many years later congratulated by the Jewish community of Zhitomir in Russia.[27] A hitherto unpublished translation, by Herbert Marshall and Mildred Stock, of a lengthy Russian critique by Sergei Durylin of Aldridge's playing of Shylock, evokes the depth and qualities he brought to the part:

Aldridge deeply understood the character and so he played it as an exploited, despised Jew whose daughter was kidnapped or spirited away after she was taught to rob her own father and to borrow money from him, and was deprived of the right to revenge for these things. He gave us a character of a Jew who was forced, under threat of death, to renounce the religion of his forefathers ... Shylock has much money but he has more insults and abuse. He is the bearer of the sorrow and tragedy of his hunted people ... he desires revenge for what he considers violated pride as a Jew ... he belongs to the oppressed, powerless people who are never forgiven anything.[28]

Shylock was the Shakespearean role that, apart from Othello, Aldridge played most frequently (Macbeth, Richard III and even Lear were also in his repertoire).[29] Yet there is virtually no contemporary comment on these performances apart from the occasional mention in the provincial press, and nothing anywhere which demonstrates, as Durylin's commentary does, the way in which Aldridge's consciousness and experience of racial oppression must have informed his art. Only his Othello and sometimes his Zanga ever seem to have been reviewed in depth by the English press. Was the black actor playing the white role simply beyond comment when he stepped outside the allotted boundaries? It seems so, except, interestingly, in those more peripheral regions of the British Isles, such as Wales and Ireland, where Bernth Lindfors has uncovered a number of brief commendations and one more considered review which finds Aldridge's Shylock to be modelled on that of Edmund Kean, and 'far above' that of Charles Kean.[30]

Much of the material developed for Aldridge appears now to be lost, such as *The Negro's Curse*, by H. M. Milner, performed with success at the Coburg, but of which no trace can be found.[31] Lost, too, are *The Libertine Defeated, or African Ingratitude* and *Savage of the Desert* by W. Roberds, though presumably these would have capitalised on the themes of slavery and vengeance still deemed appropriate for a black actor. Nor do we have many details of the composite entertainment that Aldridge put together while performing in Ireland in the late 1830s. Similar in format to Mathews's *A Trip to America*, but apparently more serious in intent, it included a 'brief introductory LECTURE on the DRAMA . . . a Memoir of the African . . . His Scene in ROLLA . . . and amusing Anecdotes of Mathews's well-known Trip to America',[32] as well as extracts from *Othello*, *The Revenge*, *The Castle Spectre*, *Oroonoko* (1695), *The Padlock*, etc. Unlike Mathews's, Aldridge's scenes from America went on to cover such topics as 'Liberty and Equality, or the American Slave Market' and 'England, or the Negro Emancipation. The Slave's Gratitude'.[33] It is not fanciful, I think, to see in this Aldridge's oppositional approach. He took a hugely popular format, with a funny and extremely racist content, and turned it, if not on its head, into something that contradicted Mathews's formulations of the black character and yet remained entertaining.

It is true that he performed some of the minstrel songs, such as 'Jim Crow' or 'Miss Lucy Long', that were becoming so inordinately popular from entertainers like T. D. Rice. After all, he had to cater to the tastes of his audience (and this material veers wildly in how directly offensive it is). But whereas Mathews, Rice and their subsequent imitators were guying the black performer, this approach would seem inimical to a black American, who had left his own country where '[n]o qualities of the mind could compensate in the eyes of Americans for the dark hue of his skin' and who, presumably, was impelled by a desire to extend his capacities and the range of activity open to him.[34] (At the time Aldridge left for England, not even all of New York's slaves had become free under its earlier emancipation legislation.)[35] Was it perhaps also, as Nicholas Evans has suggested, 'a sly reappropriation' of Mathews's own parody of black performance – of which Aldridge was rumoured to be the occasion?[36] With his exceptional comic skills, Aldridge was also successful as Ginger Blue (one of Rice's original roles) but Ginger demonstrates much more wit and capacity than most 'minstrel' parts. One reviewer, writing in the *Illustrated London News*, was certainly conscious of the difference, citing the comedy of Aldridge's Mungo as 'differing entirely from the Ethiopian absurdities we have been taught to look upon as correct portraitures . . . his total *abandon* is very amusing'.[37]

Obi; or, Three-fingered Jack

There is, however, one extremely interesting survival of material supposedly written for Aldridge, a dialogue version by W. H. Murray of John Fawcett's pro-slavery pantomime, *Obi* (1800), in which he played the role of Karfa (Three-finger'd Jack).[38] (*Obi; or, Three-fingered Jack* was also in the repertoire of the African theatre.)[39] It demonstrates both the potential for and the limitations of rerendering and reordering a pressing issue of race and power through rewriting a popular dramatic entertainment. It also demonstrates the lengths to which Aldridge could go, within the constraints of the melodramatic format, to make the black villain not only the most dynamic but also the most imaginatively involving character in the play. Of necessity, given the subject matter of the whole, Karfa/Jack is forced into the mould of full-blown villainy, but what is impressive is the way that he threatens to explode that mould.

The play closely follows the sequence of events in Fawcett's pantomime, with the happy, hierarchical world of the plantation threatened by the lawless outsider, Karfa (Jack is his slave name). The plantation owner, Ormond, is presented as kind and benevolent. His slaves dance and sing and, on his first entrance, 'all the Negroes crowd round shouting, and expressing great affection for him'.[40] The plot hinges on Karfa's capture of Rosa, the planter's daughter, and of her fiancé, Captain Orford. Aldridge first played Karfa in the former slavetrading city of Bristol in 1830, not long before one of the largest and most serious of slave rebellions in the Caribbean broke out, in Jamaica, in 1831–2, immediately preceding abolition. At first Karfa, who dwells in a cave with a bunch of brigands, is presented by Ormond as evil incarnate for having first attempted to violate Ormond's wife and then murdered her. He is a 'monster' of 'giant strength' who has 'burst his bonds' and escaped.[41]

Karfa, however, is allowed to tell his story differently and in doing so recites once again the tale of betrayal, capture and loss that motivates the avenging figure of the enslaved African. For him, the murder of Ormond's wife was a 'sacrifice' to the memory of his 'beloved Olinda',

whom they tore lifeless from these arms as they dragged me from my native land; can I forget? can I forgive? Never ... As Africa receded from my gaze I swore that the first white man who purchased Karfa's services should also feel his hate ... I will sacrifice his every remaining joy to the memory of my broken-hearted wife, my helpless infants, and the wrongs of my poor country.[42]

While Orford, Rosa's husband-to-be, is out hunting, he is seized by Karfa and taken captive. Rosa, determined to find Orford, disguises herself as a boy and is, in turn, captured. Karfa is a powerful and outspoken character, who continually threatens to burst through his stereotype. Openly contemptuous of his superstitious mother's traditional Obeah magic, the sense of modernity he projects is exhilarating – and unlike anything else in the play (which, perhaps because it stays so close to its pantomimic origins, has a somewhat old-fashioned air):

Jack [Karfa]: Your white man, I am told, can soar into the air, fathom the deep, ransack the mine, and enslave in every clime where his accursed arts find access. Here, here alone, no white man finds an entrance, but as Karfa's slave . . . obey me! the times have changed, and the white man must now labour for the black.[43]

The latter speech is all the more shocking in that it is spoken to the captured Rosa, for the audience is aware that she is a vulnerable woman, even if Karfa is not. That a black actor, from a slave society, was playing this role must surely have added to its charge.

While Karfa's is the strongest and most dynamic part in the play, it is apparent that the mould of stage villainy only allows of such a forceful counterblast to accepted values and mores because it is so fixed and defined an identity. It is safe to let Karfa express such wild ideas because they are contained within and decontaminated by his status as a racialised black villain. How else can one account for what is, to modern eyes, the glaring imbalance that allows Quashee, the obedient plantation slave with his inarticulate broken English, his gratitude to Massa and his inability to dispose of Karfa/Jack without the help of two others, to carry the dramatic weight of restoring the status quo? Quashee's reaction to Karfa's taunt that he is a slave serves only to underscore this. 'Me *no* slave! me free!' cries Quashee, 'me *gentleman*, me Mr. Quashee now, and no care a button for you or Obi either.'[44]

Karfa is finally defeated by Sam and Quashee in a desperate struggle and despatched on stage with a blunderbuss and two swords. Assurance is made doubly sure. The powerfully argued justification for Karfa's fury is, in the event, outweighed by the hierarchy of the plantation, by the granting of the rewards of freedom and basic human status – a status that is undermined even as it is asserted by the very manner in which that assertion is made. Only a culture in which the assumption of racial superiority and inferiority is becoming endemically ingrained could accept that the Karfa/Quashee equation is valid; that Quashee's obeisance to his 'master' is of more weight than Karfa's independence; that Karfa's

3 **Karfa about to kill Quashee in** *Obi* Frontispiece, Dicks, no. 478, Malcolm Morley
Library, Senate House Library, University of London

rebellion is even lower in the human scale than Quashee's manifest
inferiority.

The play remained long in Aldridge's repertoire, despite the ultimately
rather anachronistic setting from which Karfa's indictment was hurled.
Perhaps it allowed him to express, through Karfa's rebellion, something of
his own struggle. As late as 1857, the play is listed in the *Theatrical Journal* as
due to be performed during Aldridge's last week at the Britannia.[45]

But there is an interesting omission from the Britannia performances.
Less than six months earlier, in December 1856, Aldridge had played the
eponymous hero in *Dred*, based on a real slave leader who had attempted to
instigate a slave rebellion in the American South, as depicted in Harriet

Beecher Stowe's novel *Dred* (1856). *Dred* is discussed in more detail in chapter 7 but suffice it to say here that Dred, like Karfa, is a powerful and dynamic character, eloquent for his cause, and, like Karfa, he has to die. But, while Karfa's was a personal vendetta, Dred's was a political cry for freedom. What is significant is that Aldridge had played the role in Ireland, which, throughout the nineteenth century, was conducting, in myriad ways, its own struggle for liberation and whose people – apart from the Anglo-Irish ruling class – were also the targets of a sustained racial prejudice that had intensified since the Great Famine of 1847.[46] This again is one of those tantalising indications of an oppositional undercurrent. Did the political climate in Ireland perhaps enable the black American actor to deal with such issues more openly there? One enthusiastic review of Aldridge's performance at the Theatre Royal, Belfast, could be read in this way. *Dred*, termed by the reviewer 'one of the most successful dramas on the stage for the promotion of liberty and justice', was met with 'approving cheers'. He went on: 'The love of freedom is diffused, and the heritage of liberty, bought by the blood of our fathers, is doubtless safe in the keeping of their sons . . . we must congratulate Mr Aldridge on his acting [as] "Dred". It was all that could be desired; and *he seemed endued with an enthusiasm even uncommon with himself.*'[47]

Othello and after

However, the role with which Aldridge came to be most closely associated and which dominated his acting life was that of Othello. Although his provincial performances as Othello were generally acclaimed, it was not until almost the end of his career and after a long and bitter struggle that he received, on the London stage, anything like acceptance in the role. It was a struggle that had much to do not only with the proprietorial reverence that the English felt for much of Shakespeare's work, including *Othello*, but also with the way in which that play was viewed and the challenge that Aldridge, as a black actor tackling a role that was weighted with cultural, social and political significance, posed to the dominant racial hierarchy. Indeed, the history of the staging of *Othello* is, in itself, a reflection of changing racial attitudes and mores.

From Shakespeare's time up until the early nineteenth century, Othello had traditionally been played in the blackest of makeup and black gloves. Leman Rede in *The Road to the Stage* describes the transition: 'Othello used not in former days to sport a coloured countenance, but wore the same sables as Mungo . . . but this, as . . . preventing the possibility of the expression being observable, has become an obsolete custom. A tawny tinge is now the colour used for the gallant Moor, for Bajazet, and Zanga; Spanish brown is the best preparation.'[48]

However, there was more to it than supposedly simply allowing greater transparency to the facial expression. Why, after all, had this only now become a problem? One of the greatest eighteenth-century Othellos, Spranger Barry,[49] had played Othello as black, for which, of course, there is ample textual evidence. As the early twentieth-century theatre historian William Winter put it (his evidence is close to the mid- to late nineteenth-century portrayals), revealing in the process more than he realised: 'Barry made *Othello* a black man, but as his person was tall, – more than five feet eleven inches – and absolutely symmetrical, his countenance expressive, his smile winning, his voice rich and sweet, and . . . his demeanor and motions . . . graceful, he was able to overcome that disadvantage.'[50]

It was, in fact, Edmund Kean, whose Othello was termed by William Hazlitt 'beyond all praise'[51], who displayed 'the most terrific exhibition of human passion that has been witnessed on the modern stage',[52] and whose voice was described by the American tragedian Junius Brutus Booth as 'like the moan of ocean or the soughing of wind through cedars',[53] who first played the role as a 'tawny' Moor. While for Kean (a class outsider, as Othello was a race outsider), the lighter makeup may have allowed greater play to his finely expressive face and eyes, it also chimed with a growing distaste for physical blackness. That was now associated, indelibly, with slave status and all the ingrained, systemic inferiority structured into that status. Hazlitt, as has been pointed out, made the link in his review of Kean's Oroonoko, with his sudden outburst against the 'cargo' of blacks who made up the play. That Othello explicitly declares himself to have been sold into slavery and redeemed was passed over.[54] Again, it is Winter who makes the line of thought overt:

A Moor is not necessarily black; he is tawny. *Othello* is not a Negro and he should not be represented as one. Kean was the first among actors to recognize that fact . . . the actor should consider the imperative requirements of facial expression and dramatic effect . . . 'Othello' . . . should be acted in a poetical spirit. To take a cue from such expressions in the text as 'thick lips' and 'Barbary horse,' and make *Othello* a Negro is, necessarily, to lower the tone of the interpretation.[55]

In the words of Paul Robeson (whose 1943 performance as Othello perhaps 'approached the greatness attributed to actors in other times'[56]):

Shakespeare meant Othello to be a 'black moor' from Africa, an African of the highest nobility of heritage. From Kean on, he was made a light-skinned Moor because Western Europe had made Africa a slave center, and the African was seen as a slave. English critics seeing a black Othello – like my Othello – were likely to take a colonial point of view and regard him offhand as low and ignoble ... Othello's personal racial dignity is involved in his love ... he is intensely proud of his color and culture.[57]

That the nineteenth-century burlesques or 'travesties' of *Othello* lampooned the character as a thick black in thick black make-up assaulted the notion of a dignified but unmistakably black-skinned Othello from yet another direction.[58]

Moreover, the play itself, like other Shakespearean works, was in some ways too much for the sensibilities of its early nineteenth-century audiences. *King Lear* had had its ending rewritten; *Titus Andronicus* had been adapted in the seventeenth century by Edward Ravenscroft and even in this version was rarely staged, while *Othello*'s explosive mixture of profound sexual passion, jealousy and barbarous nobility had already been 'refined' by excision to meet the taste of its eighteenth-century audiences.[59] Add to this the racial theme of the whole, in an increasingly race-conscious age, and one can see not only how deeply disturbing audiences would find the play but how provocative any portrayal might be that would shake the frame within which it was experienced. Yet, and this is the apparent contradiction, *Othello* was not for those reasons rarely performed; highly venerated as one of Shakespeare's greatest works, it was, rather, one of the most frequently performed of his plays during this period.

Thus by the time Aldridge came to play Othello on the London stage in 1833, there was a whole complex of motivations – political and psychological – ready to be mobilised to belittle and attack him. He had had several successful years in the provinces and the reviews had been highly favourable. J. Cole of Scarborough was moved to publish a small pamphlet on Aldridge's Othello, 'a performance enriched with the brilliancy of genius' after witnessing him,[60] and he had a letter of commendation from Edmund Kean, who had seen him performing Othello in Dublin.[61] This time, the invitation was not for one of the minor theatres, but to one of the patent theatres, Covent Garden. Battle was swiftly joined. For here was not one of the sable brethren who could be safely patronised and pitied overseas and who, in that capacity, did so much to bolster English national pride in its benevolence, but one who was attempting to engage, on equal terms, with two national shibboleths at once – Shakespeare and the home of legitimate drama, a centre of national prestige. The reaction was furious, swift and devastating.

Even before Aldridge's appearance at Covent Garden in April 1833, there seem to have been rumours that he was to perform at Drury Lane. In September 1832 *Figaro in London*, Gilbert Abbot à Beckett's trenchant critique of contemporary politics and contemporary theatre, reported as follows:

[I]n the way of novelty there has been a stupid looking, thick lipped, ill formed African calling himself the African Roscius, and posting placards about Lancaster saying that he appears there previous to the fulfilment of *his engagement at Drury Lane Theatre*. Now we suspect this to be a hoax, but if this vain glorious [*sic*] *Niger* is positively engaged at Drury Lane, we have little hopes that Captain Polhill [then lessee of Drury Lane] will ever be instrumental to the regeneration of the Drama. Is it because the man has a black skin that he is a ready made Othello? . . . If a sooty face, we mean, of a naturally black complexion of necessity implies an aptitude for parts such as Othello, Zanga, etc. why has not the old Commodore been long ago dragged from his crossing in Tottenham Court Road, and thrust upon the boards of Drury Lane Theatre as Oronoko [*sic*] or some other of the numerous Moorish parts in the Drama.[62]

There is much more in the same vein. What lies behind this story is impossible to say – it is not mentioned by Marshall and Stock, and I have seen no other references to a possible engagement at Drury Lane. It seems unlikely, on the face of it, that the *Figaro* writer (probably à Beckett himself) would have witnessed, as he claims, a performance by Aldridge at Lancaster, though he may well have seen him earlier in London.[63] Might there be any connection with this rumour and C. M. Westmacott's staging of his travesty of Othello, *Othello, the Moor of Fleet Street* (in which Othello is a crossing sweeper) at the Adelphi in January 1833?[64]

When Aldridge did finally appear, at Covent Garden (10 April 1833), *Figaro*'s vituperation reached even more hysterical levels:

a further act of insolence is to be perpetrated, by the introduction to the boards of Covent Garden theatre, of that miserable nigger, whom we found in the provinces imposing on the public by the name of the *African Roscius*. This wretched upstart is about to defile the stage, by a foul butchery of Shakspeare, and Othello is actually the part chosen for the sacrilege. Is it because nature has supplied the man with a skin that renders soot and butter superfluous, is it on the strength of his blackness that he considers himself competent to enact the part of the Moor of Venice. We have before jammed this man into atoms by the relentless power of our critical battering ram, but unless this notice causes the immediate withdrawal of his name from the bills, we must again inflict on him such a chastisement as must drive him from the stage he has dishonoured, and force him to find in the capacity of footman or street-sweeper, that level for which his colour appears to have rendered him peculiarly qualified.[65]

So it goes on, in issue after issue. *Figaro*, after having been accused in placards of attempting to drive Aldridge from the stage without fair trial (Aldridge received support from the Garrick club[66]), assumes a pious air of critical impartiality, citing once again the poorly attended performance in Lancaster.[67] The magazine, claiming credit for having 'hunted the Nigger from the boards of Covent Garden', went on to excoriate his performance as Mungo at the Surrey.[68] He is accused of using foul language outside the theatre: 'that he should not have the manners of a gentleman cannot surprise us, seeing that he was once a slave, then a footman, afterwards a Roscius, and now, thanks to us and to the Times, a quack detected'.[69] He is accused, as Mungo, of slurping beer off the stage floor (*Figaro* faints at this) and derided for attempting a white part.[70] And the black crossing sweeper once again makes his inevitable appearance in all the farrago.

That Aldridge should attempt to continue in London, despite the barrage of hostility, suggests strength of character of the most steadfast kind. *Figaro*'s (untrue) accusation of Aldridge's former slave status is, perhaps, the nub of the matter. The abolition of slavery in Britain's overseas possessions was imminent (to be effected in 1834), but the pro-slavery interest, propagandising the inability of blacks to exist without white tutelage, together with the necessity for immense reparations for the planters, was still powerful. After Aldridge's appearance as Othello, the pro-slavery, ultra-conservative *John Bull* (funded by the West India merchants) had a few snide words to say:

The City Theatre produced a black man as *Tom Tug* in the *Waterman*. An example which Covent-garden followed on Thursday by exhibiting another *Whango Iang* in *Othello*, as if, because a man's face is black, he could act that particular part ... The City Blackamore got unmercifully hissed – the Covent-garden nigger considerably clapped. This is all a matter of taste.[71]

The presence on the London stage of a black actor, performing one of the most revered and highly charged roles in the Shakespeare canon, gave the direct lie to the argument of innate black inferiority that the proponents of slavery so assiduously peddled. Nowhere outside London, heart of the West India interest, did Aldridge ever meet such dedicated hostility.

But what were the qualities of Aldridge's performance itself, following on as it so closely did, the last of Edmund Kean as Othello? *The Times* was, of course, disparaging. The house was thinly attended and the reviewer found his accent 'vulgarly foreign' and his performance 'weak'. It conceded, though, that 'Mr. Aldridge was extremely well received' by the audience.[72] (Throughout Aldridge's career reports of audience enthusiasm were often at variance with critical opinion.) The liberal literary journal the *Athenaeum* was outraged, for reasons of class, race and national pride, and sexual propriety:

Mr. Henry Wallack's black servant in the character of *Othello – Othello*, forsooth!!! *Othello*, almost the master-work of the master-mind – a part, the study of which occupied, perhaps, years of the life of the elegant and classical Kemble; a part, which the fire and genius of Kean have, of late years, made his exclusive property: a part, which it has been considered a sort of theatrical treason for anyone less distinguished than these two ... to attempt; and this is to be personated in an English national theatre, by one whose pretensions rest upon the two grounds of his face being of a natural instead of an acquired tint, and of his having lived as servant to a low-comedy actor. It is truly monstrous ... it is extraordinary, that under all the circumstances, a natural quickness and aptitude for imitation, should enable him to get through such a part as *Othello*, with so little of positive offence, as he does ... It is impossible that Mr. Aldridge should fully comprehend the meaning and force of even the words he utters ... In the name of propriety and decency, we protest against an interesting actress and lady-like girl, like Miss Ellen Tree, being subjected ... to the indignity of being pawed about by Mr. Henry Wallack's black servant.[73]

   None of this suggests much about Aldridge's performance, after which 'Mr Sheridan Knowles, the great dramatist' is said to have 'rushed into his arms, exclaiming, "For the honour of human nature let me embrace you."'[74] The conservative *Spectator* seesawed wildly between praise and censure, concluding:

He evinced a great deal of feeling and nature in his performance; these, indeed, were its redeeming qualities; but they could not reconcile us to its numerous and glaring defects. Its beauties, however, surprised us more than its faults ... In the most violent bursts of passion, he was deficient in energy and power; though in depicting the struggles of mental agony and suppressed emotion, he was vigorous and natural ... It was upon the whole a failure ... the applause bestowed on his ... *Othello* induced the Manager to announce its repetition.[75]

   The *Morning Post* was cool in its assessment, claiming to be '[p]rejudiced neither in his favour nor against him', following the campaign of 'several publications ... tending to condemn, or rather to annihilate, him unheard':

His ... face ... is not capable of very varied expression. His figure is tall and noble, and his manner of walking the stage is dignified ... Mr. ALDRIDGE's enunci-ation is far from correct or pleasing ... but he possesses a fine, full, melodious voice, which might with practice be turned to more advantage ... To sum up ... it was not an *Othello* for Covent-garden Theatre, where we do not ... go to witness mere curiosities ... there was not any audible expression of disapprobation throughout the whole of his performance.[76]

More enthusiastic were the *Standard*, which expressed 'unqualified delight with his delineation of this masterpiece of the divine Shakespeare' – his 'representation all through was watched with an intense stillness, almost approaching to awe' – and the liberal *Globe*. For the *Globe's* reviewer, there were 'beauties throughout his performance' which more than compensated for the occasional lapse into 'rant' and 'some vulgarisms of pronunciation'.[77]

Aldridge's engagement at Covent Garden was, however, curtailed and he gave only two performances (an epidemic of 'flu shut the theatre for some nights). He never gave the planned performances of Zanga and Mungo, but moved for a period to the Surrey, one of the more adventurous of the minor theatres. Here he continued to be hounded by *Figaro*, though apparently ignored by the rest of the press. His own version of events was given in his *Memoir*:

> Certain of the public Press – a few individuals – were inimical to the histrionic pretensions of the African ... Miss Ellen Tree was the Desdemona of Mr. Aldridge's Othello, and certain admirers of that lady ... were envious of the Moor's familiarity with her fair face, and ridiculed his privilege ... Men who have since grown older, and, if we may judge from their literary pursuits, wiser, took a pleasure in scoffing at 'the idea' of ' a nigger' filling an intellectual character, and surpassing themselves among others in his delineation of poetry, pathos, and passion ... Had Laporte [lessee of Covent Garden] persisted in his undertaking, Mr. Aldridge would soon have been established as a generally known, popular, and extraordinary actor ... Prejudices, too, will come even across the great Atlantic.[78]

Aldridge returned to provincial touring, and his next major London engagement was some fifteen years later, in 1848, again at the Surrey. In 1852 he appeared at the Britannia, a large popular East End minor theatre with a working-class audience, which had had less success than the Surrey in broadening its appeal and remained the home of old-fashioned melodrama. Shortly after, Aldridge left for his first tour of mainland Europe, where most of his subsequent successes were to be and where he would be loaded with honours for his brilliant performances – despite the difficulties inherent in his acting in English, with supporting casts who acted in the vernacular. His other documented appearances in London were at the Britannia in 1857 and the more fashionable Lyceum, in London's West End, in 1858, for which he was praised by the *Athenaeum* and lengthily dismissed by *The Times*;[79] his last was at the Haymarket in 1865.

Across Europe he attracted huge interest and dazzled audiences. Théophile Gautier was one who praised his ability, as Lear even more than as Othello. 'In the former he acted; in Othello he was just himself . . . [as Lear] his outbursts of indignation and anger were superb, but at the same time there was a feebleness, and senile trembling . . . such as one would expect from an old man on the verge of his eighties who is being changed from an idiot to a madman by the weight of intolerable misfortunes.'[80]

The Black Doctor

If playing the great roles of the Shakespearean canon across Europe – and receiving widespread acknowledgement of his abilities – was one way in which Aldridge transcended the barriers erected against the black artist, back in England the situation was different. Here, although he played many of these roles, he was limited to short runs in provincial theatres and his performances, except as Othello, were little commented on. There is not space here to trace Aldridge's career in detail. However, certain developments stand out, characterised by their opposition to the prevailing trends of the time, through which one can interpret Aldridge's career as a counter to the growing virulence of racial stereotyping. One was the addition to his repertoire, in the late 1840s, of what was probably the first contemporary melodrama to deal seriously with issues of race – 'a play in which colour prejudice was the motivating factor and not simply a comic ploy'[81] – *The Black Doctor*. Jack Gratus, in his historical analysis of cultural racism, sees the play as a white response to the notion of black equality 'by making the latter the victim of humiliation'. He continues, 'On the stage where [the white man] can play out his fantasies he punishes the black man for presuming to be his equal.' But, in the context of its time, *The Black Doctor* is more progressive than that implies.[82] In the 1840s much contemporary popular theatre and entertainment was dominated by images of happy stupid slaves, singing the songs of 'nigger minstrelsy'. In 1846, when *The Black Doctor* was first performed, the Ethiopian Serenaders were also in England, following on from and giving further impetus to the Jim Crow vogue initiated by Rice in 1836.

　　The Black Doctor, however, is an intense, highly melodramatic, interracial love story. An adaptation from the French, it survives in two versions, one by Bridgeman and one attributed to Aldridge, with an (incorrect) first performance date of 1841.[83] The French setting has been retained, perhaps to circumvent any potential discomfort were *The Black Doctor*'s theme of interracial love, between (former) slave and white mistress, to be brought nearer home. Aldridge's role in the play, set in the prerevolutionary period, in the French colony of the Isle of Bourbon, was that of the black doctor, Fabian, a mulatto who has saved the life of his erstwhile master's wife, Madame de la Reynerie, and fallen deeply in love with her daughter, Pauline. It should be noted that though Fabian is described as a 'mulatto', he is not endowed with the evil characteristics of the mulatto, derived from a mixed parentage, as portrayed in a number of other mid-century dramas. In Bridgeman's version Fabian is described as 'very dark brown, with glossy straight black hair', but in the version attributed to Aldridge there is some attempt to distance him from such a dark skin colour; he is 'not a black man, but ... yellow and brown'.[84] Throughout the play he is known as both the 'Black Doctor' and 'the mulatto', suggesting little distinction between the terms in this instance.

Pauline de la Reynerie brings her servant Lia, who is languishing from some unknown complaint, to Fabian for diagnosis. Fabian recognises the syndrome:

Fab: The sickness that oppresses her is of the heart.
Lia: (*Rising in terror.*) Fabian, Fabian! Oh, be silent ...
Fab: And this love, pure and chaste, you would hide from all, as if it were a shame for you to love one whom you have no right to love, and who despises you ... Because he is not of your accursed race; because he is a European ... he is a good and worthy young man; but his skin is white (*To Lia.*), and yours is dark as mine; therefore you have not the right to love him. Suffer, poor sister, suffer, and despair, for yours is a malady for which there is no remedy.[85]

Pauline is appalled and pledges to make it possible for Lia and her beloved to marry: 'You say he is not of her race; what is that to me, since she loves him – would die for him?'[86]

Transported with joy that Pauline should utter such sentiments, Fabian is cast into the depths of despair when he encounters St Luce, the husband intended for Pauline – a man whom he has just rescued from a poisonous snake. Struggling between his desire to kill St Luce and his desire to kill himself, he goes to meet Pauline at a prearranged spot, to further Pauline's plans for Lia. Walking along a wild and rocky cliff path with her, Fabian determines that he and she will die together, rather than he surrender her to St Luce:

Fab: Listen, then. There lived in St. Louis, a poor mulatto – a slave, who ... received his freedom! the generous gift should have made him happy, but it was otherwise; for once free he was compelled to leave his master's dwelling, and under that roof dwelt his better angel. At length he went forth, more wretched in his freedom than in his slavery! for he loved – yes, madly loved – adored that master's daughter. (*Wind heard.*)

Paul: (*Alarmed.*) How dreadfully the wind howls.

Fab: (*Not heeding her.*) He would have buried his love in his heart, though it had crushed it . . . He thought himself beloved – and though respect to the pride of her race forbade her to be *his*, he thought at least she would never be another's. The fool was dreaming; one word awoke him, she was about to marry – to marry! she had deceived him, had sported with his agony; she should not have done so – it was imprudent, for then the wretched man took an oath to unite himself to her by the solemn, dreadful, awful tie of death.[87]

It is interesting that Fabian is allowed to go to the very brink of murder, while Pauline is pleading to be let go, and yet still retain his heroic status. Unusually, Pauline returns his love and, in peril of imminent death,

4 **Fabian and Pauline in** *The Black Doctor* Frontispiece, Dicks, no. 460, Malcolm Morley Library, Senate House Library, University of London

pledges herself to him, even as he repents of his plan. The two contract a
secret marriage which has to be kept from Pauline's mother, in whom the
pride of race and class runs strong. The household, with Fabian now in
attendance as a servant, returns to France, where Pauline's mother insists
that Fabian be sent back to the Isle of Bourbon and Pauline marry St Luce.
St Luce suspects Pauline and Fabian, and is insolent to him, ridiculing his
status:

> *St. L:* No doubt, in Bourbon 'twill be necessary to doff these trappings of the
> gentleman, which appear rather strange; here 'tis only laughed at, but in
> Bourbon ... this insolence would be chastised, particularly the sword,
> which sits but ill on a mulatto, who could not dare to raise it even to
> ward off the planter's whip![88]

At this baiting of her husband, Pauline reveals the truth and threatens to
take her life with poison. Fabian, while insisting on the validity of their
marriage, renounces Pauline: 'you would have died for me, you shall live
for your mother!'[89] Fabian is incarcerated in the Bastille thanks to the
machinations of the marchioness; St Luce is also incarcerated (more
comfortably) for getting in a fight. The Bastille is stormed, St Luce escapes
and Fabian is liberated. Fabian, by now driven mad with grief, is brought
together with Pauline but fails to know her; yet it is important that she be
acknowledged as his wife, rather than St Luce's, for as an aristocrat her life
is forfeit to the mob. Only as she is about to be shot does Fabian's reason
return, and he sacrifices his life, taking the bullet that was meant for her.

The whole is highly charged, with Fabian as the centre of interest
throughout. In its sustained melodramatic tone; swiftness of pace (it is
terser and punchier than Bridgeman's more prolix version); dramatic
incident (the rising waters on the rocky shore, the storming of the
Bastille and the shooting of Fabian); and clarity of opposition between
the haughty aristocrats and their humbler fellows (the scene in the Bastille,
of comfort versus rags, is explicit), it would have been highly effective.
Fabian is a serious character, with an emotional range – albeit expressed
within the conventions of melodrama – that the black character of this
period is not often endowed with. Nowhere does he lapse into minstrel-
type speech; an achievement in itself for the black character at this time.
With his commanding presence Aldridge no doubt made an excellent
Fabian, and he was sufficiently associated with the play for its publishers,
Dicks, perhaps for publicity reasons, to attribute it to him. Although there
are frequent (and, from the context, favourable) mentions of his performances of *The Black Doctor* during 1847 and 1848 in the *Era* in, among other

places, Bath, Dumfries, Norwich, Dover and London (at the Surrey), I have discovered no proper reviews of them.[90]

It is indeed frustrating that this is so, for there are several notices, some fairly detailed, of his 1848 engagement at the Surrey, which, of all the minor theatres, did attract regular press attention. Reading one such notice, it is impossible not to feel for Aldridge. Did he believe himself to have finally broken through the metropolitan barrier to acceptance, after years of short-term, strenuous engagements across the country? Perhaps a climate of opinion in which the Chartist movement, with its emphasis on popular rights, was mobilising for a mass rally on Kennington Common, very close to the Surrey, only a week or two hence, might have emboldened Aldridge to speak out. After an excellent performance as Zanga, one of the radical magazines of the time reported:

Mr. Aldridge was called for, when he came forward and made a pathetic and eloquent address, and stated that 'the twenty years' struggle he had made, was amply repaid by the reception he had that night received, and hoped the prejudice was fast dying away, when one man should be deprived of a hearing on the stage, because his face was of another colour, seeing the black man and the white were both the work of the same Creator,' and which brought down the most deafening applause.[91]

The Chartist breakthrough failed, however, and so did Aldridge's. His engagement at the Surrey (long flagged in the *Era*) did not, in fact, make any fundamental change to his status. His next metropolitan engagement was not until March 1852, at the Britannia. Here, as well as his other roles, he played Fabian, of which the *Theatrical Journal* said simply, 'Mr. Ira Aldridge ... has given us further proofs of his histrionic abilities by his powerful delineation of the Black Doctor, it was an artistic performance, nor did it escape the reward it merited.'[92] *The Black Doctor* appears not to have stayed long in the repertoire; its mode and style, already somewhat dated, would soon have seemed terminally old-fashioned. The class polarities, clearly evidenced in the Bastille scenes, that might have seemed so pertinent in 1848, presumably no longer had the same rallying power in the 1850s. Not long after his Britannia engagement, Aldridge left England for the first of his lengthy and successful continental tours.

Titus Andronicus

The Black Doctor, however, was not the only vehicle that Aldridge used to extend his repertoire and promote an alternative view of black potential and capacities. In Edinburgh, in July 1850, on the last night of his engagement at the Adelphi, was 'performed for the first time it is believed that it has ever been acted in this city, Shakespeare's Tragedy of *Titus Andronicus*, Carefully revised and altered from the original text'.[93] The first London performance was at the Britannia in 1852.[94] Of this ground-breaking adaptation, the *Theatrical Journal* has only this to say: '*Titus Andronicus*, has been produced here for the purpose of giving Mr. Ira Aldridge an opportunity to show his versatility of talent. The tragedy was well acted, and mounted with care and propriety. Mr. Aldridge's person-ation of the Moor was exceedingly clever and effective; his performance was remarkable for energy, tempered by dignity and discretion.'[95]

To present *Titus* at all was a bold undertaking, given the horrors of the original, though Ravenscroft's seventeenth-century adaptation caused many of these to be performed off-stage, rather than on.[96] Ravenscroft also emphasised the role of Aaron and his dramatic death on the rack, in flames, as he refuses to confess. Aldridge's revision must have been of the most drastic kind, for he made Aaron the hero. J. M., writing in *Notes and Queries* twenty years later, recalled it thus: 'In the present century an attempt was made to bring *Titus Andronicus* on the stage. The revolting scenes of necessity were omitted, and the catastrophe changed, so that, excepting the title, Tamora the Queen of the Goths, and some other characters, it had a very small resemblance to the original … The repre-sentation of Aaron was good but the adaptation was ineffectual.'[97]

Another correspondent to *Notes and Queries*, J. J. Sheahan, remembered that 'at least one great scene from a play called *Zaraffa, the Slave King* (written in Dublin for Mr. A –) was imported into it'.[98] The play was 'prepared for the stage by Mr. C. A. Somerset',[99] and a letter from him to Aldridge indicates some of the changes.

I … think you will alter your intentions in not having the child revive at end of Act 3rd when you come to read Act 4, and I have the opinion of a very competent judge here that nothing superior to my Act 4 has been written for many years. In Act 5th you will see to what an unparalleled powerful situation for Aaron the abduction of the child by the spies of Saturninus will lead – I will venture to say that there is not a play on the stage with a more powerful climax: besides with terrific action, incidents which form its ground action, we preserve in a mitigated form one of the greatest features of the original play, and give Shakespeare only divested of the Horrors of the scene – I care not for the Critics, my Answer is, 'Titus Andronicus' as written could not be acted at all – hence the necessity of remodelling the plot entirely – Aaron will grapple the Emperor by the throat and strangle him, but not before he has himself been poisoned at the banquet table –

Can anything be more interesting than the scene between Lavinia and Titus (who is evidently deranged in the original), or more noble than the conduct of

Aaron in my 4th Act – ? and in crowning him King of the Goths we add dignity and importance to his character . . .

Still I repeat – only enable me to come to Edinburgh to recopy and alter the play to your entire satisfaction, and you shall have no reason to regret it.[100]

What this shows is Aldridge's continuing desire to extend the range that was open to him, not only – as he so radically had – by taking on roles that were not racially determined, like Lear, or, at a lesser level, parts in *Valentine and Orson* (1804), *Bertram*, *Rob Roy* (1818) or *The Brigand* (1829), or by taking on the persona of the outcast Jew, as Shylock, but also by extending the repertory of powerful black roles. Indeed, he is reported to have said as much to the reviewer from the *Brighton Herald*:

Mr Ira Aldridge tells us that being as a man of colour limited in his repertoire, he was ambitious of adding *Aaron*, the Moor, to his list of characters, and therefore 'adapted' *Titus Andronicus* for modern representation . . . In point of fact, Mr. Aldridge has constructed a melodrama 'of intense interest,' of which *Aaron* is the hero. The character is a strong one, and not unsuited to his powers.[101]

In taking the archetype of black villainy and turning him into a heroic figure, Aldridge was perhaps doing more than he realised. This is not so much an extension of the range of black roles as the subversion of one of the most enduring black stereotypes, the murderous and evil-natured Moor.

The *Era*, reviewing his performance as Aaron after his *Titus Andronicus* had been revived at the Britannia in April 1857, was complimentary and its account demonstrates the range of emotion and expression that this adaptation had made available to Aldridge. His Aaron was obviously not constrained within the straitjacket that bound most black roles (Othello is the notable exception):

Aaron is elevated into a noble and lofty character . . . Mr. Aldridge's conception of the part . . . is excellent – gentle and impassioned by turns; now, burning with jealousy, as he suspects the honour of the Queen; anon, fierce with rage, as he reflects upon the wrongs which have been done him – the murder of Alarbus and the abduction of his son; and then all tenderness and emotion in the gentler passages with his infant. All these phases of the character Mr. Aldridge delineated with judgment and great force of expression.[102]

At least Aldridge was now being taken seriously by the reviewers – after more than twenty-five years. The *Era* was one of Aldridge's most consistent supporters throughout his career and frequently argued that he should be given more opportunities to perform in London.

ALDRIDGE'S LEGACY

Not until near the end of his career (he died suddenly in 1867) did Aldridge
gain recognition at the more prestigious London venues of the Lyceum
(1858) and the Theatre Royal Haymarket (1865), for his performance as
Othello, a part he had been working on almost without ceasing for nearly
forty years. And, since his Othello did attract more sustained notice from
the reviewers than any of his other roles, it is possible to trace, however
indirectly, the development of certain qualities in it. For example, the
Morning Post had said of his 1833 Othello at Covent Garden that he was
'dignified', his voice 'fine, full, melodious', but that there was 'nothing
sufficiently great or original' in his performance.[103] *The Times* had found
that it was only 'by chance' that his 'drawling and unimpressive' manner
rose to 'a higher strain', in which the reviewer detected 'the elevation of
rant, not the fiery dignity of soul-felt passion'; Aldridge 'wanted spirit and
feeling' and was weak in the third act.[104] Similar complaints were made by
the *Spectator* and the *Athenaeum*, that he did not understand the words he
was saying, that his emphasis was false.[105]

But, by the late 1840s, his Othello is 'a very superior piece of acting, well
considered and well developed; the latter part, where after the death of
Desdemona he becomes conscious of her innocence, his desperation, and the
abandoning of himself to the furies of his mind, were touches of the highest
excellence'.[106] The *Era*, similarly, called him 'very fine in the character':

In Othello he delivers the most difficult passages with a degree of correctness that
surprises the beholder, and, at times, he ascends, to a pourtrayal [*sic*] of the
conflicting passions of the jealous husband in a manner both artistical and
true ... The workings of his mind, and sensations of his heart, were conspicuous
in his swarthy visage, and depicted in his every gesture.[107]

So much for his inexpressive countenance and failure to understand his
lines. In the provinces comment was even more enthusiastic. In 1846 the
Era reprinted a lengthy and laudatory piece on Aldridge from the *Warwick
Advertiser*: his acting was 'consummate', 'impressive beyond ... description' and 'we have seen Edmund Kean, Young, Macready, and other
masters of the art, in the character of Othello'.[108]

By now, Aldridge has begun to win plaudits for the originality of his
conception of Othello. Witness the *Era* again, this time citing a review of
his performance in Devonport:

Mr. Aldridge's Othello was a very superior piece of acting; his readings were good,
his action well-regulated and graceful. In the subdued portions of the tragedy his

gentleness contrasted admirably with the force and power he showed in the more terrible conflicts of passion. In this he was highly original, and when to the merit of originality is added that of judgment, the commendation cannot be mean. We believe he possesses the elements of a great tragedian.[109]

By the time of his next London performances – as Aaron at the Britannia in 1857 and as Othello at the Lyceum in 1858 – he can no longer be ignored or straightforwardly despised by the luminaries of the *Athenaeum* or *The Times*. It is true that neither noticed his performance as Aaron at the Britannia (despite its innovatory quality, which, as we have seen, was highly praised by the *Era*), but the Lyceum was a different matter. Having had to 'subdue' a 'repugnance' to this Othello's 'labial peculiarity' (i.e., his thick lips), the *Athenaeum*'s reviewer is won over, finding that 'not only does the sable artist pronounce our language distinctly and correctly, but with elocutional emphasis and propriety':

One small peculiarity, too, soon subtly indicates itself with remarkable significance. We have before us an Othello, with his hands ungloved, and the fingernails expressively apparent. We begin to perceive the play and action of the hand, and the remarkable assistance which its variety of gestures may give to the meaning; and then to recollect with some surprise that this is an advantage of which Othellos have been in general deprived ... to the critical observer it is wonderful what additional animation this unwonted sign of life gives to the entire man.[110]

Here is not only an acceptance of Aldridge's skill, but a recognition of what he, as a black actor, could bring to the part of Othello. Elsewhere, the reviewer comments (though not uncritically) on the originality of Aldridge's conception and this is one of the most thoughtful and informative reviews that he ever received from that journal. So encouraged was Aldridge by this response that he wrote to the *Athenaeum* from Russia, requesting the journal to mention his progress there.[111] Even *The Times*, that most consistently hostile of organs to Aldridge, while condemning his delivery of the speech to the Senate as that of an 'elocutionist' who does not understand the connection between meaning and gesture and is unable 'to sustain a strong emotion', concedes that 'if his acting throughout had been up to the level of the utter despondency with which he exclaimed, "fool, fool, fool", in the last scene, there would have been little to desire as far as one side of the character is concerned'.[112]

The black theatre historian Errol Hill locates Aldridge as one of those who originated a more naturalistic approach to acting, alongside Charles

Fechter in his 1861 Hamlet. He refers, among other things, to Aldridge's performance as Aaron at the Britannia in 1857, citing the *Era*. For the journal's reviewer:

He rants less than almost any tragedian we know – he makes no vulgar appeal to the gallery . . . he is thoroughly natural, easy, and sensible, albeit he has abundance of *physique* at his command when the exercise of it is required. In a word, he evidently knows what he is at, and there is as little 'fustian' about him as in anyone.[113]

In relation to Aldridge's Othello, however, Hill disputes Madge Kendal's account, in her memoirs, of his pulling her as Desdemona out of bed by her hair and dragging her round the stage before he smothered her. This was in his last major London performance at the Haymarket in 1865. 'So brutal did it seem that the audience hissed the business vociferously.'[114] Hill claims that this ran counter to the nobility which Aldridge would have wanted to inculcate and that the recollection has been confused with a similar piece of business in the popular dramatisation of *Oliver Twist*, in which Bill Sikes dragged Nancy round by her hair. It is not mentioned in the *Athenaeum*'s review, which praised Aldridge's 1865 performance (and the whole production): 'He plays with feeling, intelligence and finish . . . We may claim this black, thick-lipped player as one proof among many that the negro intellect is human, and demands respect as such.'[115] But according to another review, 'In the third act he was pointed and happy; and, as most of Othello's action was novel, the temptation scene had an air of originality seldom realised. Miss Madge Robertson was excellent in Desdemona; and had to undergo some new business in the bed-scene which added to her murder some incidents that were extremely striking.'[116] This would imply that Kendal's memoirs (and she was acting opposite him) were correct. Moreover, in this Aldridge was developing a precedent that was later taken up by the Italian actor Salvini who, according to Marvin Rosenberg was 'one of the theater's greatest Othellos'.[117] Salvini, too, 'drags her [Desdemona] to her feet . . . grasps her neck and head with his left hand, knotting his fingers in her loose hair, as if to break her neck'.[118] Rosenberg acknowledges Aldridge (and even mentions the hair-dragging) but more as a 'novelty' than as an actor who added anything to the interpretation of Othello.

Possibly more with Aldridge than any other actor, it is difficult to gain a true picture of his stature, amid so much biased comment – certainly in the earlier stages of his career many of the English press reviews give the impression, even when favourable, of being somewhat grudging; accounts of enthusiastic audiences sit alongside a certain disparagement. The review of his 1865 performance by the *Athenaeum*, with its assumption that membership of the human race still had to be proved for those with black skin, is a case in point. On, the other hand, a certain hyperbole informs other reviews which, one feels, probably also has to do with the colour of Aldridge's skin; witness the ardent review, quoted earlier, from the *Warwick Advertiser*. One has often to read into and against the grain of the text.

Yet there is one evocative account of a performance by Aldridge which does not have to be read in this way, for it is by the black abolitionist William Wells Brown, himself a former slave, who first visited Britain on a lecture tour between 1849 and 1854 and whose daughters remained here to be educated. Wells Brown became a playwright, novelist and man of letters and met many of England's literati. He describes the scene; it is probably the 1858 performance at the Lyceum:

Though the doors had been open but a short time, when I reached the theatre, the house was soon filled, and among the audience I noticed Sir Edward Bulwer Lytton ... As the time approached for the curtain to rise it was evident that the house was to be jammed. Stuart, the best 'Iago' since the days of Young, in company with 'Roderigo', came upon the stage as soon as the green curtain went up. 'Iago' looked the villain and acted it to the highest conception of the character. The scene is changed, all eyes are turned to the door at the right and thunders of applause greet the appearance of 'Othello'. He seemed to me the best 'Othello' I had ever seen. As 'Iago' began to work upon his feelings the Moor's eyes flashed fire, and, further on in the play, he looked the very demon of despair ... I watched the countenance and every motion of Sir Edward Bulwer Lytton with almost as much interest as I did that of the Moor, and I saw that none appeared better pleased than he.[119]

On his death in 1867, the *Era*'s obituary of Aldridge praised an achievement that it saw as enhancing the 'credit of English literature' and 'the reputation of [our] ... National Poet'.[120] To this, it could be added that Aldridge did so as the perennial outsider from English society; never achieving the position that would have been commensurate with his talents; never achieving anything like a lengthy run with any one company; always on the move; always the 'novelty', never the local 'favourite' of any particular theatre.

What the *Era*'s obituarist could not have envisaged, steeped as he was in a culture that was not only saturated with racial beliefs but in which such beliefs were taking on an ever more 'scientific' authority, was how significant the life of this American-born black artist would be to future generations. Aldridge's example inspired black troupes of players in America. There is an Ira Aldridge theatre at Howard University; a chair is dedicated in his honour at the Shakespeare Memorial theatre in Stratford-upon-Avon; a monument was erected to him in Poland, where he died; there have been innumerable exhibitions in which he has been featured.

But it is not the monuments or museum pieces, valuable as they are, that are the real point. Aldridge's lifelong, arduously won personal achievement can be set alongside those of the great American black liberationists of the period, who fought so perspicaciously and to such purpose against slavery. There are, though, differences. Not only was Aldridge's a fight on the cultural front and so less clearly defined in its focus and target than the political battle against slavery, it was also fought almost entirely alone. One black actor, Morgan Smith, followed him to England in 1866, the year before Aldridge died. James Hewlett of the African theatre may *possibly* have performed once or twice in England in 1824/5 – the period of Aldridge's debut.

So, single-handedly, and with great courage and determination, Aldridge gave the lie to the racist assumptions of English society. He not only struggled to achieve, as a black, the height of fame in one of the most valued and popular cultural arenas but attempted to extend the range available to the black artist. He did much to retain within popular culture that wider vision of the black influenced by the values of the Enlightenment, giving vent to the injustices of slavery while he attempted to extend the emotional repertoire of the black character to include tenderness and gentleness as well as passion and, as Fabian, self-sacrificial love. He did not recognise the fixed and tightly defended barriers that were meant to keep him in his place, hence the vituperation he sometimes met with. In his person and his practice, he challenged a racism that had become endemic but, although he was finally allotted a limited space in the nation's cultural life, could apparently do little to dent that racism – at least as expressed in the middle- and upper-class commentary that is now our main contact with the period. But while comment and reviews can be analysed, the effect on the hearts and minds of ordinary theatregoers who witnessed him at the height of his powers is unquantifiable. On that night in 1858, as Wells Brown records, 'The audience with one impulse rose to its feet amid the wildest enthusiasm. At the end of the third act "Othello" was called before the curtain and received the applause of the delighted multitude.'

Nonetheless, a more powerful cultural tide had swept in. Its beginnings can be seen in the development of the comic black persona that ran in parallel with the earlier stages of Aldridge's career – a persona that, crucially, was derived from the American experience of slavery and that had a substantial and lasting impact on how blacks came to be perceived.

CHAPTER 4

The comic and the grotesque: the American influence

If Ira Aldridge's career can be seen as a fight against ingrained notions of black inferiority, the early years of that career were punctuated by a cruel parody, first promulgated in 1824 by the famous comic actor Charles Mathews, in which he attacked the perceived incongruity of 'black' and 'high culture'. It was a stereotype that continued to linger in various 'comic' guises long after its original perpetrator had died in 1835. Indeed, it could be argued that Mathews's real influence in perpetuating various derogatory images of the black lay nascent until the arrival of Jim Crow and Crow mania from America in 1836. For Crow inaugurated a new trend in English racial attitudes. It was a trend that incorporated a new conception of the black individual as no longer the vengeful African of yesteryear but a comic black American slave, grotesque in appearance, manners and language. Its effect was to render the black as a species apart; it was a conception that quickly rooted itself into popular culture and continued to grow there.

It was, I argue, the influence from America, which Crow crystallised and focused, that altered the tendency of English racial attitudes and beliefs, channelling them in new ways. This was achieved through the medium of comedy – far more effective, because more insinuating, for inculcating a world view than any amount of high seriousness. However far the descendants of Othello and Oroonoko might have become degraded from their originals, a link, albeit often of the most tenuous kind, can still be traced back to them; some connection with a general humanity. They are still informed by an English perception of the enslaved African; a perception born out of commercial slavetrading and slaveholding, yet where those back home rarely witnessed the visceral terror of slavery. It was a perception in which lay buried a deep moral unease which expressed itself in the philanthropic stereotype of the suffering, pitiful claimant on white humanity, the noble slave, the unbridled child of nature – or the inhuman monster. But whatever it was, it was not, for the most part, based, except initially, on a direct, domestic relationship. In that sense, there was not so pressing an intimate, psychological necessity for individuals to justify themselves personally in terms of their activities *vis à vis* black enslavement. Both the practice of slavery and the attempt to justify it in moral terms were held at one remove; hence slavery could be the more easily condemned, or its philosophical justification more readily contested, by the conception of a universal humanity. In America, however, slavery was a domestic issue, imbricated in the very fabric of this new nation rough-hewing itself out of Native American dispossession and black enslavement, even as it proclaimed the fundamental freedom and equality of man as the nation's founding principle. Here the racism really *was* personal, as well as structural – there was so much more at stake – and was that much more pointedly vicious because of it. The black slave in your field or your kitchen had to be imaged as a total grotesque, nonhuman, not just an inferior being.

Increasingly, America had come to exercise a certain fascination over the English mind, as it expanded its commerce and trade, and territory. It offered such contrasts – the new against the old, the republic against the monarchy, a people's militia against the soldiers of the Crown. Then there was its vastness, its hectic flux of competing values and experiences, the cultural and linguistic backgrounds of its immigrant inhabitants – and it had, in the Anglo-American War (1812–15), sometimes known as the Second War of Independence, even won *naval* battles against the greatest naval power of all.[1] All of which combined to attract, repel and seize fast hold of the English literary imagination. Harriet Martineau, Frances Trollope and Frederick Marryat all visited America and published accounts of their impressions in the ten years or so before Dickens followed suit in 1842. The 'memoirs' of made-up characters such as Sam Slick of Slickville (the production of a right-wing American judge) with his homespun philosophy and humour were published and widely quoted.[2] In the 1830s American actors such as George Hill portrayed such characters on the English stage with much popular success. Much contemporary journalism and commentary on America portrayed it in terms of comic stereotypes: the roads, the manners, the food, the lodgings – and those who inhabited them, the alarmingly boastful backwoodsman, the calculating Yankee, the stolid Dutch American.

These were all among the stereotypes of the American character, including, notably, the risible black, popularised by Mathews.[3] But even by the time of Mathews's first American entertainments (1824), much of the material he dealt in was overfamiliar to his audience, as this review from *The Times* of his performance makes clear:

The fact is, that the very stories which have excited curiosity as to America, have, in a great degree, used up the means of administering to its gratification. The points to be laid hold of were so broad, and we have had tourists in such abundance, that they have almost all been described and caricatured into the bargain already. Coarse meats, and coarser manners; short commons, and no bows; we have had in print, over, and over, and over again.[4]

What was new, however, was 'the negro theatre' which Mathews incorporated into his act.

CHARLES MATHEWS

The most popular comic actor of his day, Mathews was famed not so much for his ability as an actor and mimic as for the skill with which he persuaded his audiences that he *was* the incarnation of each (wildly varying) character presented to them. As well as playing in conventional drama, he also performed in a series of 'At Homes', one-man shows in which he impersonated a series of characters, the whole woven into a single story and ending usually with a 'monopolylogue' – with all the characters conducting a dialogue through the medium of Mathews alone. In 1822–3 he visited America, where he not only performed but also built up his source material, recording scraps of speech and turns of phrase. After disparaging America generally, in his letters home, as a source of comedy for its 'universal sameness' – 'It will require all your ingenuity, all your fancy (and more than ever I possessed) to find real materials in this country for a humorous entertainment' – he went on, nevertheless, to assert, 'I shall be rich in black fun. I have studied their broken English carefully. It is pronounced the real thing, even by the Yankees. It is a pity that I dare not touch upon a preacher . . . I have a specimen from life, which is relished highly in private.'[5]

Here Mathews concocted a travesty of a black sermon – the preacher's main concern is getting his 'wordy bredren' to put more money into 'de plate dan de white meetum houses', and so on. This has been accepted fairly uncritically as based on Mathews's acute ear and direct experience of the type of oration in question. However, as Sam Dennison argues:

[It] strains the imagination to consider this . . . authentic . . . By his own testimony, Mathews was unable to pierce the surface of any American characteristic . . . One who could not condescend to frequent the porterhouses would hardly extend

5 Charles Mathews's American characters, including Agamemnon courtesy of V&A Images/Theatre Museum

himself even further down the social scale to mix with blacks ... His memoirs, so detailed in other respects, does [*sic*] not, in fact, mention a single instance of a visit to a black church.[6]

Dennison goes on to demonstrate how the so-called black dialect of Mathews's sermon has more in common with the version of English that would be spoken by an Italian immigrant, with one or two German and possibly Native American features. The preacher did not make it into Mathews's entertainment – that would have been far too disrespectful of religion – but two other black characters did: Agamemnon, a lazy fat runaway slave, and an ignorant but self-important actor. It was the latter parody that was used as a stick with which to beat Aldridge, though there is no evidence that it was based, however remotely, on any performance he might have given while still in New York. Here is an account from *The London Mathews*:

Mr Mathews next informs us that he went to a theatre called the Niggers' (or Negroes') theatre, where he beholds a black tragedian in the character of Hamlet; and just enters as he is proceeding with the speech, 'To be, or not to be? That is the question; whether it is nobler in *de* mind to suffer, or tak' up arms against a sea of trouble, and by *opposum* end 'em.' No sooner was the word *opposum* out of his mouth, than the audience burst forth, in one general cry, '*Opossum! opossum! opossum!*' and the tragedian came forward and informed them, that he would sing their favourite melody with him greatest pleasure; when, to please his audience, he gave them '*Opossum up a gum-tree.*'

When he had finished his song he walked up the stage, and when he got up the stage he soon came strutting down with, 'Now is the winter of our discontent made glorious summer by the sun of York;' upon which a person in the boxes exclaimed, 'You should play Hamlet, and not King Richard.' 'Yes! yes!' says the man in black; 'but I just thought of New York then, and I couldn't help talking about it.'[7]

In another, possibly later, version, the humour is grosser and more heavy-handed. 'Hubble bubble' substitutes for 'trouble'; 'Opposum up a gum-tree' is described as 'the national air, or sort of "God Save the King" of the Negroes'; the black actor is referred to as 'the Kentucky Roscius'; this 'versatile genius' struts 'with one arm akimbo, and the other spouting out in front, just for all the world like a black teapot'; and Shakespeare's lines are rendered 'Now is de winter of our discontent made de glorious summer by de sun of New York.' And the tragedian refers to himself as 'him', a convention that became *de rigueur* for the comic black.[8]

The fruits of Mathews's trip were first presented to the London public at the English Opera House, on 25 March 1824, as *A Trip to America*; it was 'received with the warmest applause from all quarters of the theatre'.[9] The runaway Agamemnon made an appearance, as did the black tragedian. According to *The Mirror of the Stage*, this 'specimen of negro tragedy' exceeded his other representations.[10] The character types to which Mathews gave flesh and voice had a continuing life in popular theatre. For example, *Monsieur Mallét (or, my Daughter's Letter)*, by W. T. Moncrieff, first played at the Adelphi on 22 January 1829, is a direct spin-off from one of the sketches in *A Trip to America*. Included in the cast of characters is 'Oroonoko, a Negro. Loves acting and misquotes Shakespeare in the vein of Mathews' Negro tragedian, all in Negro dialect'.[11] Given how closely the characters echo those in the 'At Homes' (even Mrs Bradish's boarding house is there), it is probable that the page of closely printed monologue given to Oroonoko, in which he acts out a performance of 'Romo and Jewlet' at 'de African play-house', welcomes the audience, breaks into song and dance as (in)appropriate and then has to flee because he sees his master enter, was based closely on Mathews's live performances, and reflects his manic energy.[12] All the humour lies in Oroonoko's pretentious, energetic stupidity and misuse of language. Frederick H. Yates, as Oroonoko, was praised by *The Times*: 'This is one of the most amusing parts in the play, and its original pleasantry lost nothing by the performance of Mr Yates.'[13] But, popular and oft repeated as his 'At Homes' were (Mathews continued to perform his American characters almost until his death in 1835), they did not spark the long-lived craze for 'black fun' that was to follow. That was set off by the American actor and comedian T. D. Rice at the Surrey in July 1836.

BLACKFACE PERFORMANCE

Blackface performance is generally held to have emerged in America in the late 1820s (though W. T. Lhamon cites an earlier period of origin), at a period of growing racial polarisation.[14] Slave insurrections, the nightmare of the slaveowner surrounded by a large and hostile population, had begun to increase in intensity and frequency. Denmark Vesey, a free black who identified completely with his enslaved brethren, led a secessionist religious movement that, under the relentless suppression of the white authorities, became, in 1822, a planned wide-scale revolt across South Carolina. The planning and organisational skill that led to hundreds being recruited for the uprising proved its undoing, and the plot was uncovered. On the day Vesey was executed in Charleston, another attempt at insurrection was made that had to be contained by troops.[15] In Alabama, fugitives were organising and arming themselves in the swamps in 1827 until the fort they were in the process of building was attacked and captured by whites.[16] Then in Virginia in 1831 came the insurrection led by Nat Turner, in which the insurgents, after killing the plantation owners, aimed to capture a cache of arms; heavily outgunned by the white militia, the rebels were rapidly and bloodily defeated. Turner was eventually captured and hanged, but not before another planned insurrection in North Carolina and the threat of the formation of a servile army of thousands.[17]

The rapid growth in the popularity of blackface minstrelsy was, perhaps, a way of containing, defusing and rendering safe this volatile and dangerous presence. It can also be seen, at least in its early stages, as a way of tapping into (even if by grossly distorting) vigorous African musical and dance traditions that had survived the middle passage.[18] Much of the more recent commentary[19] has seen early blackface performance as a kind of sympathetic bonding between the lowest stratum of a white working-class which had not yet been fully racialised into a belief in its complete superiority and an urban black population which was, in some northern states, becoming free through Manumission Acts. There is no doubt, however, that, as it developed, blackface performance became more rigidly racist in its portrayal of the black. And indeed, the very concept of white assumption of the guise of blackness, in comical fashion and for comic purposes, whatever lip service was said to have been paid thereby to black cultural practices, represents in itself yet another violation, another mockery of an already violated people; they were good for a laugh as well as good for labour, and exploitation could take many forms.

I see the assumption of the black mask, to reveal the comical and grotesque buffoon that animated it, as one response to the threat posed by the presence of so large and alienated a black population; a way of laughing off, and so making safe, the black bogeyman. It also created a forum in which the boundaries of what was said or enacted could be drawn far more loosely than would have been the case for the same performer in *propria persona*: under the mask he could safely take on some of those dangerous and despised attributes of the black; he could go slumming. Alexander Saxton has argued persuasively that blackface minstrelsy 'propagandized metaphorically the alliance of urban working people with the planter interest in the South', even as the shows operated as a kind of 'underground theatre in which the blackface convention rendered permissible topics that were difficult to handle explicitly on the Victorian stage or in print'.[20] But, whatever the balance between black and white represented in the very earliest days of blackface performance, whatever the relationship between, in Eric Lott's phrase, 'love and theft', no comparable subtlety of interpretation can be posited for its effect on racial attitudes in England. There was no equivalent real black slave presence against which to set the image that was presented; no widespread strain of authentically different black cultural practice that would have shocked, fascinated and enticed. The black presence in England at the time was much, much smaller and more completely absorbed into the lowest strata of English society.[21]

Blackface performance and the development of the Jim Crow persona are indelibly associated with T. D. Rice, who specialised in comic song and dance. Born into a poor working-class family in 1808, he entered the theatre world as a supernumerary at the Park theatre, New York, and then, in his late teens, became a member of Drake's touring company whose circuit included Pittsburgh, Cincinnati, Louisville and Lexington. The exact date of the first Jim Crow performance is contested, though it was probably sometime in 1828 or 1829.[22] One version of the legend has it that Rice, then aged about twenty, based his Jim Crow song and dance routine on an imitation of a crippled and deformed black ostler he had seen, crooning to himself and doing an odd shuffling dance as he worked. At the end of each verse, to the refrain of 'Wheel about, turn about,/Do jis so,/An 'ebery time I wheel about/I jump Jim Crow', the man would give 'a peculiar step, "rocking de heel"'.[23] Another version has it that Rice copied it – and took the clothes – from a black steamship porter, Jim Cuff. Cuff was kept, half-naked in the wings, waiting for his costume to be returned, while Rice took encore after encore, until, able to bear it no longer, he rushed on stage: 'Massa Rice, Massa Rice, gi' me nigga's hat, – nigga's coat, – nigga's shoes, – gi' me nigga's tings! . . . STEAMBOAT'S COMING!'[24] All highly droll, but according to Lhamon both stories miss (or rather falsify) the point – that Jim Crow originated not from any one source, but from a trickster figure, 'a black folk pattern glimpsed here and absorbed there'; he argues that the myths of origin later imposed on Crow reflect a middle-class appropriation of an early, complex and culturally subversive identification of lower-class whites with the black.[25] Certainly both stories, in attesting to the supposed authenticity of Rice's representation, frame that authenticity in a highly specific way. It is an authenticity that is derived from a deformed geriatric or a half-naked buffoon. Even when a black provenance is necessary, it has to retain a derisory quality; it has to be held at arm's length.

Jim Crow swept American audiences by storm. While the songs (and this is very much a generalisation, for they proliferated rapidly, using scraps of nonsense verse, folk song, occasional topical references, and the like, and

6 **T. D. Rice as himself and as Jim Crow** courtesy of V&A Images/Theatre Museum

drew their music from old world airs as well, perhaps, as slave songs) reflected a happy-go lucky, witless character with few cares and an eye for the ladies, the dance routines that were developed are believed to represent more genuine African-derived survivals.[26] Dennison, who has analysed the Jim Crow songs extensively, shows how '"Jim Crow" symbolizes white attitudes towards the black in the late 1820s. "Jim Crow" describes himself in terms which point up, always pejoratively, his insolence and blustering . . . In the main [the songs] . . . show the degree to which whites had removed themselves from the actual condition of black life in existence during the period.'[27]

In 1836 Rice brought Jim Crow to England.

<h2 style="text-align:center">CROW MANIA</h2>

What was it about Jim Crow that so seized, and held on to, the English popular imagination? Part of the answer must lie in the general cultural climate that was so fascinated by America, so ready to ridicule it in all its manifestations, so ready, too, to triumph as a monarchy that practised liberty over a republic that practised slavery. The figure of the black was, and continued to be, a conduit for English attitudes to America. Crow was a figure to be genially scorned and, on occasion, patronisingly identified with:

Nothing like it was ever before seen or known in England. To use a common phrase, 'it took like wildfire.' The famous dancing mania of the Middle Ages cannot have been a worse epidemic than this was; and the small beggar-boys of the streets . . . drove a flourishing trade by imitating the fashionable comedian of the Adelphi, and 'jumping Jim Crow' in the public thoroughfares by day and by night. It became an indescribable nuisance . . . But, worst phase of all in its unhappy history, its popularity was so great that it became the first of a series, which has lasted . . . until the present day.[28]

Or again:

Rice in due time arrived in England: and from that moment the *crowing* mania spread like wildfire; the king and queen, and all the ministers, danced like mad to it; the butcher sung it as he stuck his mutton, and the baker had a *batch* of it as he drew the rolls; and briefly be it spoken, the great globe itself was for a time lost in one clear delightful transport of Jim Crowism . . . T. D. Rice . . . reigned triumphant.[29]

Jim Crow was one of a number of exotic novelties put on stage by George Davidge at the Surrey and Yates at the Adelphi (a West End theatre, known for its comedy). The Pavilion in London's East End rapidly followed suit.

There were the Bedouin (known to the gallery as 'Bedgown'[30]) Arabs,[31] Bihin the Parisian giant,[32] the amazing dwarf Signor Hervio Nano.[33] Yet none had the staying power of Crow: spoof biographies were rushed into print; politicians were accused of 'wheeling about' and 'turning about' like Jim Crow; cheap editions of Jim Crow songs were brought out; the songs themselves turned up in all sorts of apparently unrelated entertainments;[34] Jim Crow cigars and hats were sold.[35] According to James Dormon, 'A Jim Crow club was formed in London, and at one of its luncheon sessions Rice himself presented the membership with a large picture ... "of various portraits of members of the Club, all representing crows, Jim Crow being in the centre".'[36]

But dwarves and giants had long been the staple of fairs and street entertainments; the troupes of Arab and Native American and Hindu dancers, while imparting a flavour of the exotic and marvellous, still fell into recognisable categories of entertainment and could be equated with the splendours of pantomime. Jim Crow, however, must have been like nothing else that had gone before. This was not a black entertainer like the genuine street performers who played on the fiddle or those who played in army bands.[37]

First of all, there was the weirdness, to English eyes, of the dance. Marshall and Jean Stearns attempt to recreate what this must have been like, quoting here from the scholar Hans Nathan:

While singing the first four measures ... Rice probably moves cautiously along the footlights. In the refrain ... he began to dance ... in windmill fashion, he rolled his body lazily from one side to the other, throwing his weight alternately on the heel of one foot and on the toes of the other. Gradually, he must have turned away from his audience, and, on the words 'jis so,' jumped high up and back into his initial position. While doing all this, he rolled his left hand in a half seductive, half waggishly admonishing manner.[38]

They go on: 'The ... phrase "jis so" simply calls attention to the all-important style – the cramped yet rhythmic circling *before* the jump, which is a syncopated hop in the flat-footed Shuffle manner rather than a jump "high up" as [Hans] Nathan suggests.'[39] Most analyses of Jim Crow's phenomenal success in America attribute it to the dance, rather than the song. This must, indeed, have been what first fascinated English audiences. Perhaps the reaction to Rice's dance can be compared with that of Charles Dickens, some years later, to the great black American dancer Juba. Dickens's dazzling description of Juba's artistry in *American Notes*, of his 'Single shuffle, double shuffle, cut and cross-cut; snapping his fingers, rolling his eyes, turning in his knees, presenting the backs of his legs in front, spinning about on his toes and heels' suggests how inimitable the genuine article was.[40] Rice, by contrast, spawned an imitative craze for Jim Crow that reached, apparently, the highest levels of English society. Even the Duke of Devonshire was said to have had himself taught to "'wheel about and turn about, at his country seat'".[41]

Then there was the grotesquerie of Rice's costume and facial makeup, combined with what purported to be genuine black dialect. In all, Jim Crow combined the shock of the new with, devastatingly, a racially debased presentation of the black from America, couched in the greatest of fun and good humour, and leavened by Rice's physical artistry as a performer. The genuineness of his impersonation was often commented on in the English press, so it must have met some preconceived expectations. Contemporary prints show something of what Rice's 'authenticity' consisted of – a grinning imbecilic image, outlandishly dressed, in a kind of one-legged stance, with one hand raised. The performance is delineated in one of the most interesting of the English Jim Crow-inspired publications of the time, the abolitionist novel *The History of Jim Crow* by John Briggs, which reveals considerable knowledge of the reality of race legislation and racial attitudes in both the North and the South of America.

A heavily ironic, somewhat grandiloquent work, it purports to be Jim Crow's own memoirs, written with the aim of correcting 'the prevalent though erroneous opinion, that the semi-savage representation now so frequent throughout the British dominions and the United States ... is a true picture of Mr. Crow'.[42] In the novel Crow is a skilled and educated man, though born into slavery, who proves himself brave and resourceful and is taken into the service of a benevolent master who travels to England. His master, fond of visiting the Adelphi, agrees to take part in a benefit performance for an actress, Mrs Duncan, and to play the part of Romeo to her Juliet. Crow decides to assist by performing a comic song as an afterpiece. He then adopts a stage persona for his performance that is totally at odds with his own character, but is, he knows, what his white audience expect of a black man. What follows is a closely observed account of a Jim Crow performance that is of particular interest in that it does not follow the usual approbatory line of comment. First comes the description of the costume:

[My stage dress] consisted of an iron roan-coloured Monmouth cap, with a hole on one side that showed some of my hair through it; – a light grey serge frock-coat, out at the elbows, and without buttons ... the cape, cuffs, and mouths of the pockets being soiled with grease and soot; – a brick-coloured cloth waistcoat, with only one button, about midbreast ... a pair of deep blue shorts, without button

events the execution must be exceedingly limited.

"JUBA," AT VAUXHALL GARDENS.

7 **Juba performing in London in 1848** *Illustrated London News* (5 August 1848),
courtesy of Senate House Library, University of London

or any other fastening at the knees, the fronts of the thighs greasy ... and a hole rubbed through ... the right thigh ... a pair of yellow stockings, secured under the shorts so that they might not fall, but hang in folds about my legs.[43]

And so it goes on, to the holes in the shoes and stockings and the plantain string tie.

The performance Briggs describes is so coolly delineated that it reads as an authentic account of how this figure must have appeared when not viewed through the lens of comedy:

When I stuck my left-hand thumb into the arm-hole of my waistcoat on the same side, – moved forward in a sneaking gait, with my right hand held up and fingers spread out, – my knees bent to an angle of fifteen degrees, – and began, 'From old Virginny I come,' there was a general slight moving of bodies on their seats; but when I finished the first verse with a jump, and brought myself into an attitude somewhat like a frog on one foot, by giving the knee that I rested on an angle of about forty degrees, the transport of pleasure was uncontrollable, *and the whole audience of judges gave a hearty clap ... at the rich justice I had done to what they thought a black man ought to be.*[44]

The rest of the novel is taken up with Jim Crow's further exploits, which culminate in his manumission, marriage, retirement to a country estate and assumption of the office of Justice of the Peace. The target of Briggs's scorn here is the white view of the black, as represented by Crow, though this particular aspect of the novel is not remarked upon by the *Athenaeum*'s reviewer, who sees its moral as that 'a good-for-every-thing Black is better than a good-for-nothing White'.[45]

However, by this time, the Jim Crow figure seems to have been accepted as expressing some kind of reality. Shortly before Rice came to London, the editor of a Mississippi newspaper expressed the hope that Rice would 'do something towards opening John Bull's eyes' to 'the real character ... of the race ... by giving a genuine specimen of the "nigger"'.[46] The *Athenaeum*'s reviewer certainly found it so:

Mr Rice, an American actor, has been filling the house for some weeks past, to witness his representation of a Yankee nigger. We are to presume that it is a correct one; and, indeed *it is so utterly unlike any other human being, either black or white, that we can hardly doubt its being like the race, or the individual, it is meant for.*[47]

For *Figaro in London*, Rice was the 'most perfect representative of nigger characters; that is to say, if niggers have any characters at all, which we are inclined very much to doubt'.[48] In other words, the grotesquerie proved the authenticity; the less recognisably human, the more valid the portrayal.

JIM CROW PLAYS

Although 'Nigger minstrelsy', which became an enduring feature of popular entertainment well into the twentieth century, is derived from Rice,
the focus here is on stage performance, rather than minstrelsy's subsequent
development, which has been extensively documented elsewhere.[49] The
vehicles in which Rice appeared (devised by himself) and in which Jim
Crow songs and routines were interspersed were, to begin with, of the
slightest. One of the first he is credited with is *Bone Squash* (Surrey, 9 July
1836), an 'Ethiopian' opera that guys the contemporary elite taste for Italian
opera. It is a thin tale about Bone, a chimney sweep (a 'gemman ob color
what lives wid de sweat ob de chin'[50]) selling himself (cheaply) to the devil
(a Yankee businessman – another stock character) and trying to choose
between his two sweethearts.[51] It is, however, full of movement, song and
dance, playing in its opening chorus with notions of 'Niggers dat do de
White Washing Oh', as well as the obligatory jokes about Warren's blacking. It is characterised by a liveliness of dialogue derived from its obvious
Americanisms and heavy-handed malapropisms illustrating the pretensions of the blacks. Here is a fairly typical sample of dialogue:

Spruce: Well I neber sperienced such condensed weder, de transcending streaks
             ob de bright effulminating sun, pours down upon me like de watery
             element of de shower bath.
Junietta: . . . Oh Mr Pink look at dat man on de corner he actly got a segar in his
             mouth, stop till I put dat down in my journal. Mr Pink how you spell
             segar . . . Tank you I always put down ebery diculous custom ob de white
             folks.[52]

There is here a certain fluidity that within a short space of time would
almost completely disappear. How ridiculous of the absurd Junietta to
term smoking a 'diculous custom ob de white folks' – or is it? But such light
(and infrequent) touches of a mockery that could cut either way soon
vanished.

Bone Squash was followed a couple of months later, in September, by
The Black God of Love, also at the Surrey, in which Rice played a Negro
Cupid and of which 'it would be idle to say anything in commendation or
censure; it is a ridiculous but very laughable travestie [*sic*] mythological
fable'.[53] Apart from the broad and vigorous farce of the piece, the humour
obviously lay in the bizarreness of this black stereotype having anything to
do with matters of the heart: 'The whole merit of this exhibition consists in
the (in its way) inimitable acting of Mr Rice; his representation of an
enamoured negro is in itself sufficient to secure the success of a worse farce

than that of last night.'[54] The entertainment was concluded with four encores of the Jim Crow song and dance.

Further Jim Crow plays included T. Parry's *The Peacock and the Crow* (Adelphi, 3 February 1837)[55] and Rice's own *The Virginia Mummy* (Covent Garden, May 1837).[56] In the latter (which is similar in plot to a one-act farce by W. B. Bernard, also played at the Adelphi, in June 1833),[57] Rice played an obstreperous black waiter, Ginger Blue. Ginger agrees to be disguised as an Egyptian mummy that is to be brought back to life by a wonderful elixir devised by an antiquarian doctor. The ruse is designed to introduce the lover of the doctor's daughter, Captain Rifle, into the house, posing as a merchant. Ginger is a lively mixture of cunning and (sometimes assumed) stupidity:

Captain Rifle: You don't understand me, a mummy is a dead man preserved in spices – put into a coffin, deposited in a tomb, and never moulders away.

Ginger: And do you want to pickle me up in dat way, Child de wedder is too hot, dis ole nigger wouldn't keep from now till Sunday.

Rifle: I only want you to have the appearance of it – to make people think you are a mummy when you are only Ginger Blue.

Ginger: Well did you ebber hear de like? You is to [*sic*] debbily for de nigger.

Rifle: Come along after me to my room, where I will dress and paint you, and give you a lesson to show you how to keep still. . .

Ginger: Massa, put plenty of turpentine wid de white paint so it wont rub off, I like to make em believe I'm white man too.

Rifle: Above all don't breathe loud.

Ginger: I mind dat, for ebery time I gwan to breathe, I put my hand right up to my mouth.[58]

Ginger, it should be said, does have a certain life and vigour – which must have been emphasised when Aldridge, with his great comic flair, played the part – and is by no means as appalling a representation of the American black as some that came later. Nonetheless, he betrays one aspect of the stereotype that was to become increasingly developed – a certain animal quality. All he is bothered with, while in this guise, is eating and drinking whatever he can find, especially whisky. Much of the comedy involving him is physical in the most basic sense. Everyone who comes to see this wonder wants to chop off a bit as a souvenir, to which Ginger responds in kind by biting or kicking. According to Lhamon:

Blue is not a real black servant in a frontier hotel, and was not to be taken as any real black servant by the white working publics to whom Rice played . . . What did people see when they watched Rice perform? Everyone but the most remote yokels saw Jim Crow, Ginger Blue, Bone Squash ... They brought together what his public thought of themselves with taboo behavior they imagined incorporating.[59]

Even for the most unsophisticated publics, Lhamon seems to be saying, these characters reflect a liberatory fantasy of the self that is perceived as quite separate from any interaction in the real world (though he undercuts his argument somewhat by citing instances of audiences who did not realise that blackface minstrels were not blacks and therefore did not have access to the whole complexity of the experience). But even if such sympathetic identification could be argued for America – and surely it overlooks the fact that, by this period, America is already essentially structured as a fully racialised society, whatever the cross-cultural borrowings or pockets of exceptions – how could such an awareness be assumed for an English audience?

While there may well have been uproarious and not unsympathetic delight at the antics of Ginger and his like, an English public would not, in my view, have displayed such a sophisticated awareness. This is not to say that they would necessarily have viewed Rice's act as the literal truth; they were inveterate theatregoers, so they would have known that this was a performance, a heightening of a version of reality. But Rice's creations did not reflect the lives of the audiences at the Surrey or the Adelphi or the Pavilion in any recognisable way. The only touchstones against which to judge them were those attitudes and conceptions, already formed, of the strangeness of America and the inferiority of the black. And the ubiquity of the Jim Crow phenomenon, the continued reiteration of Crow's outlandish attributes, not only cohered, extended and solidified those preconceptions, but also fixed them firmly into place as the only lens through which to see blackness. As Dormon puts it, attempting to account for Rice's phenomenal and ongoing success in his native country: '[U]ntil the Rice emergence the stereotype of the "typical" black was still inchoate and unformulated. The arrival of Jim Crow would do much to fill this void. He was to provide the final ingredient in the total pattern of antiblack prejudice.'[60] Indeed, it is often hard to account for the apparent continuing success of what often seems quite thin material, unless one accepts that it catered to ingrained expectations which flattered the audience, enabling it simultaneously to maintain an easy sense of superiority while indulging in the comic release offered by Crow.

Many of the Jim Crow plays involve some element of disguise – a kind of double masking – the comedy coming from this lively simpleton being decked out, if not as a mummy, then as a wealthy native chieftain who has inherited a country estate (*The Peacock and the Crow*) or as a white heiress (W. L. Rede's *Life in America*).[61] The latter, written for Rice, displays links with Charles Mathews's American caricatures. There is the same galaxy of types, the comic fussy Frenchman (one of Mathews's staples) the self-important Yankee, the calculating Dutchman, the fighting turkey-cock Virginian, the linguistically grandiloquent blacks. Crow, in his patched and torn clothes, distinguishes himself from 'dam ugly black nigger' as a 'Gemman ... not to be sneezed at';[62] he wants to enter 'de holy state of Hemlock'; to ''splain de sediments' of his heart to Sally Snow, for whom he 'hab infection'.[63] If refused, he threatens to 'commit suetside from trumpery arrangement'.[64] For once, the malapropisms show some humour. The play includes the set piece of the grand ball and black procession, held annually on 5 July, with Crow mounted on a white horse to celebrate manumission, or what he and his fellows insist on calling 'Bobolition'. Such annual parades, according to Shane White, had first begun in Boston in 1808, to celebrate the end of the slave trade. 'Bobalition' [*sic*] was a derisive term coined by whites to ridicule blacks both for their language and their love for liberty.[65] The broadest humour of Rede's piece is contained in a scene in which the six-foot-six Crow, heavily veiled, is disguised as the heroine to fool her money-grabbing Virginian suitor.

In this play, as in others devised by English authors, the liberty-loving nature of the English is a frequent refrain. Here it emerges in the person of the Englishman Blenkinsopp, a man utterly susceptible to female charm, including that of the black maid Sally Snow. Out of sheer goodness of heart, Blenkinsopp rescues his former beloved from the mercenary clutches of her wicked uncle and is the means of effecting the freedom, and marriage, of Jim Crow and Sally.

Blenkinsopp: Now I say young fellows cut all your tricks you know – no larking ... after female ebony – and for you Sally if he doesn't make you a good husband complain to me...

Juliette: We'll take you to Old England with us and as a token of 'um good humour on this occasion – we–'ll even now dance at your wedding.[66]

It is Blenkinsopp who fights physically alongside Jim Crow, buys his freedom and officiates at the wedding ceremony of Sally and Crow (performed by jumping over a broomstick). Interestingly, there is even a reference to a mixed-race liaison. Pirouette, the comic French dancing master, meets his estranged wife, Mrs Mangold, in America only to quarrel violently with her – and have her run away with 'nasty Copper Charley'.[67] She is thematically linked to the black characters by her fine airs and misuse of language, and at one point resolves she won't be 'made a nigger slave of'.[68] Quite what remained of the complicated and confusing plot when it was 'judiciously compressed into one act'[69] is uncertain, but the Jim Crow dance remained and probably the spectacular procession, which harks back to pantomime (cf. *Obi, or, Three-fingerd Jack!*).

THE NEW AND THE OLD

Of course, the references to the English love of liberty for all were highly topical. It was only two years since Britain had abolished slavery and the Royal Navy was busy patrolling the seas against slavers of all nations. It was a factor of which Rice/Crow himself was well aware. The lyrics of the Jim Crow song could easily be adapted to any situation and one version, performed at the Surrey, was popular. Entitled 'Jim Crow's trip to France', it voiced the national self-congratulation over slavery. In the style of the old joke, a Yankee, a Frenchman, an Irishman and an Englishman are debating which is the best country. After listening to it all, Crow chips in:

> Now, I says, look here, white folk,
> De country for me,
> Is de country whar de people
> Hab make poor nigga free
> *Wheel about, and turn*
> *about, an do jist so,*
> *Ebery time I wheel about, I jump Jim Crow.*[70]

In Lhamon's view, as well as recognising Britain's role in slavery's abolition, this is also a celebration of the fact that manumission had been achieved in the state of New York even earlier, in 1827.[71] Whether this is so or not, certainly no Surrey audience would have been aware of it, and would have responded to the lines as applying solely to England.

A similar theme emerges in a play written to display Rice's talents by W. H. Oxberry and J. Gann, *Mr. Midshipman Easy!*.[72] The play, based on Marryat's comic novel,[73] can, perhaps, be seen as combining two genres, the familiar tar drama with its celebration of English heroism and the new, 'black' comedy. Here it is the nobility of the young naval lieutenant Jack Easy, with his comical devotion to abstract ideas of liberty, that makes him the natural master of the Rice character, Mephistopheles Faust, or Mesty:

Mesty: Oh massa Easy – I so glad I go wid you ... I tick for 'quality! It tarnation shame, cause I a black man dey tink I not equal! Black heart bad – black face not so. Only tink, massa – I 'blige to boil kettle, and am a prince in my own country! Berry degrading![74]

As is obvious, this speech has it both ways – with lip service paid to equality and Mesty's racial inferiority demonstrated. His name, of course, relies on the age-old notion of the devil as black and his comic potential is doubly ensured by larding his speech with stage Irishisms:

> *Gascoigne*: He is an African by birth, and a prince, he says, brought to America and sold: he learned English in New York, if his English can be so called, for all the emigrant labourers nearly being Irish, he has learned English with the brogue, and from his long stay in America, has a dash of the Yankee . . . Here comes the black anomaly![75]

Mesty is, in fact, an epitome in his antecedents of the stage black. He is drawn quite closely from Marryat's original, where he also has a cartoon-like and 'stagey' quality. On the other hand, the Jack Easy of the novel has more lifelike qualities than are evidenced in the play, perhaps because Marryat is more interested in him and his development than in Mesty. The play itself, with its bizarre and muddled plot ('a mess of improbability and nonsense'[76]) was not particularly successful but is interesting in the amount of agency allowed to Mesty. This is also in Marryat, but Mesty does not take centre stage in the novel to anything like the extent that he does in the play. It is Mesty's ingenuity, bravery and resourcefulness that, in the play, solve all the difficulties that beset Easy. However, most of Rice's Jim Crow characters, as played in England, were strictly under white tutelage and direction.

At some point, Rice returned to America. According to a memoir about him in *Actors by Daylight*,[77] he went back in 1837 after playing in the provinces, but he was certainly appearing in *The Virginia Mummy* in Covent Garden in May 1837, in June 1837 he was in Cork,[78] and in December 1838 he was back at the Adelphi in *Jim Crow in His New Place*, by T. P. Taylor;[79] he appeared at the Adelphi during 1839 and in Liverpool in 1840.[80] Rice spawned a number of imitators – the American comedian Ned Harper[81] and 'the English Jim Crow', Benjamin Dunn. There was even an Irish performer, Bateman, excoriated by the great black abolitionist, Frederick Douglass.[82] But, though fairly successful, none achieved anything like the popularity of Rice himself. What this meant, however, was that even in Rice's absence Jim Crow carried on, through the likes of Harper ('his dance, though destitute of the ease of Rice, is charac-teristic and decidedly clever'[83]) and Dunn.[84] In all the vehicles the Crow character displayed, in different proportions, variations on the same themes – Crow's grossly misplaced airs of superiority to other blacks; his misuse of language and insistence on calling himself a 'gemman', at odds

with his usually tatterdemalion dress and grotesque appearance; his faithfulness to a good master; his mixture of (generally good-hearted) cunning
and stupidity; and the way in which he serves as a foil of the crudest kind to
the white characters. In Taylor's *Jim Crow in His New Place*, for example,
Crow's stupidity is carried to the most tedious lengths since, gaining a
position as a servant, he obeys all orders literally. An order to recruit 'five
hands' to work on the estate, for example, results in Crow hiring two able-
bodied men and one one-armed man; to get some laundry mangled results
in Crow tearing it to pieces, and so on. A cross between a child and a
zoological specimen, and an excuse for boisterous physical farce, Crow
expresses the extremes of the black stereotype, but robbed of any of the
threat that underlay earlier portrayals of enslaved African characters. More
than simply a natural inferior, he is of a different order of beings. This
quality becomes even more pronounced as the character takes on an
independent life in England from the early 1840s onwards.

Nonetheless, while Jim Crow swept almost all before him, there were
still survivals current from the earlier modes of black representation. The
differences can clearly be seen if one compares the Crow character with the
image presented in E. Fitzball's *The Negro of Wapping*,[85] first performed at
the Garrick on 16 April 1838 and while Crow mania was still strong. There
is an echo of *Bone Squash*, in that the first scene opens with builders at work
on scaffolding, only in *Bone* it was a chorus of black painters on the
scaffolding, but that is the only resemblance. In its language, theme and
tone, the play harks back to those earlier treatments of the black avenging
figure. Although Fitzball, a prolific writer for the minor theatres, later
adopted the minstrel figure in his *Uncle Tom* adaptations, here he is still
working in a much earlier mode. The central character Sam is a black
beggarly street sweeper. At first fawning and wheedling, he turns into a
figure of real melodramatic menace, 'all clad in black so as to resemble a
Demon' when he robs and then kills an old miser who had earlier spurned
him.[86] In the course of the struggle, he is interrupted by the miser's
nephew, Philip who, entering

rushes towards him. Sam *recovers the sword . . . and drawing himself up in an attitude
of defence, the lightning through the window gives him an appalling supernatural
appearance . . .*

Philip: What see I? – man or devil?
Sam: (*Pointing with sword*) Begone![87]

It is difficult to imagine Jim Crow ever uttering such a sentiment, even
when translated into a comic register, though at times he will fight doughtily

for a good master. When Sam and his white accomplice are finally cornered, Sam echoes the old, familiar and powerful motive for his hatred:

Sam: ... the African, torn by the hand of cruelty from his native home – dragged
on board a ship, and doomed to labour, till his once proud limbs become
warped and feeble, then left to beg, or rob, or die of famine in a stranger [*sic*]
land, might well be pardoned his disbelief of the white man's sincerity were
it true as heaven![88]

He is even allowed a genuine motive – and final repentance – for his misdeeds:

Sam: ... famine made me desperate – I stole for the first time – one crime led to
another ... by a little charity he [the miser] might have saved himself – and
I – but the negroe's story is told – oh! (*Music – He falls and dies – Picture.*)[89]

It was, declared *Actors by Daylight*, 'a decidedly good melodrama ... [which] afforded much amusement to the holiday people in the East'.[90]

A NEW RACISM?

Sam's links were to the past. His was language that could have been uttered at any point in the previous forty years; it lacked the startling neologisms that the Jim Crow characters perpetrated, as well as the attendant debasement of the black image. Sam was significant enough to be morally culpable. Dangerous as well as inferior, he was still allowed a certain dignity – but he had become increasingly threadbare. He and his history were being overwhelmed by what purported to be a representation of actual black life and mores, not as derived from a semi-mythical Africa, but in a modern, white-dominated society; a representation claiming to be based on observation and truth. Crow, for all his weirdness – or, rather, because of it – represented the future.

No doubt, the sense of a peculiarly American authenticity conferred on the Jim Crow figure was part of its appeal. There was, too, its novelty – the startling figure Crow cut on the stage; the catchy songs with their simple refrains, easily adapted by the performer to different situations; the athletic and imitable dance; the outlandish farce; the scope afforded for verbal humour and malapropisms of the most heavy-handed kind (such humour being a nineteenth-century predilection); the comical portrayal of endemic racial inferiority – inferiority which assumed grandiose airs and to which even the most lowly denizens of the gallery could feel superior; all combined, on occasion, with a sympathetic (but patronising) identification with Crow when he attacked the elite.

These demeaning caricatures, all the more demeaning for being affectionately played and received, were taken by many as a basically accurate portrayal. According to Douglas Lorimer, 'The minstrels appealed to a wide variety of theatre-goers, and provided not only lively music and droll comedy, but gave, at least in the early stages of their development, what the mid-Victorians considered to be a realistic portrayal of Negro life and character in the United States.'[91] Lorimer goes on to cite the belief of Frederick Douglass that the minstrel shows had exacerbated racial intolerance in England.[92] Douglass frequently attacked the practice of blackface performance and, in his abolitionist journal *North Star*, condemned such performers as 'the filthy scum of white society, who have stolen from us a complexion denied to them by nature, in which to make money, and pander to the corrupt taste of their white fellow citizens'.[93] Philip Foner, using unpublished letters written by Douglass on his last visit to England and continental Europe in 1887, summarises his views thus:

The mass of people in England and France were 'sound in their convictions and feelings concerning the colored race.' But the 'leprous distilment of the American prejudice against the Negro' was having its effect in Europe. In part it was caused by 'Ethiopian singers [from America] who disfigure and distort the features of the Negro and burlesque his language and manners in a way to make him appear to thousands as more akin to apes than to men' – a 'mode of warfare ... purely American.'[94]

Sarah Parker Remond, another prominent black abolitionist, would have concurred. R. J. M. Blackett, historian of black abolitionism, cites an article she wrote after the Civil War in which she 'observed that Ethiopian minstrels, those "vulgar men", were like the proslavery British press, deliberately distorting the character of blacks'.[95]

Of course, it is difficult, in all the welter of writing and commentary from early Victorian England, to pinpoint when this change of tone took place, to identify that fresh emphasis that marked this new stage of English racialism. But one can, perhaps, see the influence of American racism in an article on 'Uncle Sam's peculiarities' in the popular *Bentley's Miscellany*, published in 1839. One of a series from a travelogue, it opens by asserting the natural inferiority of black to white – if all the other 'upwards of fifty' anatomical differences were absent, 'the rank odour of a nigger' alone would be quite sufficient 'to place an insuperable bar against the "amalgamation" [interracial union] ... which the blacks, and some eccentric white enthusiasts ... are professing to desire'.[96] Although the article expresses a certain English superiority over American ways – on witnessing a 'drunken nigger' being mercilessly beaten by a mob and 'nearly murdered', the writer

declares, 'no English mob would have used a dog so' – this does not extend
to the general treatment of blacks.[97] To 'amalgamate' the 'two species'
would be 'sacrilegiously to break down the law' of nature.[98] 'I never met an
Englishman, who, after being six months in the States, did not agree that
the plan of treating the blacks as natural inferiors was unavoidable, and that
the amalgamation doctrine is an abomination too hideous ever to be
entertained except by the blacks themselves, and the most degenerate and
frantic of white men.'[99] Where would Oroonoko and Imoinda, or Trudge
and Wowski, have fitted within this frame of reference?

The travelogue continues with what purports to be reported dialogue,
consisting mainly of abuse directed at various blacks on board the boat.
This is the opinion of a Tennessean:

> *TENNESSEE*: ... The licence these niggers have in these infernal free States
> sickens any one from the south. Look at that fellow eating clams.
> You don't see such an ugly nigger as that every day ... There's
> the other, too! Why, sir, I wouldn't give a hundred dollars for both
> of them in one lot. What a broken-winded, spavined pair! What
> a sprawling, lame-handed, loose-jointed pair! Shame on the
> proprietors to have such rascals on board![100]

Several pages of dialogue follow between a merchant and an old black
fruit seller. Although described with some dignity as a 'white-headed,
stout-looking old fellow' with a laugh that 'would not have disgraced ...
Falstaff', none of this dignity is left the fruit seller in the dialogue, in which
he is ridiculed as 'you rum Hottentot nigger you', 'you exaggerated piece
of darkness', 'you woolly tortoise', ' old Flourhead', 'you immortal niggar'
(*sic*), 'you live elephant's leg'.[101] Meanwhile, a 'dandy nigger, technically
termed a "long-tailed blue"' – a description suggestive of nothing so much
as a zoological specimen – is dancing Jim Crow on the deck.[102] This is
followed by a squabbling dialogue between the blacks themselves (Long-
tailed Blue, Caliban and Zip Coon) that demonstrates inferiority and
pretension in equal measure, until the captain intervenes. 'D'ye think
I'm going to turn my boat into a zoological institute, and have nothing
but chattering scratching apes in her?'[103]

All this, expressed in the most coarse and pungent language, gives force
and penetration to what is a racist diatribe under the cover of travel writing.
Jim Crow dances, jokes, songs and terms are a constant reference point
in the *Bentley's* article, binding together this harsh, unmediated racism
with one of the most popular (and long-lived) entertainments. *Bentley's*
expresses a racism which, in its lively intensity and unveiled nature, sounds

a new and striking note in English commentary. And it appears even more starkly when set in the jovial inclusiveness of *Bentley's* brand of entertainment-cum-instruction. If the savagery of 'Uncle Sam's peculiarities' did not feed directly into the Jim Crow craze that swept England in the late 1830s, the grotesqueness of the portrayal of American blacks certainly did, as becomes clear when the image's subsequent development, at the hands of English dramatists, is examined.

CHAPTER 5

The consolidation of the black grotesque

By the late 1830s, popular racial commentary on the character and abilities of the black had undergone a major shift in tone; a shift that had long been prepared for through the medium of comedy, Charles Mathews's 'black fun'. It may seem somewhat arbitrary to distinguish between the impact of T. D. Rice in the late 1830s and the further development, in the 1840s, of the type of black image he popularised, but it is, I think, necessary for an understanding of how the black stereotype developed. Rice's conception of the black may have been some distance from reality, but those that followed were even more remote and more pernicious. Overall, one can trace in the England of the 1840s a greater expansion of the notion of the grotesqueness of the black figure. Expansion is the right word, for this image oozed out of minstrelsy to fill almost every gap in which the black dramatic character functioned. This was especially so in relation to the black woman, who now came under attack for her bizarre mimicry of every quality that defined proper womanhood.

Rice himself made his last appearance in England at the Adelphi in Edward Stirling's *Yankee Notes for English Circulation*, which was set in a New York hotel, à la Charles Mathews.[1] Dickens's account of his travels in America, *American Notes*, had appeared some three months before, but though Stirling's title seems to attempt to capitalise on this, there is no echo of *American Notes* except in the drinks that are called for (mint julep, cobblers sherry, gin sling) and a speech at the end where the Rice character, Julius Caesar Washington Hickory Dick, threatens, "Em go upon a grand tower to England, make a book maself, and tell about de white trash in dis country like Massa Boz and Missee Trollops.'[2]

Yankee Notes is in fact the same collection of caricatures already familiar. Hickory is the general factotum of the hotel and his sweetheart, Miss Zip Coon, serves in the bar. Hickory declares himself 'no common niger' (*sic*) – 'em a prince in his own country'; the girls all 'fall in lub wid me ... yah! yah! de poor tings can't help themselves – dese fine legs win dere hearts'.[3]

He goes mad with jealousy when two of the male guests start making free with Zip Coon in front of him. In this there are deliberate echoes of Mathews's absurd black tragedian; Hickory is a grossly parodic amalgam of Hamlet and Othello (with perhaps a hint of Lear thrown in – 'I shall go mad', 'Golley, I'm mad'[4]). 'I'll hab revenge – like de colored gentleman in a play, I'll hab revenge.'[5] Witnessing one attempt to kiss Zip Coon, Hickory *'appears at Door in Front very wild in manner, dress disordered, and hair erect ... he starts and stamps on the ground'*:

Hickory: ... Oh, you white debil! I hab cotched you two times wib da white trash hab I? Golley, ma loife! I hab a mind, like Massa Ot-ello in da *trashedy* to give you a slockdologer.[6]

'Look on dat ugly picter – den look ob dis,' he tells her, dragging her to the wing and pointing to his own face. Hickory's passion is uncontrollable – in that lies the comedy of the piece; the juxtaposition of such irrepressible and absurd self-importance with the grand passions of love and jealousy:

Hickory: No, Miss Coon – 'em requires no expl-a-ni-cum-shi-cum – it is too dam bad! (*She follows him.*) Stand ob 'ooman ... I am all red-hot, and shall burn your fingers! Kiss a white boss! Oh, I shall ashsasinwate maself.[7]

'[C]hock full of gunpowder', he threatens violent revenge against his tormentors – planning to 'hide in da passage – run up against 'em and squeedge 'em flat in da dark'.[8] The denouement to a series of confusing and complicated events comes when Hickory (who is now attempting to impersonate a white major and run off with his sweetheart in order to wound Zip Coon's heart fatally) has to hide himself by standing on a pedestal in place of a statue of George Washington (who, of course, could never tell a lie).

It is noticeable that the 'markers' of black speech among Jim Crow characters have become even more confused. From, in the early stages, calling themselves 'me', they move to designating themselves as 'him' and, on occasion, as ''em' – a variant of 'them' and used variously for me, him, you. While 'me' may be a valid dialect usage, by the time ''em' is in play, the effect is to suggest near imbecility. There is, too, the all-purpose syllable 'cum' which is increasingly used and is inserted into any word of three syllables or more to suggest ignorance and pomposity in equal measure. Rice was praised by *The Times* for his performance as 'the most perfect representation of the emancipated negro of the United States that can be imagined' – demonstrating the continuing belief, frequent in English commentary, that there was some reality in Rice's depiction.[9]

Rice's last season ended in January 1843 – coincidentally, the same year in which the restrictions were lifted on minor theatres playing 'legitimate' or spoken drama. It was followed not long after by the arrival of the Virginia Minstrels, one of the most famous of such troupes and the first to visit England. They performed at the Adelphi for a month, from 19 June.[10] Whereas Rice's blackface theatrical entertainments had, in America, been a crucial factor in the development of 'nigger minstrelsy', in England the obverse happened, with the themes and images suggested by visiting minstrel troupes from America all proving grist to the jobbing dramatist's mill. As American minstrelsy initially fed off Rice's theatrical productions, so writers such as the prolific 'theatrical opportunist'[11] Stirling were inspired – if that is the right word – by the performances of minstrel troupes. Although it is not possible to include here an account of the course of minstrelsy itself, it is worth noting the type of image that the Virginia Minstrels presented of the American black. It was, by and large, one which fed straight into the latest variant of the stereotype, despite their use (much debated by scholars) of certain debased elements of African American culture.[12] R. C. Toll describes their impact in America; in Britain they must have been seen as a further exaggeration of the already exaggerated Jim Crow:

The Virginia Minstrels combined the raucous qualities of the frontier with what audiences believed were Negro song, dance, dialect, and humor and presented them with a vitality, exuberance, and rapid-fire pace previously unknown on the American stage . . . They burst on stage in makeup which gave the impression of huge eyes and gaping mouths. They dressed in ill-fitting, patchwork clothes, and spoke in heavy 'nigger' dialects. Once on stage, they could not stay still for an instant. Even while sitting, they contorted their bodies, cocked their heads, rolled their eyes, and twisted their outstretched legs. When the music began, they exploded in a frenzy of grotesque and eccentric movements.[13]

By the mid-1840s, the music, the jokes, the image had become omnipresent. In the view of the journalist Charles Mackay, the worst thing about the Jim Crow song and dance routine was the way it spawned imitations 'to disgust and plague the real lovers of music'.

The thing must have been in vigorous existence from 1836 to 1841, when two or three competitors of a similar kind, but somewhat better in quality, began to struggle for a . . . hearing. These were 'Old Dan Tucker,' who was always told to get out of the way . . . 'Buffalo Gals,' who were entreated to . . . dance by the light of the moon; and 'Sailing down the River on the Ohio.'[14]

When Fanny Kemble appeared on the Liverpool stage as Lady Teazle in *School for Scandal* in March 1847, she brought the house down by making her entrance (as stage directions prompted) 'humming an air of the period' – nothing other than 'Oh! Hi! Ho! de boatmen row – /Going down de Ohio!'.[15] That perennial favourite *The Wood Demon* was updated (in April 1844 and again in April 1847 as a burlesque) to include a troupe of minstrels, including Bones, Ginger Blue and Dandy Jem, pressed into service to celebrate Count Hardandcute's feast day:

Picklewitz: ... I've made an acquisition
        That beats Tussaud's magnificent addition.
        The Holstein Ethiopian Serenaders,
        A fresh detachment of those black invaders.[16]

This was after the Ethiopian Serenaders, an immensely popular troupe, had come to England in 1846 and catalysed the next mini-boom in stage mock blackery. Unlike the Virginia Minstrels, the Serenaders veered more to the refined and sentimental in their music, and were criticised for it after their return to America, where 'the *Spirit of the Times* warned them that they were too elegant and sedate in their formal wear and their musical manner to compete with the humor of the Christys [another minstrel troupe] who "accomplish what is the legitimate object of their costume and colored faces, namely the personation of the witty Negro"'.[17]

Little of this refinement seems to have filtered through into English stage portrayals, but it may well have made minstrel musical entertainments acceptable to a wider range of the English public, including those respectable religious elements for whom the theatre was of dubious morality.[18] In this the more refined minstrel shows may have acted as a conduit for the

THE ETHIOPIAN SERENADERS.

8 **The Ethiopian Serenaders** *Illustrated London News* (24 January 1846), courtesy of Senate House Library, University of London

greater acceptance of the more grotesque images. *Douglas Jerrold's Weekly Newspaper* commented wrily on the widespread taste for such minstrel refinement and its effect: 'If the patronage of *blackened* songsters increases at its present rate – to meet the taste of the town, Grisi, Mario, Lablache, and Fornasari, must bedaub themselves with burnt cork.'[19]

Yet it was the grotesque that increasingly dominated, and reached into new areas that had hitherto remained, if not untouched, at least unreconstructed for the latest taste. Even as Ira Aldridge was acting the lead, as Fabian, in the serious, if intensely melodramatic, interracial love story *The Black Doctor* (1846), an image of the black woman was being developed that was as bizarre as anything Jim Crow had presented for the black man.

DINAH AND HER SISTERS

Perhaps Jim Crow had gone almost as far as he could go; perhaps a new twist to the novelty was needed. Whatever the reason, a number of minstrelsy-based entertainments started to focus on the black woman as a caricature figure of fun. The Ethiopian Serenaders popularised a highly sentimental ballad about a slave girl, 'Lucy Neal', but Lucy's was not the image that, by and large, was featured on stage. Maybe, though, it suggested the idea. In the weird amalgam that is G. D. Pitt's *Toussaint L'Ouverture or the Black Spartacus*, written for the Britannia, a completely extraneous character, Cuffa, is introduced, with her 'beansome babby', solely, it seems, for the purpose of ridiculing her inability to pronounce a long nonsense word that three white comic characters have made up as a name for her baby. As the rest of the play involves the Haitian rebellion and an unlikely (but very noble and properly spoken) Toussaint doing his utmost to save his white master and family from the slave battalions while, at the same time, leading the revolt, this episode seems even less related to the general plot than most such vignettes.[20]

This ridicule is mild, however, compared to that meted out to the black 'Jenny Lind' in A. L. V. Campbell's *More Ethiopians!! or 'Jenny Lind' in New York*, performed at the Grecian in the East End of London on 17 May 1847.[21] An attempt to capitalise on two current crazes – opera singer Lind, the 'Swedish nightingale', had taken audiences by storm – this Jenny Lind 'enchants ... with the bones ... which [performer] will prove the most attractive is yet to be seen'.[22] The plot is of the slightest and involves the usual lovelorn Englishman, Tom Manders, who has pursued his beloved to America (a frequent device in such vehicles) where her father, Alderman Grubbins, has just come into an estate comprising plantations and slaves, whom he immediately intends to set free after a grand ball to celebrate his birthday. It is a compact amalgam of English pride in the bestowal of liberty and good-humoured contempt towards its recipients, with plenty of 'characteristic' dancing and singing. Jenny Lind's garrulousness accounts for much of the dialogue and, although she is initially established as a crucial part of Tom's scheme to forward his suit, she actually plays only a minor part in the plot. What we do get instead is an extended, would-be affectionate mockery of Jenny Lind's pretensions and abilities. First encountered 'shuffling across the stage', she is introduced by Tom to his friend Fred as a curiosity.[23] Fred politely says he is proud to make her acquaintance, to which she responds:

So [illeg.] ought to be Sar – I am no common nigger like dem nigger ou meet ebery day, Sar – I am partikler nigger, berry great faborite ob ebery body, 'trive to please ebery body . . . can sing, Sar, like [illeg.] ebery ting – my name Sar is Jenny Lind, and I can play de bones like noting at all, Sar.[24]

She invites them both to Grubbins's ball, to hear her on the bones – 'we shall 'stonish your ears' – as long as they come properly dressed, in which case she will introduce them to her friends.[25] All this is pretty much par for the course. What is emphasised about Jenny Lind, however, and strikes a newer note, is that she is a complete travesty of any of the qualities or sentiments that were held to be appropriate to womanhood. Whereas earlier comic vehicles might have guyed notions of romance or sentiment between black characters, Jenny Lind is on another plane altogether. Most bizarre is her account of her marriage to 'Jack Slack' and the death of their only child. Such a tale would, in another context, be occasion for an outpouring of melodramatic emotion.

Jenny:	I used to do all I could in de whitey trade, while Jack did de blackey one.
Fred:	In what way?
Jenny:	I was washerwoman, I whiten de clothes, while Jack black de shoes, Sar.
Fred:	Any children?
Jenny (crying):	One piccaniny, Sar, as lubly a babby as ever lived – Curiosity Sar – I've got him in a bottle now, Sar.
Fred:	A what! A bottle.
Jenny:	A bottle, Sar – He war de handsomest crittur eber you see – Him hair war blue – his eyes yellow – I thought Sar, he might be some use – for dere never was noting ever made, but has some use as it grows up – but he war too beautiful to live, Sar, so when de crittur's health was gone, I popp [*sic*] him in a bottle, Sar, and keep him in remembrance of poor Jack Slack, de blacking man.[26]

While it could be argued that this type of image represents a subversion of sentimentality, or a harking back to an older folk humour, in which physical characteristics become grotesquely exaggerated and develop a life of their own, as in traditional clowning, its effect here is to dehumanise Jenny completely. What woman, even a comedy one, keeps her dead baby in a bottle? And what kind of specimen is he, with his blue hair and yellow eyes? Jenny's lack of any feminine attributes is again stressed when she is on stage with Tom's fiancée, purporting to pass on a letter from Tom. The drunken raucous Jenny, swigging from a bottle of rum that she hoicks out of her petticoat – 'a drop of labender water; dat I always use when I go among de niggers' – and singing of her long-lost love, whose 'heel stuck out an inch or two behind his lubly foot' and who taught her to 'blow 'um cloud and smoke a short . . . black pipe' stands in stark and obvious contrast to the gentle and concerned Fanny.[27] Such images were part of the stock-in-trade of many of the comic Jim Crow songs, and no doubt informed this and similar caricatures of the black woman. But the impact of seeing, in the flesh, this gross physical travesty would have been much stronger than the updated folk humour presented in the songs.[28]

That a sophisticated attack on sentimentality was not part of Campbell's intention is obvious, not only from some of the anti-slavery utterances that Grubbins makes, but from the conclusion to the whole piece:

Grubbins: Thanks, thanks friends – tomorrow will be the last day of your slavery! Tomorrow I shall publicly and legally give you all your freedom. (*A general rush takes place of all the niggers, who shout with delight, and cling round his legs – Group – while the band play the chorus of Rule Britannia!*) And now proceed with your sports. (*The ball commences. . .*)[29]

This is the story, of Britain bestowing freedom on grateful slaves to the tune of 'Rule Britannia', that has been told since the end of the eighteenth century.

Only a couple of weeks after this production, a whole bevy of black females featured at the Queen's in *Somebody's in the House with Dinah, or the invitation to the Nigger Ball* (31 May 1847).[30] Again, there is the hit at black self-delusion and self-preening, 'dem white trash . . . not so genteel and delicate as us colored ladies', 'our lubly faces quite fascinutinuate the John Bull Englishers';[31] the usual jealous misunderstandings as Dinah attempts to handle two beaus while looking after another woman's child; and an older black woman, Julia, who is rendered even more bizarrely, since, under emotional stress, she also refers to herself as 'him', in an extension of this all-purpose pronoun's 'black' usage. The effect is to rob her of gender entirely; and if she does not even have this basic characteristic, then how can she be fully human? She is simply, in Dinah's condescending phrase, a 'poor nigger crittur'. That Dinah goes on to add that if Julia 'was only a bit more genteeler I might let my fader marry her',[32] evokes Dinah's unwarranted assumption of gentility more than it humanises Julia. It implies, too, that there is a closer bond between Dinah and Julia than Dinah realises: that Julia is what Dinah will become. Still, even the ugly Julia is suited in the end, accepting the 'jolly old' Corio as her 'chum chum'. 'Oh yes, yes – him [i.e., herself] am not ticklar, as chum chum of any sort am better than none.'[33] This presumably was the most an older black woman could hope for.

The image of the predatory black woman whose sexuality is grotesquely expressed spilt over into plays that were of more serious intent than the entertainments of minstrelsy. One such is Stirling's *The Cabin Boy*, first performed at the Adelphi (9 March 1846). The play, which J. S. Bratton has termed 'an extraordinary piece full of masochistic sexual suggestiveness',[34] perhaps because Madame Celeste in the title role is always being threatened with whipping, revolves around the issue of slavery as experienced by light-skinned and more refined characters and will be discussed more fully in the next chapter. However, one crucial scene involves a black woman, Clara, and mocks, in the most degrading context, her physical appearance and sexual rapacity. A slave sale is taking place. Ballandier, a Parisian dealer, is congratulating himself on having acquired 'A young white slave, for they are all whites in this Island, born into slavery like the blackeys ... I shall introduce her in Paris as foreign produce for home consumption. (*walks round*). A nice figure, and not too much of it, my love!'[35]

A scene of coarse and unpleasant comedy ensues, for the goods are closely veiled:

Bal: 'Clara Claminta Clouts'. That's your name I believe?
Cla: Issa. Oh dearee! (*sighs*).
Bal: I'm your wholesale and retail proprietor.
Cla: Poor Clarry knock down.
Bal: To me – now let me look at your face.
Cla: Me shame, massa (*simpers and laughs*) ...You so berry much too pretty, eh? Oh! (*sighs*) ...
Bal: ...'pon my soul, this is a sensible girl! If she's smitten now, wait till she removes the curtain. I should like another lot at the same price ...
Cla: Oh! oh! massa (*she refuses*) don't.
Bal: I will – I will – give me a kiss, you little dog. (*he casts off the veil, and discovers a very ugly negress. Cla laughs; he stands aghast.*)
Cla: Issa kissa, massa.
Bal: (*running from her, catching up a chair to keep her off*) ... I'll have my money back, it's a fraud, a robbery; I bought a white – you're a black.[36]

He flees, pursued by the now roused Clara. If one compares Clara's response to her white proprietor, and his to her, with the mutual loyalty and loving hearts shown by Trudge and Wowski in *Inkle and Yarico* (1787), one can see how diminished has become the notion of any romance between black and white.

HAVING IT BOTH WAYS

There was, not surprisingly, some reaction against the tide of blackface performance. G. D. Pitt, whose attempt at a serious melodrama on Toussaint L'Ouverture foundered on even greater improbabilities than usual (as well as Cuffa and her baby, it included, in the role of an overseer, a comic Yankee who had formerly blacked up as Jim Crow and was no doubt destined to do so again in the working out of the plot), also wrote a parody of the genre, *The Black Bayaderes, or the Rival Serenaders*, performed at the Britannia (26 April 1847).[37] Pitt managed to have it both ways. The play revolves around a dispute between Alderman Coddle, who prefers 'the bones and banjo of the blacks'[38] and his wife, who prefers opera, while their servants, both male and female, are also smitten by the craze for blackface entertainment. Of course, both men and women end up putting on rival entertainments, under false identities, in what becomes a contest between the Alderman and his wife. Pitt includes a not very funny minstrel-style stump sermon, delivered by one of the 'Negro Nickerbocks':

Now broder dem say there's no good taters in England – but dere is, Dick-Taters and agetaters – de common-tater, and I hope we shall find plenty of speck-taters, Jim Crow come here and built a wigwam for himself, broder blacks, and now him broder blacks come take up dare lodgings to prove dat black is white.[39]

One of the servants, Tancred, combines a passion for the old-style 'black' entertainment and the new. This is how Coddle's manservant, Jim Scrump, describes it:

Jim: ... the girls are all jumping Jim Crow, the Stable Boy is climbing up the Poplars singing 'Possum up a gum tree' and the Footman is 'Sitting on a Rail' all day long; then there's Mr. Tancred Tickle, as we calls our Butler, as is a sort of Jack of all trades, is play mad – has made a play-house over the coach house, and ... he fancies himself, Othello, Zanga, and three-finger'd Jack – till I think he'll go crazed.[40]

Tancred's speech is larded with quotations, particularly from *The Revenge* (1721). Presumably Pitt would have expected some sort of audience recognition for lines such as: 'He struck me, while I tell it do I live' and

'Hear me, tis twice three years since that great man – great let me call him for he conquered me', though it would have been many years since *The Revenge* had been played.[41] In this Pitt exemplifies the long historical memory of popular theatre. To locate the craze for minstrelsy in a continuum like this shows an unexpected and sophisticated awareness of the historical development of the black image on the part of the dramatist, and an expectation that his audience would be sufficiently well versed in that earlier material to respond to it. It is interesting, too, that this play should be performed at the Britannia, which remained the home of traditional melodramas, though these were less and less played elsewhere; the Britannia's more old-fashioned stance suggests a retention, almost by chance, of the residue of earlier dramatic histories.

The whole scenario of *The Black Bayaderes* is mixed in with Coddle's opposition to the marriage of his daughter Caroline with Adolphus Crosby. Crosby speaks for honesty and native talent in the face of this and other foreign onslaughts and, in doing so, becomes the mouthpiece not only for his author but for others disturbed by this trend.

Adolphus: Why is not native talent encouraged in preference to Bedouins – Blacks and other foreign supporters, that have vitiated our good old English taste, and aided by Elephants – Mameluke cavalry, and monster processions – driven tragedy and comedy from our major houses – to seek an humble shelter in the limited means of domestic drama.

Caroline: Yet merit, my dear Adolphus, should be welcomed in whatever guise it appears.

Adolphus: You say truly – whatever guise, for disguise is the order of the day, and impostors abuse a too good-natured public – the old fable of washing the Blackamoor white is now illustrated in the dressing rooms of most of our places of entertainment.[42]

Crosby's critique of foreign performers was picked up in reality the following year, so it must have reflected some underlying public mood, among theatre people at least. In June 1848 (only a few months after the mass Chartist protest at Kennington) occurred the 'Monte Cristo' riot, at Drury Lane (still seen as a national theatre), in protest against its staging of a Parisian company's production of Alexandre Dumas's novel. Jim Davis and Victor Emeljanow, quoting from the *Spectator*, describe '"large placards" being posted everywhere, "which at first looked like new manifestations of Chartism, but on closer inspection they turn[ed] out to be appeals to the British authors and actors, calling upon them to resist the foreign invasion by petition"'.[43] A number of actors were subsequently found guilty of riot and Benjamin Webster, then proprietor of the

Haymarket, petitioned the House of Commons about 'the great hardship' caused by the country's 'being overrun by foreign dramatic performers'.[44]

Not that this stemmed the minstrel tide; it was too popular and, presumably, financially worth while for that, at a time when the theatre was suffering the effects of the financial crisis afflicting the country.[45] Nor was Pitt alone in tackling the 'Ethiopian' theme. A similar idea, though without Crosby's social criticism, informs George Wilson's slight one-act farce, *The Male and Female Serenaders, or Native Talent's Best*, performed at the Royal Albert (8 May 1847).[46] Here it is a troupe of travelling actors needing work who pose as the 'Ethiopians', ousting the 'real' troupe, who burst in too late. The actors have made life somewhat more difficult for themselves by pretending to hail from Pondicherry, the former French-controlled enclave in India. One can only assume that this has been done to extract the maximum amount of comedy from the maximum amount of foreignness. There is the obligatory tilt at slavery – again, just one slight indication of how removed, by now, the whole concept of such 'black' entertainment had become from even the most tenuous connection with reality.

Crosby's criticisms went unheeded at the time, at least by the public, who retained an appetite for 'black fun'. That same year, 1847, also saw Stirling's popular *The Buffalo Girls*, which took, as its *raison d'être*, the famous song (which I remember as still current in the 1950s). This is *Obi* well and truly Jim Crowed. *The Buffalo Girls* is set on a plantation in New Orleans and opens with all the blacks singing, as they work, the first chorus, in praise of the 'good massa' of *Obi* – another historical retention. Here even the master, after threatening them with a whip (because they are happy and he is miserable), flings it down, declaring, 'A man's no man to strike the unfortunate, black or white.'[47] He follows this up by declaring a holiday. There is an uppity black, Mark Anthony Napoleon Alexander Wellington Tom Thumb (as the caricature gets more exaggerated, the names become more grandiose), who pays court to the owner's daughter, and looks thoroughly ridiculous when he does so (the humour lies in his blindness to the gulf between them). He is mortified when she threatens to have him horsewhipped:

Mark: ... Horsewhip a coloured gen'lemans! Me – me dat was stole a piccaninny from home where I was a prince! I'll marry Lucy Neal, and break da white gal's heart into immortal smash! Whip me? Oh, ye immoral gods, my blood is tingling wid de smart – my hair stands up stiff, like da each particular hair ob da fretful porcupine. She said whip! She, dat ma tender soul melted like tallow for. Oh lub! lub! what a riddlecumree you be![48]

Like so many black characters of this period, when thwarted in love, his language echoes that of the absurd black tragedian first called into existence by Charles Mathews. However, Mark Anthony consoles himself with his devoted Lucy, who fell in love with him 'when I seed him jump Jim Crow, and play wid his beautiful bones'. They plan to escape the plantation, along with the other female slaves, aided by a Yankee ship's captain. And where do they plan to go?

Silas: . . . I hope they are the genuine article . . . If they can sing, and will, they'll do tarnation well in London, I calculate. Folks there are running wild for niggers – there's a thunder and lightning sight of money persuaded out of their pockets by this trading. Folks take to it kindlier than to bread stuffs, cow hides, or Pensylvanian [*sic*] bonds. Oh, yes![49]

Just as Crosby in *The Black Bayaderes* commented, though critically, on the fashion for 'Blacks and other foreign supporters', so Stirling draws his audience's attention to a phenomenon in which they are participating and of which *The Buffalo Girls* is a part. Towards the end of the century, Mackay reflected in his memoirs on the fashion of the period for minstrelsy. Writing of the songs around which *The Buffalo Girls* was constructed, he indicated the fashion's disconnection with reality: 'People who would have been very sorry to associate with negroes, acted (musically) as if they themselves had been negroes of the woolliest and blackest kind; and nothing was to be heard but their vulgar jargon, until Mr. Henry Russell, popular vocalist and composer, managed to stem the tide of niggerism in some small degree.'[50]

AFTER CROW, WHAT?

Through Jim Crow and his acolytes, seriousness or depth of content had been emptied from the black figure in popular entertainment. At best a sentimental songster, at worst a grotesque buffoon, he had become commonplace throughout society – Henry Mayhew calculated that there were some fifty 'Ethiopian Serenaders' working the streets of London in the midnineteenth century.[51] No longer uprooted from his homeland, no longer a figure of menace or, however rarely, of potential tragedy, the black figure had become the jolly golly, serving a flattering racial fantasy to his audience. In the characteristically trenchant words of Gilbert Abbot à Beckett (who had done so much to excoriate Ira Aldridge some years earlier):

The old constitution-loving and sentiment-spluttering Stage Nigger is . . . rapidly disappearing from the stage; and we get, in these days, very few of those cutting allusions to the traffic in slaves, and those tender appeals to the equality of the human race, which were the charm of the dramatic negroes of our infancy. The Stage Negro has become a vulgar dancing brute, with a banjo in his hand ... a wretch constantly jumping about, wheeling about, and turning about, but wholly devoid of that solemn admiration for the British Constitution ... which we once used to hear with a feeling of pride at being natives of a land that admitted of so much puffing on the part of our dramatists. The Stage Negro of the present day can only indulge in frivolous allusions to Miss Lucy Long, Coal Black Rose ... or call upon some imaginary individual, of the name of Josey, to Jim along – a process that we are utterly at a loss to form any conception of.[52]

Yet, despite à Beckett's dissection of the 'physical peculiarities' of the stage black, with his different coloured hands, face and legs, he, and now she, is still considered somehow to represent a black reality.

This allusion to reality, or the claim that their performances were derived from original black music, dance, folk humour, and so on, was often adduced by minstrel performers as evidence of their 'authenticity'. A claim originally made by Rice, it was repeated by later exponents of minstrelsy, notably by the American G. W. Moore, 'Bones' of the Christy Minstrels. The Christy Minstrels were one of the most popular troupes in England and in 1865 Moore opened St James's Hall in London, which became one of the best-known minstrel venues. In his account of his career, Moore made much of his quasi-sociological account of the 'black population of the United States'. He saw them as

quite different from the white, in the way they pronounce the English language and also in their actions ... All negroes are very jealous of each other, and you seldom hear them speak well of one of their own colour who is well-to-do in the world ... All blacks are very superstitious and easily frightened ... There are no people under the sun who are so polite to the fair sex ... very fond of gambling ... very fond of dress.[53]

Out of such differences, the kernel of whose (limited) validity is largely attributable to distinctions of status, cultural background and belief (Moore's 'superstition' might well be another man's religion; 'fond of dress' might be the only allowable outlet for self-expression; pronunciation of English would initially have derived from the patois created by different linguistic groups thrown together on the plantation, and would have also developed into a dialect designed for slave to slave communication, not slave to master communication, and so on), an image had been created which was devoid of human depth. Nearly all the 'characteristics' Moore cites are evidenced, in much-exaggerated form, in the plays and entertainments of minstrelsy. Moore concluded his summary, which is far less gross than the actual persona presented on stage, 'no offence is meant towards those who may happen to be of a different colour to myself'. Yet it was what people saw and heard on the stage, not the gloss put on it by minstrelsy's exponents, that influenced their views of what blacks were like. It is significant that when a group of real black ex-slave entertainers made their way to England, in the wake of the minstrel troupes, they fared less well – until they 'blacked up' and exaggerated in the manner of the minstrels.[54]

In the theatre the black character had become so debased a stereotype that it was, by and large, no longer capable of functioning in a serious dramatic vein. So much so that the 'serious view of the Nigger', evidenced in *The Black Doctor* and other French dramas, is 'one that can never enter into an English head'. The weary-sounding reviewer of a French production of *Le Docteur Noir* continued:

Fun and a corked countenance are so inseparably connected in our ideas, that a black man – though, for the sake of form, we admit him to be a brother – can never draw tears other than those of laughter. It was under this difficulty that we laboured when we recently saw 'Le Docteur Noir,' at the French Plays, especially as the St. James's Theatre is hallowed by the reminiscences of the activity of old Joe, and the unwillingness of the Buffalo Gals to come out ... Whenever [the hero] came on, he appeared to us imperfect, without either bones, banjo, tambourine or accordion.[55]

No wonder Aldridge's attempt to retain *The Black Doctor* in his repertoire after 1850 seemed destined to fail. Black equals comic equals Nigger minstrel.[56]

Yet the themes traditionally associated with blackness – slavery and revolt – are powerful dramatic foci. Slavery was still very much an issue of concern, though that concern, in the campaigning sense, had now shifted to the anti-slavery struggle in America; the final official remnant of British colonial slavery, 'apprenticeship', had ended in 1838. Race matters and race theories came increasingly to the fore in a context in which political struggles involving black peoples were understood in terms of biological theories and criteria. In 1845 Robert Knox, one of the major proponents of scientific racism, began travelling the country to give the lectures that became *The Races of Men* (1850), which decreed that 'Race is everything ... civilization depends on it'[57] and which updated Edward Long's polygenist view of man's origins.[58] Long's view of blacks as 'brutish, ignorant, idle, crafty, treacherous' and much else besides, expressed in his *History of Jamaica* (1774), continued to be the basis of much proslavery propaganda.[59] Thomas Carlyle's vituperative masterwork of racist prose, *The Nigger Question*, expressed the quintessence of racist belief, as adumbrated by slaveowners and pro-slavery advocates in the 1830s, and elaborated the *right* of blacks to be compelled to work. After bestialising the freed blacks of the West Indies as sitting 'with their beautiful muzzles up to the ears in pumpkins' and with 'little labour except to the teeth, *which* surely, in those excellent horse-jaws ... will not fail', he continued:

Do I, then, hate the Negro? No; except when the soul is killed out of him, I decidedly like poor Quashee; and find him a pretty kind of man. With a penny-worth of oil, you can make a handsome glossy thing of Quashee ... A swift, supple fellow; a merry-hearted, grinning, dancing, singing, affectionate kind of creature, with a great deal of melody and amenability in his composition ... The black African, alone of wild-men, can live among men civilised. While all manner of Caribs and others pine into annihilation in presence of the pale faces, he ... lives and multiplies, and evidently means to abide among us, if we can find the right regulation for him ... I say, if the Black gentleman is born to be a servant, and ... is useful in God's creation only as a servant, then let him hire not by the month, but by a very much longer term.[60]

It was Carlyle who made the most pungent and brutal expression of racist belief in the endemic inferiority of the black not merely acceptable, but worthy of respect among respectable men.

Moreover, in a decade marked by sharp economic fluctuations, hunger and social unrest among the poor, bad harvests, terrible famine in Ireland and the mass demands of Chartism, slavery as an analogy, as an image of the lot of the English working classes, was a constant reference point.[61] Yet, even as Jim Crow, presenting the happy, sometimes irrepressible, face of the sometime slave, wheeled and jumped and grinned and sang, black freedmen and escaped slaves, fighting for the repeal of slavery in America, were visiting Britain in increasing numbers to put their case and appeal for support at mass meetings across the country.

From the late 1840s to the early 1850s, more black abolitionists visited Britain than at any other period, and a figure with the presence and power of, for example, Frederick Douglass, was lionised at every level of society. And the fugitive former slave William Wells Brown described how he 'had eaten at the same table with Sir Edward Bulwer Lytton, Charles Dickens, Eliza Cook, Alfred Tennyson'.[62] This was perhaps in part a reflection of the continuing fascination with America that had made England such a ready market for Crow and all his works. But there was also a genuine and widespread appreciation of black abolitionists' struggles, attested to, as Blackett has shown, by the large audiences, drawn from both the middle and working classes, that they attracted across the country.[63] This widespread interest may then, at another level, indicate a growing debate and polarisation of views within society at large over issues of slavery, abolition-ism and black capacity.[64] Catherine Hall has demonstrated the ways in which abolitionist sentiment could dovetail with a view of racial hierarchy, even among those white abolitionists most committed to establishing a free and independent black society in the sugar colonies.[65] The decade had opened with the holding of the World Anti-Slavery Congress in London, in 1840; at its close came Carlyle's *Occasional Discourse on the Nigger Question*. As Hall puts it, 'If all England had been abolitionist in 1840, it certainly was not by 1850.'[66] Nancy Stepan has stated that interest in Knox's prophecies of 'a war of race against race' increased after the revolu-tionary outbreaks in Europe of 1848.[67] Although the heyday of scientific theorising on race did not come until the 1860s, one can detect during the 1840s the beginnings of a greater, more conscious elaboration of views and theories on racial issues.[68] Carlyle both marked this process and dramati-cally advanced it.

In many different ways, therefore, slavery pervaded the popular con-sciousness. It was an issue that dramatists continued to tackle. Yet Jim Crow or Quashee no longer had any purchase on the subject; Dinah never had had. All endowed with nothing but comic or animal qualities, how could they feature with emotional complexity or force in any work on the subject that most closely concerned them? In fact, they could not. Even as the black-skinned character was becoming ever more closely confined to the Jim Crow ghetto, the lighter-skinned mulatto was taking on his or her serious dramatic functions. It was for the mulatto now to pick up the baton of protest against slavery. The nature of people of mixed race – perhaps again owing to the influence of America and obsession with degrees of 'black blood' – became in the late 1840s and 1850s a subject of intense interest and concern. Knox had revived the old polygenetic canard, pro-mulgated by Long in the eighteenth century, that 'races' could not inter-breed.[69] The ways in which dramatists worked in this area, and in particular developed the image of the mulatto woman, reveal how black-ness came to be elided from the context of slavery.

CHAPTER 6

Slavery freed from the constraint of blackness

In sum, by the late 1840s serious dramatic intention was scarcely compat-
ible with the black-skinned character, apart from those in the repertoire
of Ira Aldridge. The influence of the comic Jim Crow figure, in all its
manifestations, was pervasive. It chimed well with a growing belief –
apparently evidenced by the continuing economic decline of the sugar
industry in the West Indies, following slavery's abolition, and propagandised by the planter interest – that responsibility and freedom were
incompatible with a black skin. Thomas Carlyle had expressed this most
forcefully, arguing, in effect, for the reintroduction of slavery. The image of
the irresponsible, carefree and indolent black was one that, at the popular
level, the Crow figure reinforced, though never with the level of vitriol that
Carlyle brought to it. The issue of slavery retained currency in other ways –
comparisons between the lot of slaves and the lot of the English working
class were frequently resorted to – and much attention was focused on the
American situation. At the level of cultural expression, the theme of slavery
continued to drag in its wake all those other, multilayered notions of the
Englishness of liberty and freedom. But what was new was the way in
which American quasi-'scientific' notions of race came to be filtered down
to a wider English public through the agency of the theatre.

It is worth recalling that it was not only the abolitionists or the com-
mentators on American mores who made their way across the Atlantic.
Plays, actors and entertainers also travelled between England and America.
Ira Aldridge may have seen Edmund Kean perform in New York; the
English actors James and Henry Wallack, whose stories were linked with
Aldridge's, pursued their careers in New York and built theatres there.[1]
Stephen Price, manager of the Park theatre in New York, who had helped
to get the African theatre there closed down, became lessee of Drury Lane
in the late 1820s. Charles Mathews had used America as source material
and had toured there; T. D. Rice's popularity in England was the subject
of comment in America.[2] However, it was not only Rice's anti-black

stereotyping that made its way to England to impart an extra dimension to already ingrained ideas of black inferiority, but also more subtle elaborations of the racial theme, particularly in relation to the light-skinned or mulatto character.

That character was used both to bear the dramatic burden of slavery and as a conduit for the racial ideas propagated about his and her status. The medium of the drama was one way in which specifically American racial theorising passed, if only tangentially, into English thinking. In a different context Philip D. Curtin has argued that 'In the transatlantic exchange of ideas, Britain gave the anti-slavery crusade to America in the 1830's and received back the American racism of the 1850's.'[3] In plays which deal directly with the American situation, two of which are discussed below, this is evident. Others reflect some correspondences, though the exact derivation of the new ideas they present is hard to determine. Racial thinking on the nature of the mulatto had also developed within the West Indian context, where there was an established practice of concubinage, as well as within the American.[4]

What the emphasis on the mulatto also did, however, was to pave the way for a certain interiority on the part of the mulatto protagonist. Caught between two worlds, the mulatto is forced to reflect on his or her position as marginal in both. The black character, on the other hand, is never marginal in the same way; he or she can never 'pass' – they are simply beyond the pale. This becomes clear in the contrast between the mulatto drama and that which, though contemporary with it, reverts to the time-worn theme of slavery, and liberty as in the English gift.

The process of removing from the black protagonist his traditional authority as a character uniquely qualified to contend against and pronounce upon the evils of slavery began fairly early, and was first hinted at in that most enduring and popular of genres, nautical melodrama. The prolific E. Fitzball who, according to *Figaro*, knew as much about 'real life as a donkey does of the theory of gravitation',[5] nonetheless frequently captured the prevailing froth of popular culture in his output. In his 1836 drama *The Koeuba; or, the Pirate Vessel*, performed at Sadler's Wells and at the Surrey, he broached the threat of slavery to white characters, in a context which specifically excluded the black as involved in the issue at all. The play is a rich mix of pirate drama (under the murderous captain Ali Mahone);[6] reunion of long-lost siblings (one of them reputedly dumb) with each other and their father, the wealthy Diego di Montaldo; and safely concluded romance between Montaldo's niece Isabella and the Scottish officer Donald Maclain.[7] Isabella and Montaldo have embarked on a

Spanish vessel, which is wrecked in a storm. They are saved by an English tar, Mat Maintop, who had taken service with the pirate Mahone on the *Koeuba* in ignorance of its true nature. He braves the raging storm in a jolly-boat to rescue them. Mahone is furious at the rescue, but his anger soon abates when he realises that he now has Montaldo's riches on board.

Mahone, as is the case with many pirate villains, has a 'legion of black slaves'[8] ready to do his bidding, and who serve mainly to amplify his wickedness. His chief black henchman and drinking companion is Ciprus, whose function is somewhat similar to that of Hassan in *The Castle Spectre* (1797). Ciprus offers, for example, to murder one of his crew-mates – 'Speak but the word, captain, and – '. 'My brave and trusty Ciprus!', Mahone responds.[9] The loyal band of slaves, too, though treated with violence by Mahone, show no hesitation in fighting at his behest. In recompense for which they all perish alongside Mahone and Ciprus, when British marines from the frigate *Albion* 'appear on the rock, and fire a volley' at the end of the play.[10]

Stirring nonsense, yes, but what is of interest in the representation of this servile and serviceable black villainy is that it is set, without any aware-ness of contradiction or inconsistency, against two other factors. One is Isabella's singing, while still on board the Spanish vessel and without any prior or subsequent contextual link, a sentimental anti-slavery song:

> Astride o'er the maindeck, oft lash'd by the spray,
> A poor little child of misfortune was seen.
> His worn limbs were cold, and his garments were wet,
> His heart, too, a stranger to comfort or joy;
> And the rain as it dripp'd from his ringlets of jet,
> Sadly mix'd with the tears of the negro boy.
> Poor, poor little negro boy![11]

Yet Mahone's blacks have been completely dissociated from this pathos; they are simply excluded from the catalogue of slavery's evils.

The other factor that denies the slave crew's experience of slavery is the course that Fitzball's plot takes. Part of Mahone's evil design consists of making for the nearest slave coast, once he has relieved Montaldo of his papers and valuables, to dispose of Maintop and the rest 'to the highest bidder'.[12] Maintop exclaims, 'A pirate! – and have I let myself to serve a confounded pirate! – A British sailor to fight under the colours of a scoundrel like this! Sell me for a slave, will he! I think I see myself being sold for one!'[13] Mahone then orders the black slaves – who willingly obey – to load his white captives with slave chains.[14] All this is presented unpro-blematically; shock value lies not in slavery, but in the possibility of trading in whites. It could be argued that the status of the white-skinned Imoinda in Thomas Southerne's *Oroonoko* (1695) is a comment on the enslavement of whites. However, the discussion of slavery and its ills is there mainly the prerogative of Aboan and Oroonoko. Oroonoko's authority and seriousness is not demeaned by Imoinda's European status – rather, it is enhanced. Similarly, Mug, in George Colman's *The Africans* (1809) is a slave. But, here again, the serious issues of the drama are carried forward by the African characters, though Mug has a comic and choric role. The Africans are not belittled or sidelined by his status; the purpose and effect is to add to the indictment of slavetrading as practised against a noble and dignified African people.

It is no coincidence that the transference of the slavery theme to white-skinned characters should be made in nautical drama. This genre more than any other was associated with the concept of liberty; the English tar was often a kind of working-class everyman, a spokesman for individual valour and against oppression. At the same time, he was at the lowest level of the strict naval hierarchy, subject to a captain's tyranny. The linking of class injustice with racial injustice has already been briefly discussed, in relation to *My Poll and my Partner Joe* (1835). Fitzball's *The Koeuba* goes further and, by removing any vestige of humanity from the African slaves, is able to turn the whole notion of racial injustice upside down, effecting a reversal of what had hitherto passed as dramatic 'reality'. Of course, the play is by no means as cerebral and conceptually worked out as that analysis might imply – but this, nonetheless, is the effect of what doubtless suggested itself as a good and exciting (if highly improbable) dramatic 'wheeze'.

THE 'SIGN OF THE BEAST'

More frequent than the enslavement of whites as a theme during the period under discussion is the enslavement and liberation of light-skinned characters. Usually, at least when a serious, moral attack on slavery as an institution is envisaged, these are young and beautiful women, designated as octoroons or quadroons in the status-conscious, spuriously scientific jargon of the day, and often unaware of their slave ancestry. In America, in particular, as justifications for slavery became more elaborate and articulated under the pressure of a militant and many-sided abolitionist movement, pro-slavery racial theorists returned increasingly to the polygenist view of human origins, under which the different races were regarded as different species. Hybrids (that is, those of mixed race) were believed to be sterile. One of the most prominent of these thinkers was Josiah Nott, who, along with Dr George Morton, a leading ethnologist, made the theory more credible by arguing that such hybrids were not sterile outright, but that their fertility would simply decline over time until they died out.[15] That notorious architect and propagandist of scientific racism, Robert Knox, who was lecturing and writing on race from a polygenist perspective in Britain around the same time, concurred: 'cross as you will, the mulatto cannot hold his ground as a mulatto: back the breed will go to one or other of the pure breeds, white or black'.[16]

This was a period, as Curtin has demonstrated, in which the foundations of the later scientific racism were being laid, with the establishment of the Ethnological Society in London in 1843;[17] the growth of phrenology and its transition from an instrument for the analysis of individuals to the analysis of racial groups;[18] the development of the view, propounded most notably by Thomas Arnold in 1841, that certain races were doomed to extinction and that this was now the period of Anglo-Saxon ascendancy.[19] Knox's ideas were taken up, as Curtin has shown, by some of the liberal quarterlies in the early 1850s,[20] and Benjamin Disraeli's famous statement that 'All is race', made in the course of arguing against the wisdom of slave emancipation, was 'Knoxian'.[21] The polygenist view was to retain currency and influence throughout the 1850s and early 1860s, largely through the work of James Hunt, Knox's most significant follower, and the Anthropological Society, until, finally, Charles Darwin rendered it irrelevant, scientifically speaking.[22]

Thus, in relation to the serious drama of slavery of the 1840s and 1850s, two cultural tendencies came together and reinforced each other. On the one hand, the vacuity and imbecility of the black stage character meant that a black protagonist was no longer available to carry the weight of more serious dramas, except to those who, like Aldridge, had their own reasons for swimming against the tide. On the other hand, there was a growing awareness of the significance of the mulatto presence, both in the West Indies and in America. The emancipation of the slaves in the West Indies had drawn attention to the substantial mixed-race populations of the islands and their often ambiguous status.[23] In America the growth of racial theorising in defence of slavery led, as I have said, to the development of polygenist ideas which focused on the mulatto as a degenerate hybrid. The threads of such notions can be traced in the plays; they were what dramatists used to explore their subject, if not deliberately and programmatically, as materials lying ready to hand.

To add to the transcontinental mix, a number of the plays under discussion here are derived from French originals. France, of course, had its own experience of colonisation and slavery to explore and promulgate, and it is a truism that the hard-pressed or fledgling British dramatist would simply adapt from the French.[24] Moreover, the use of a French original possibly allowed the dramatist more licence to explore, if only implicitly, the underlying sexual nature of a transaction in which a young woman may be bought for the gratification of a man. French plays were, indeed, sometimes attacked for their lack of moral fibre – as was *Lugarto the Mulatto* (1850), discussed below. Often, too, the French colonial setting and revolutionary or prerevolutionary timescale are retained – allowing the attack on slavery to be deflected from any consideration of Britain's recent past.

An early example of the genre is B. N. Webster's *The Quadroon Slave* of 1841 – most dramatic quadroons did not really get into their stride until the late 1840s and early 1850s.[25] Although the play is set in Jamaica 'about 1830' (i.e., before the abolition of slavery), it was originally based in Guadeloupe, as is evident from corrections in the manuscript, so it probably derives from a French original. (At times, the manuscript reverts to Guadeloupe, and terms like mamselle are used.) The quadroon of the title is Julie, the beautiful daughter of a mulatto woman and European father, whose past is known only to herself. She ultimately confesses that she had been brought up by a generous mistress who 'gave me a free education, filled my heart with the germs of happiness and independence, overwhelmed me with her favours, forgot but to give me the chief thing of all, liberty . . . [On her death] her will confirmed me in the position in which her generosity had placed me as to means but I was still a slave.'[26]

Julie has escaped a servitude that, for her, would have been far worse than for those accustomed to it and has been helped by a friendly merchant to escape by sea. Washed up on the shores of Jamaica again by a shipwreck, she has been taken in by the wealthy and benevolent Mrs Heartly. Beloved by two men – the hotheaded but ultimately decent Vincent St Georges and the stern upholder of the colonial slave law, Alfred Pelham – she chooses, and marries, Pelham. The spurned St Georges, who has just inherited his own slave estate on the island, is informed by his overseer of Julie's real status, for St Georges is now her 'lawful' owner. He determines to use this knowledge to make Julie elope with him.

There are some unusual aspects to the play; for example, the attack on slavery is developed through the sentimental reeducation of Pelham. As upholder of the colonial law, he refuses a plea for mercy, made by Vincent St Georges and supported by Julie, for a young quadroon slave who has insulted a free woman and been 'sentenced to a cruel and degrading chastisement' (presumably whipping).[27] Pelham's concern is to avert rebellion: 'the yet smoking ruins of the incendiaries in St. Domingo and *their* successes form the theme of conversation among *our* Blacks'.[28] He continues: 'They compel us to use them [coercive measures] – I will yield to no man in an ardent and honest wish to see the state of the slave ameliorated and making them free as ourselves, but the time is not yet come.'[29] Moreover, the owner of the young quadroon slave who is pleading for mercy on her behalf has an undeclared interest. The governing council of the island, of which Pelham is the leader, is not likely to be swayed by the owner's pleas for clemency: 'for I blush for your friend in being obliged to tell you, that the soft blandishments of love and not the cause of humanity makes [*sic*] him feel more strongly for the woman than the slave . . . men are now so lost to shame as to fix their affections on slaves which will in some instances doubtless end in marriage'.[30]

This is an unusually frank avowal, for a dramatist of the period, of the nature of some master-slave relationships.[31] Casual and frequent rape was a constant threat for slave women and the growth of mixed-race populations in slave colonies testified to the massive disjunction between what was practised and what was preached. As the image on stage of the black-skinned man or woman became so robbed of serious content by ever more mindless stereotyping that any use of the slavery issue for dramatic purposes had to turn to mixed-race characters, so they, in their turn, engendered an unspoken but real fascination with the transgressions that had called them into being. Hence the emphasis on the beauty, purity and *desirability* of these young women, on their entrapment in a situation that is not of their own making. For, lovely as they are, they are, in the eyes of many, pollutants.[32] In the words of Henry Hughes, a nineteenth-century pro-slavery theorist from Mississippi, 'Hybridism is heinous. Impurity of races is against the law of nature. Mulattoes are monsters . . . The same law which forbids consanguinous amalgamation forbids ethnical amalgamation. Both are incestuous. Amalgamation is incest.'[33]

While this is a very extreme statement, born out of a far more polarised domestic socio-political situation than pertained in Britain, nonetheless, such subject matter carried with it an aura of the forbidden, of the intimate, shameful secret. Thus marriage to Pelham was, for Julie, 'a happiness that she had no *right* to accept'.[34] Her dilemma before marriage is whether to flee a love that she knows she cannot refuse and, after her marriage, when St Georges is asserting his power over her, whether to tell Pelham the truth. Underlying all the melodramatic language, there is a strong compound of pain, compulsion and desire in the scene between St Georges and Julie.

Her helplessness is what gives the scene an unspoken charge; her moral purity adds to her desirability.

Julie: ...Where is he? I ask of you but this, sir, the name of my master? ...
Vincent: (*kneeling to her*) At thy feet.
Julie: (*with terror*) Ah!
Vincent: Yes, at your feet; your master, who reproaches himself with having caused you one moment's pain, to shed one tear, this master whom you think so implacable is he who now humbles himself before you ... and who implores you to look with favor [*sic*] on his passion.
Julie: Mon dieu! ...
Vincent: Ah! Julie, maddened by your refusal I came to claim you as my slave but feel that in your presence I am thine! ...
Julie: I will not go!
Vincent: Recollect that he who now supplicates can compel you – (*with affection*) Julie, I beseech you, do not, oh do not drive me to exert a power at which my heart revolts ... Julie, come.
Julie: No!
Vincent: Julie! – I will wait until nine for the woman I adore – if at that hour she fail me – Here before all, I will claim my slave.[35]

Pelham, when confronted by St Georges's determination to assert his right of property over Julie – the very rights Pelham had proclaimed on behalf of other slaveowners – does yield to his love for her, accepts her slave origins, and renounces his position as delegate for the colonial council. Julie's attempt to kill herself, rather than bring dishonour to Pelham and their marriage, brings St Georges to his senses. 'I owe you my thanks for having saved me from endless remorse,' he tells Julie, tearing up her slave papers. 'Live, live for him ... In him behold the only master of your destiny.'[36] The abhorrent hierarchy of slavery has been replaced with the familiar hierarchy of patriarchy and male authority; interestingly, the reason that Julie fell in love with Pelham in the first place was that she feared his sternness.

The fascination with the white-skinned slave is also evident in Edward Stirling's *The Cabin Boy*, first performed at the Adelphi in March 1846 and said to be derived from a French play, E. Souvestre's *Le Mousse* (1846).[37] Indeed, Stirling's work exemplifies my theme: black *qua* black characters are to be used for 'fun' and merriment, while more serious topics are the prerogative of the light-skinned or white. Stirling's ridicule of the black woman's sexuality in *The Cabin Boy* has been discussed previously. However, this episode serves not only as minstrel 'comedy', but also as a foil to the plight of Jenny La Roche, a young plantation owner beset with debt after the sudden death of her father and forced to sell up to pay her creditors. Chief among them is Vincent, a wealthy planter whose aim in demanding immediate and total repayment is to get Jenny in his power and force her to marry him – and whose air of menace would have lost nothing in the forbidding O. Smith's portrayal:

Vincent: . . .When I first came to Guadeloupe, I saw and loved you; vainly I
          endeavoured to meet you; your mother refused all my overtures . . . 'twas
          then I determined to buy up all the debts incurred by your father, and
          make myself master of your fortunes . . . I wanted you in my power . . .
          and I have gained my object.[38]

If he cannot buy her in one way, he will buy her in another. Jenny determines to flee the island with her lover; Vincent, hearing of this by worming it out of one of Jenny's most loyal allies, the cabin boy Julien (played by the dazzling and popular Madame Celeste), thwarts her by getting the island's governor to ban her departure as a known debtor. But, as a minor, she cannot be compelled in this way. Vincent demands to see proof, in the form of her birth certificate, which Julien volunteers to fetch from Dominique, crossing a perilous and stormy sea (a 'capital stage effect', *The Times* called it[39]). The sale of Jenny's goods takes place; she says farewell to her slaves; all that remains is for her to leave to join her beloved Henri. But when the certificate is produced, she is more in Vincent's power than ever. There is one more item to sell – Jenny herself, 'the daughter of Monsieur La Roche, and Martha his slave'.[40] In the colony, as had earlier been observed, 'It is not their colour, but their origin makes them black.'[41] Paradoxically, blackness, a highly visible marker for perceived inferiority and low status, can be rendered completely invisible and yet still retain its polluting power. Thematically linked to the would-be comic sale of Clara Clouts by this notion, the auction of Jenny is, by contrast, highly affecting as befits her almost-white status. Jenny takes her place on the stand: 'Then my place is here – I am no longer free. (*lets her shawl drop and stands with* SLAVES; *they weep and kiss her hands*).'[42]

Impassioned pleas for Jenny's freedom – Berthault, her friend and protector offers all his fortune, Julien offers to be enslaved in her stead – fail to move Vincent, who outbids all others. 'No one offers more than the twenty thousand. Monsieur is the owner of the slave.'[43] Vincent will free her, though – on condition that Jenny marry him.

In this way the nature of auctioning human flesh is made apparent through the mode of melodrama. The explicit sexual transaction (Vincent merely seeks his 'pleasure, not the sorrows of others'[44]) is kept within the bounds of decorum only by his insistence on marriage to Jenny. Jenny's dropping of her shawl at the point of sale implies her transition to a piece of property which needs to be clearly seen if it is to be honestly sold; it also implies her disrobing for a master. The *Era* described the scene, in which the devoted Julien tried to comfort a Jenny 'now reduced to the lowest level of human degradation', as the '"ne plus ultra" of truth and feeling'. 'Anything more natural, touching, and pathetic, we never saw; there was not a dry eye in the house.'[45] But it would have been unthinkable to grant Clara or any of the black-skinned slaves such recognition that their human dignity had been betrayed. Fortunately, Jenny is saved from her fate by the timely recognition that Vincent is, in fact, a notorious pirate and wanted criminal. As is common in melodrama, he bears a scar that is the mark of his true identity.

If the sexual power of the would-be slaveowner over the beautiful, apparently white, slave woman is what gives power to *The Quadroon Slave* and *The Cabin Boy*, two subsequent dramas focused more on the internal pollution of such women by even the smallest drop of 'black' blood. This is the theme of Captain Williams's *The Woman of Colour*, performed at the Surrey theatre in November 1853. At one level, it brings before an English audience and popularises the horror of miscegenation that was at the time gaining scientific justification in America. In this the play acts as a conduit for current American racial beliefs. Williams manages, in fact, both to exploit the sense of horror and to condemn it. His play is set in America, and many of the American protagonists, both those we are expected to despise and those whose goodwill is asserted, give a practical demonstration of how socially obscene they find the offspring of miscegenation. At the same time, English values of liberty, horror of slavery and, as well, a certain puzzlement that a beautiful young woman should be viewed as an outcast, prevail in the person of the hero, Lord Everton.

The beautiful, loving, pure (yet impure) heroine, Florida Brandon, is an American heiress, who does not know the true nature of her origins. She is loved by Lord Everton, an English earl, and we learn that they met and became engaged while on voyage to New York. She was returning to her home, he was planning to investigate the realities of slavery 'at the fountain head'.[46] They have been pursued to New York by Lady Moreland, the recent widow of a West Indies plantation owner. Full of jealousy, Lady Moreland determines to revenge herself on Everton for never having returned her passion for him and finds out, through the agency of various American caricature sidekicks, that Florida is the daughter of the slave Josephine who was 'married illegally ... to a certain Captain Brandon of the British navy – on board his vessel, and [who] after long concealment in various states of this union ... accompanied him to Europe with her child born in Florida. Josephine is dead but the child born in involuntary servitude exists.'[47] There is the usual unmasking, a slave auction and, at one point, Florida is even gambled for. Her degradation is further under-lined by the desire of a recently freed black to buy her, for he 'has no prejudices ginst Malgamation'.[48]

What is of particular interest is the stress laid by a number of characters on the ineradicable taint of black blood. The snobbish, vulgar, kindly (or so we are told) Mrs Bloomberry, who took Florida under her wing on the voyage out from England, has this to say to Florida's mixed-race maid:

Mrs Bloomberry: ... Impertinent! Like all your race slaves or free, all the same, insolence and black blood are sure to go together...

Florida: My dear Mrs Bloomberry, what has happened to make you speak harshly to Marion? You know she is almost a sister to me ...

Mrs Bloomberry: Oh! I know all that, and more's the pity I know how philanthropists and free soilers spread their horrid doctrines. But no matter all their fine words won't wash out the dark drop. A nigger is still a nigger.

Lord Everton: (*smiling*) Why Mrs Bloomberry, how can you speak in this tone of Marion? It seems to me that she has as fair a skin as many of her white neighbours.

Mrs Bloomberry: ... I am sorry that you, too, are imposed on by these kind of creatures – Her skin may be a sort of white, but her nails (*whispering*) her nails, my lord, there is the sure sign of the beast – nothing can hide it.[49]

A warrant is issued for Florida's arrest, as property to be returned to its rightful owner, and the vengeful Lady Moreland ensures that this takes place at a ball (given by the Bloomberrys) while Lord Everton is absent. Before Florida is arrested, though, the rumour goes round that she is really a quadroon, and she is immediately shunned by all those present. There is considerable power in the build-up to Florida's arrest and ejection from the company, and it is, dramatically, the most effective part of the play:

Lady Moreland: (*in a haughty tone*) Will no one put an end to this scene? (*pointing to the door*)

Several voices: Out with her, out with the Quadroon! Out with the woman of colour!

Florida: (*in violent agitation*) What do they mean? Quadroon! Woman of Colour! Oh God! Oh God! ... (*She meets Mrs Bloomberry and rushes towards her*)

Mrs Bloomberry: (*repulsing her*) Don't touch me, don't put your filthy black fingers on me ...'[50]

The play doubtless capitalised on the Uncle Tom vogue, being produced about one year after that had got under way. In the words of the *Era*, it was

intended to demonstrate the working of the Fugitive Slave Law in the United States . . . the woman of colour, who has derived the slightest taint of negro blood through her mother . . . anywhere else but in America would be regarded as a charming brunette . . . it may be doubted whether [the play] will advance the cause of abolition, or strengthen the feelings of mutual regard between England and the United States . . . The sentiments are well calculated to attract the applause of an audience composed of 'Britishers'.[51]

As the *Era*'s comment makes clear, the play gave comfortable scope for English superiority, in morals and manners, over America. Even Lady Moreland is uncomfortable with the public barracking of Florida at the ball, and it is an English lord who dramatically rescues her. Yet despite all the play's good intentions, the fine speeches from the enlightened Lord Everton about the wickedness of slavery (he scarcely turns a hair over the revelation of Florida's background, unlike Pelham in *The Quadroon Slave*), and even the final repentance of Lady Moreland, its most gripping message is that of the dark secret of Florida's 'blood'. She herself accepts that she is tainted, telling Everton, 'I never can be your wife . . . alas, alas, I am then indeed the child of a degraded race.'[52] As a true-born Englishman, however, he overrides such objections, and all ends happily. But it is the 'black blood' that gives the play its most powerful charge.

The apogee of such dramas is reached with Dion Boucicault's *The Octoroon* (1859), written and first performed in America and brought to the Adelphi in London's West End in 1861. This contains elements of the *Uncle Tom* story in its narrative of an old-fashioned plantation (stocked with faithful and long-serving slaves) that has to be sold up to meet crippling debts, and combines them with a story of doomed love between the heir of this encumbered estate, George, and the beautiful Zoe. Zoe is the illegitimate daughter of the judge (now dead) who was the estate's owner. Zoe has been brought up by the judge's wife, not to slavery, but as a loved (if subordinate) member of the household. George is her cousin. All this is compounded by Yankee skulduggery (the figure of the calculating Yankee was brought before American audiences as well as English ones), which involves the murder of a young black slave-boy, Paul; the theft of letters that would have saved all; and the unmasking of the villain. The latter, with a flair typical of Boucicault, is contrived by the use of the relatively new invention of photography.

It was far more daring to present a drama involving a protagonist of mixed race in America, where miscegenation was illegal in many states, than in England.[53] There the sense of English self-congratulation in the country's status as a free nation of free people might ease any discomfort over the racial background of such a character.[54] Nonetheless, Zoe, whose subordinate status is clearly shown in her interactions with other characters, and equally clearly condemned through George's reaction to her treatment, is not allowed to fulfil her love. She is forced to revert to slave status, for the earlier free status that had been conferred upon her by her white father was invalid, since all his property, of which she was part, was under lien of debt. So she follows (though more realistically) the trajectory of Florida Brandon, in moving from the status of free individual to unfree thing. Bought at auction by the Yankee villain, whose motive is his sexual desire for her, she determines to commit suicide. The knowledge that the estate does not have to be sold after all comes too late, and Zoe relinquishes George to the Southern belle, Dora.

Some of Zoe's strongest and most affecting speeches are those in which she dwells on the shame of her origins:

Zoe: George, do you see that hand you hold; look at these fingers, do you see the nails are of a blueish tinge?
George: Yes, near the quick there is a faint blue mark.
Zoe: Look in my eyes; is not the same colour in the white?
George: It is their beauty.
Zoe: Could you see the roots of my hair you would see the same dark fatal mark ... That – that is the ineffacable [*sic*] curse of Cain. Of the blood that feeds my heart, one drop in eight is black – bright red as the rest may be, that one drop poisons all the flood. Those seven bright drops give me love like yours, hope like yours – ambition like yours – life hung with passions like dew-drops on the morning flowers; but the one black drop gives me despair, for I'm an unclean thing – forbidden by the laws – I'm an Octoroon![55]

This lyrical and passionate despair condemns the racial status quo (in which blackness is not only inferior but evil in its essence), bringing its ugliness into the light and, because it is the deepest expression of Zoe's soul, at the same time upholds it. 'Forbidden by the laws' suggests both the statutes that criminalised miscegenation and the polygenist belief that race mixing was against the law of nature. The duality inherent in Zoe's despair is reiterated by the conclusion of the piece, in which Zoe cedes George to Dora by taking poison and ensuring her own death. Thus, in the final analysis, the racial order, of white cleaving to white, is restored and reaffirmed. Yet, given the mores of the period and the seriousness with which Boucicault treats this aspect of his story, anything else would have been too easy, at odds with the depth that he had touched. According to Peter Thomson, for the first three weeks of the English run, in 1861, Boucicault retained his original ending, but finally was forced to accede to demands that Zoe be allowed to marry George.[56]

In brief, the drop of black blood that was the hidden taint of the beautiful young woman whose mother was a slave (a black father would have been completely unthinkable, given what was expected of women in a white, patriarchal society) was used by dramatists in a number of different ways. First, it could enable a serious comment to be made on the iniquity of slavery through a character who was sympathetic, attractive to the audience and sensitive; the black-skinned character was no longer available for this purpose. Second, it could be used for the dramatic frisson, unspoken but real, of enforced sexual power over a vulnerable and highly feminine woman. This is in strong contrast to the way that sexual power is exercised over the black slave Clara Clouts in *The Cabin Boy*. Third, it could be used to hint at the shameful, transgressive nature of miscegenation. And, fourth, it was, as Boucicault demonstrates most movingly, a way into the duality of the psyche of the mixed-race character; the beginnings of an exploration of her interiority. Such interiority is, I would argue, a relatively new pheno-menon in melodrama, which is built around expressivity. What a character feels is what she expresses, is what she is, is what she does. There is no ambivalence. The mixed-race character allows for the beginnings of ambiv-alence in that she straddles two worlds, yet is wholly accepted in neither. Of course, given that these are melodramas, such ambivalence has to be resolved, either through a most unlikely and busy series of events, such as a duel between Everton and two others in *The Woman of Colour*, or in the truncated and unsatisfactory nature of Boucicault's conclusion to *The Octoroon*. The misfit between the resolution and the issues raised, however, suggests a process of transition to a new dramatic mode.

'THE DESPISED CREOLE'

While a trace of black ancestry served to render those young women who carried it the more desirable and worthy of rescue, for the men, it was a different matter. Here the transgressive sexual energy that has called them into being marks them out as bitter outsiders, hostile and seeking venge-ance. The black avenger with profound moral justice on his side becomes the almost white one, with little justification except arrogance for his wickedness. Once again, the purely black character is written out of the story, except as a supernumerary. The major exceptions to this are the

Uncle Tom plays to be discussed fully in the next chapter. These tend to retain the stereotype of the black-skinned character as foolish or ineffectual and also retain the stress on the indignity of slavery as visited on the more intelligent mixed-race character. Where they differ, and counter the prevailing American stereotype of the mixed-race persona, is in the notion of that persona's innate moral goodness.

Shirley Brooks's 1847 drama, *The Creole; or, Love's Fetters*, performed at the Lyceum in the West End, was more serious in intent and approach than much of his other work. (Brooks is best known for becoming the editor of *Punch* after Mark Lemon.) It exemplifies a number of the themes discussed so far, and introduces the male character of mixed race.[57] Set in the Isle de France (now Mauritius) at the time of the revolution, it concerns the love of Alphonse de Nyon, a young officer who has recently inherited his father's estate, for Louise Fauriel, a beautiful, fair-skinned young woman who is, unbeknown to him, a slave on the estate. (He has kept his true identity secret from her.)

The preface to the drama outlines its social context:

The creole part of the population made themselves remarkable by [their] intrepidity . . . on board the fleets of France . . . the European looked with disdain upon the Creole, who, in turn, regarded the former as an adventurer . . . The condition of the Slave was of the lowest and most abject degradation. Numbers of these unfortunates had European blood in their veins, being the offspring of *liaisons* between Planters and their Slaves, but such a pedigree only increased their misfortune.[58]

Even before she realises that de Nyon is, in fact, her owner, Louise has hinted that their union is 'impossible', that a 'dreadful barrier exists between [them], which she dares not indicate more clearly'.[59] The driving force of the play is not, however, Louise's inner struggle but the lust for revenge of the poor, proud and embittered Creole, Latour. He sees this as his opportunity to humiliate the wealthy and ardent de Nyon, and does not scruple to use Louise, to whom he poses as a friend and as linked by their marginality. Of course, the term 'creole' does not necessarily imply mixed race, but there are frequent references to Latour's 'copper' skin colour and ambiguous social status. He occupies not so much an intermediate position in the social hierarchy, as one on the fringes of proper colonial society. Even if there is no explicit statement that Latour is of mixed race, the external markers of his social position, his vendetta against the power-brokers of the colonial milieu and his dastardly character, all underlined by the colour of his skin, inevitably align him with those villains who bear the taint of blackness.

Latour engineers a meeting, in public, between Louise and her new owner – the man she already knows as a lover.

Latour: This meeting will be strange. Two persons at more singularly cross purposes have hardly met ... The proud blood of the Frenchman, and the fiery current which animates our pretty friend here, may ... make the experiment hazardous. But we shall see ... If matters go as I have planned, there will fall to my share two very delightful things – money and revenge![60]

Louise is devastated at the revelation that de Nyon owns her; he recoils from her, from her slave status and what he conceives as her deception: 'the slave, whom the law pronounces incapable of uttering the marriage vow,

9 *The Creole*: **Latour (centre) witnesses the exposure he has contrived** Frontispiece, Dicks, no. 1009, Malcolm Morley Library, Senate House Library, University of London

the slave is mine! And such is the end of my day dream.'[61] But his love prevails over his initial repulsion. Prevented by the conditions of his father's will from emancipating Louise directly, de Nyon is duped by Latour into selling her to him. Latour will then, he claims, manumit her to de Nyon. Latour, however, has another haughty (and in this case prejudiced) Frenchman in his sights – the planter Damiron who is deeply in debt to de Nyon. With 'composed decision, as of triumph and power', Latour unfolds his plan to de Nyon:

Latour. ... I hate this Damiron. His prejudice has insulted me, and his hollow wealth has given him a title to do so. For that passable prettyness, his daughter, I am very anxious to wed her; less for her own sake than because the union would humble Damiron's pride to the very earth.[62]

Louise is, he reminds de Nyon exultingly, 'mine irrevocably':

Latour. You have assigned your bride to me – to me, the despised Creole. She is my slave; and if you dare to dispute my will, I may – do you hear? – I may – Her eyes, though tearful are still bright; her hair, though dishevelled, is still beautiful. Do you hear, Monsieur de Nyon?[63]

The sexual threat could hardly be more obvious, and the passage demonstrates the point made earlier about the power of the man who can buy the woman who has to be sold. The deep and malicious hatred of the mixed-race male is his most abiding feature. Even at the point of death, following a duel, the 'copper-coloured creature'[64] clings to his revenge, bequeathing his only property, the slave Louise, to his cousin, a cruel and arbitrary master. Only at the very last is Louise saved: 'By a decree of the National Convention of France, slavery is henceforth abolished in all her colonies.'[65] At which, Latour falls dead. The moral is pointed by Bellona, an active and outspoken follower of the French regiment garrisoned on the island, whose symbolism is suggested by the fact that she carries a model of the guillotine around with her, and who has attempted throughout to champion Louise and foil Latour:

[M]ay we be permitted to remind those who have sympathised in the fortunes of our poor slave girl, that at this very hour there exist, in other countries speaking our own language, thousands of maidens as young, as fair, as loving, and as liable to be bought and sold like the beasts of the field. We can perhaps do but little towards lightening their fate; but may we not remember, with a thankful pride, that our own is cast in a land where (with its faults) the claim is unknown – where God's image is unsullied by the brand of slavery?[66]

Thus Brooks, in this intricately plotted drama, interweaves a number of popular themes with a new twist. Already familiar is the equation of

England with freedom, the turmoil of the apparently white female slave and her master/lover, and the backwardness of America as expressed in Bellona's epilogue, quoted above. What is new is the dangerous nature of the mixed-race outsider, his cunning and cruelty. The play presents an interesting counterpoint to *The Black Doctor* (1846) and is certainly less daring in its 'take' on interracial mixing, given that, in a social structure governed by patriarchy and class, it is the male who raises or lowers the female to his social position.[67] The *Era* was highly enthusiastic about the play, praising it as 'a drama of pretension and performance, admirably put together ... the "Creole", with its telling points, earnest appeals to universal sympathies, and nervous, vigorous, and hearty language ... will not be shelved after the prosperous run before it has been completed'.[68] The play continued to draw full houses for a number of weeks after its opening.[69]

If the status of the Creole in Brooks's drama is somewhat ambiguous, not so that of Count Lugarto, the villain of Charles O'Bryan's 1850 drama, *Lugarto the Mulatto*, first performed at the Surrey.[70] Here is the mixed-race villain in all his devastating wickedness. Based, according to the *Era*, on a story by Eugene Sue,[71] the play is only comprehensible at all if one is familiar with the conventions of vampirism. Lugarto is a monstrous figure, the embodiment of demonic and sexual energy, bending men and women equally to his will. In the words of De Rochegune, the cousin of Mathilde de Lancry, who is attempting to prevent her from falling under Lugarto's sway: 'All he approaches are lost! If a man, he is dishonoured – if a woman, she is defiled! He is a fiend incarnate – a kind of Mephistopheles of this world, contaminating the very air he breathes!'[72]

For reasons unexplained until the very end, Lugarto has in his power Mathilde's husband, Gontran, who, though only recently married, is conducting a flirtation with Mathilde's cousin, Ursule. Such is Lugarto's absolute control that he is able to compel de Lancry to elope with Ursule (at a glittering ball, given by Lugarto), despite his earlier resolution to break off the affair. Moreover, Lugarto openly presses upon Mathilde his desire for her, before her husband and her friends. He then arranges for the distraught Mathilde to be spirited away in a carriage, not, as she thinks, to meet up with her now disgraced husband, but to one of the count's lonely chateaux, in the middle of a forest. (The wild and stormy night, the mysterious coach journey, the arrival at a gloomy mansion, are the familiar clichés of a hundred horror films.) Only a villain of the grandest and most gothic proportions could do this.

In the racial theorising of the time, the mulatto was considered far more intelligent than the black. According to the contemporary theorist John

Van Evrie, 'as a general principle the mongrel has intellectual ability in proportion as he approximates to the superior race'; he was also more vicious.[73] In Knox's view, 'When the Negro is crossed ... with the white race, the result is a scoundrel.'[74] Lugarto, then, is not the 'black gentleman' of a previous era, but an even more dangerous combination of white and black, energetic in his pursuit of evil and exultant in his power. He expresses the threat once articulated by the black avenging figures of *The Castle Spectre* or *Obi* (1800):

What a crowd! what a noise! and all this for me – a Mulatto! the son of a *slave*! This fête, this luxury, beauty, pleasure, all for me! And yet, in their hearts, they laugh at – and *despise* me! Why, then, should not I, in return, hate this vile race? Both men and women pursue me because I am rich! (*pause*) My mother was a negress and died under the blows of her master, after giving birth to me; that master, who was my father, lost his legitimate son, and then remembered his natural child, who was his slave ... [and left] me his name, and fortune. I took the fortune without the name ... I visited the great cities of the world ... Everywhere people *sell* themselves! Bazaars, markets, slaves, everywhere, only here the chain is gold, and is harder! I wished to be noble – I have purchased a name, and title; I am the 'Count de Lugarto,' a noble black! Ha, ha, ha! Nothing is impossible with five million francs.[75]

Lugarto finally dies, at de Lancry's hands, after de Lancry himself has been fatally wounded in a duel. It was, perhaps, the single-minded lust with which Lugarto pursued Mathilde, and suborned her husband to his quest, that led the *Era*'s reviewer to assert that 'the construction of the piece partakes too much of the modern French school, and the *morale* is far too questionable for it ever to became a popular stock piece'. For there is no doubting the condemnation that is heaped upon Lugarto – who dominates the action completely – at every stage of the play, so any perceived amorality could not have lain in that. Moreover, as the reviewer went on to note, the audience showed 'a high appreciation of retributive justice, for at every step where the villains of the drama were foiled, they applauded to the echo'.[76] (Presumably the hapless and debased de Lancry, along with Lugarto's servants, were included in this as villains.) The sexual energy and explicitness, couched in the language of melodrama but potent nonetheless, with which the mixed-race Lugarto hunted his white, virtuous prey was the likely cause, therefore, of the reviewer's unease.

Titles such as *The Mulatto Murderer* (1854), *Quadroona; or, the blot upon humanity* and *Quadroona; or, the man of crime* (both 1857) would suggest that the mulatto continued his career in villainy. A further twist to the career of this criminal but resourceful outsider, the product of a social transgression who transgresses in turn, is given by a dramatist of greater stature, Tom Robertson. His *The Half Caste* was first performed at the Surrey on 8 September 1856.[77] Here Sebastian Cabrera, the half-caste of the title, is an exaggerated mixture of evil and some good, a larger-than-life, highly melodramatic figure who sits somewhat ill at ease with the more naturalistic tone of much of the play's dialogue – a naturalism that pre-figured Robertson's highly successful subsequent development as a writer of socially realistic comedies for the Prince of Wales theatre. That, however, was still to come.

Sebastian Cabrera, a mysterious figure, is travelling in the Alps and exchanges identities with an English lord, Falconer, who is anxious to keep his name concealed from some other travellers. Cabrera, who we learn much later is an escaped slave and the former overseer of a plantation in the West Indies, is eager to trace his brother, from whom he was separated when young. He determines to murder Falconer, taking his identity permanently, for such a change of identity will make his travels less dangerous. Cabrera also seeks to win for himself Eugenie, the daughter (unknown to him) of his former owner, De Grandet, whom he has ruined financially. But Eugenie is engaged to a poor artist – who turns out to be that long-lost brother of Cabrera. The inevitable confrontation takes place between the now impoverished De Grandet, who is travelling in Europe with his other daughter Isabel, and Cabrera. Moreover, the real Lord Falconer has, after all, survived Cabrera's attempt at murder and reemerges to complete his unmasking. At the bitter end, all Cabrera can finally do is take his own life with the poisoned pearl that Falconer had handed him when they first exchanged identities.

Like Lugarto, Cabrera has energy, passion and resourcefulness; he even arranges for a mulatto doctor to burn off the slave brand that De Grandet had burned into his arm. Unlike Lugarto, he is not a cardboard-cutout villain but a figure of some attraction. He forces apologies from male customers insulting Eugenie and her florist friend, Fifine. When Eugenie is vigorously repelling his advances and trying to entrap him, believing him to be the cause of her father's downfall, she has to steel herself: 'There are moments that I think that had not my heart been given to Oscar, I should have loved this man.'[78] Before his attempt to get rid of Falconer, Cabrera had saved Falconer's life on a treacherous ravine. And, in the confrontation with De Grandet, Cabrera has powerful arguments on his side – arguments that hark back to the fierce moral anger of the captured slave – and a desire for retributive justice. Robertson so arranges it that there is even a satisfying moment, before that of recognition, when De Grandet, his eyes fixed on the ground, begs Cabrera for a job: 'I am used to business, write a good hand, and am clever at accounts.' Then the humility changes to arrogance and bluster: 'Wretch; when I leave this house, expect the worst!'[79] Cabrera's account of his own motives is harrowing and blunt:

Sebas: . . . I had a little brother on whom I doted. I had a wife, who gave me hopes that she might one day bless me with a child. One summer's day, my wife, my little brother, and myself, were at work in your plantation – working for you – when you passed with Mademoiselle [*sic*] De Grandet by your side, and a friend – a visitor who had just arrived. My wife was handsome. – Your friend remarked it. You answered him gaily, 'Well, as she seems to suit your taste, take her – I give her to you.'

De Grand: Ruffian! you threw your arms round my wife's neck with the fury of a lion!

Sebas: I did, and pressed my slave's lips to her patrician mouth, and shouted to you – 'Can you now feel what a man feels who sees violence offered to the wife of his bosom – the mother of his child?' You ordered me to be branded on the arm with a red-hot iron. Your wife had my wife whipped so cruelly that in three days she died, bearing with her to the grave the fruits of our unhappy union. On the day of her death, you sold under my eyes my poor old father and my little brother . . . I then stood in this world alone! . . . I still toiled on, until you made me your overseer. All appeared forgotten – pardoned. When you spoke to me you called me 'friend.' Monsieur de Grandet, there are abysses so profound, that cast a stone down them you cannot hear the sound it makes when it has reached the extremest depth below. My soul was such an abyss. You heard no sound or wail of grief; the stone you cast had reached the bottom of the gulf. (*with fury*) Now hear its echo in the ruin of your fortune! – the dying wail of your expiring wife! – the blasted prospects of your child! – your own last cry for mercy and for life![80]

This has elements of the stories of Hassan, of Three-fingered Jack, of Couri: it reprises all that history of the black presence on the stage. Yet it is also a cry of heartfelt, deeply personal anguish that is more than a reiteration of those former laments. In this Cabrera is echoing Boucicault's Zoe, laying bare the movement of his soul. It is at the point where he speaks of his own internal abyss that the speech moves, I believe, from an impassioned but familiar account that could almost have been penned by Douglas Jerrold for Couri, to a specific, interior anguish.

What is also different is that it is the story of a mixed-race character, a quadroon. Only such, it seems, could have the resourcefulness, energy, intellectual capacity and individual personality to carry out Cabrera's daring deception. The black-skinned slave, the buffoon of minstrelsy, was now rarely linked to so keenly felt a degradation – he, and she, did not possess enough human depth to recognise it or individuality to suffer it. Instead, he might follow a performance of, say, *Lugarto* in the guise of an Ethiopian Serenader, to give his usual 'amusing' performance on the bones or his 'vehemently encored' 'plantation dance'.[81]

OLD ENGLAND AND LIBERTY

This strand of my narrative began with a nautical drama and it is to that genre that I now return, with a play that combines many of the elements discussed so far – the English love of liberty and destruction of slavery; the degradation inflicted by slavery on the light-skinned; and the stupidity and acceptance of their lot by the black-skinned. Yet it does it in a way that harks back to the past, rather than exploring the new avenues of personality and motivation that the mulatto figure is beginning to open up.

Colin Hazlewood's *The Staff of Diamonds*[82] was first performed at the Surrey in 1861, where the prolific Hazlewood was then resident dramatist (his melodramas were later associated most closely with the East End theatres, the Britannia and the Pavilion). This was also the year that saw the first performances of *The Octoroon* and that the Civil War began in America. And it was a period when British naval efforts to suppress the slave trade had shifted to policing the Arab slavetraders who continued to supply the sugar plantations of Cuba and Brazil.[83]

The Staff of Diamonds exhibits the same dichotomy between the light-skinned slave and the black that characterised Stirling's earlier *The Cabin Boy*. The action is set in Brazil on a planter's estate and in the diamond mines of Minas Gerais, in the lawless interior of the country. The location of the drama is yet another instance of the facility with which hard-pressed dramatists plundered their contemporary milieu – for by the mid-nineteenth century, Brazil's (mostly slave-produced) commodities, including precious minerals, had become extremely important to the British economy.[84] In the play, an honest English tar, Tom Trunnion, whose unlikely and frequent presence on the estate is explained by his captain's friendship with the owner, befriends a young quadroon slave, Namettah. She is married to Palmedo, a Creole 'who has good [Spanish] blood in his veins, although he is a slave', and they have a small child.[85] Namettah is pursued by the villainous overseer, Diego, whom she resists doughtily. Although their owner, Signor Riccio, is reluctant to split the couple, he gambles Palmedo away to Cordillera, a mineowner. No one, it is said, ever leaves the mines alive. Comic interest is provided by Sam Sliddery, a Londoner who has inherited a plantation complete with slaves and spends his time in terror lest they attack or murder him: 'I can't eat for fear of being poisoned, – I can't drink for fear of being dittoed, – I can't sleep for fear of being stabbed, – I can't stay at home for fear of being shot, – and I can't walk out for fear of being pushed into the river.'[86] Slave revolt was the constant nightmare of slaveowners; Sam renders it absurd. When the black slave Gus tries to give him a message, he flees, crying 'murder'.[87] (His terror at being out of his native element also validates the implied message that nowhere really equals London – no doubt a sentiment to which the Surrey audience would have responded.)

When Tom sees Diego about to whip the defiant Namettah, he leaps to her defence and, having seen Diego off, offers to splice himself to her 'in a brace of shakes'.[88] Learning that she already has a husband who is a slave and a child born into slavery, he remarks, 'Well, bless the old British Lion we've none of this sort of fun in England ... d – e if they *do tax* you a little, they don't *sell* you body and breeches.'[89] Such direct comments include the Surrey audience within the comfortable aura of English superiority. It becomes Tom's altruistic object to enable Namettah and Palmedo to gain their liberty.

The working out of plot and incident makes clear Hazlewood's, and presumably the audience's, racialised conception of who is worthy of freedom, for what type of person it is appropriate. It is a conception that can only be explained in terms of skin colour, the lightness of Palmedo's and Namettah's being stressed. The very first scene of the play features the villainous Diego and his black henchman, Gus. Unlike Palmedo, who speaks in the language of melodrama of the tribulations and humiliations of slavery, of being 'doomed to a life-long labour for nought but food and shelter',[90] Gus has all the markers of 'black' speech; 'iss' for yes, 'de' for the; 'gib' and 'lib' for give and live; self-referral in the third person; confusion between him and his, am and is, and so on. Jealous of Palmedo's light skin – 'if *I'm* black, *he's* yellar, and black's a good standing colour, much better dan a washed out nankeen like Palmedo' – he is happy to see him sent to the mines.[91] When Namettah escapes to join Palmedo, Gus eagerly helps to hunt her down. His treachery is matched only by his lack of intelligence:

Gus: Look eberywhere, and when you've looked eberywhere look nowhere, in
      case they should be there ... Hark! Gus, hear something. Hush! Don't
      breathe, – don't wink, – don't think while him listen ... Yes, yes, one, – two
      footsteps, – hush, step back, – more back yet, – backer! backer![92]

When Tom, as he frequently does, expresses directly his commitment to liberty – 'I hate slavery, and would give liberty to all, barring neither creed nor colour'[93] – no consideration is given to Gus. He is simply not part of this equation. Unlike Namettah and Palmedo, he is not linked to any expressed desire for liberty; he is just a self-important and unpleasant plantation slave.

That racialised conception of who is worthy of freedom and who is excluded from it is also evidenced by Tom's first scheme for liberating Palmedo and Namettah. He intends to raise the money to buy their freedom from Sliddery – by getting him to sell *his* unwanted slaves who had already been promised freedom by Sliddery's uncle before he died. There is no awareness of the contradiction in trading the many to liberate the few. The plan fails, so, Palmedo concludes gloomily, 'the slight ray of Freedom that broke in upon our souls has vanished for ever!', as it would also have done for Sliddery's slaves had Tom's plan succeeded.[94] Tom then borrows the money from his captain, against his next year's wages (true tar generosity), but by that time events have overtaken him, for Palmedo is being sent away.

After a series of stirring incidents, chases, fights and imprisonments, in which the unheroic Sliddery plays a crucial role alongside Tom, all are recaptured and about to be shot. Tom, defiant to the last, declares, 'Oh, pull away, and be hanged. An Englishman would as soon be without brains as without liberty.'[95]

Then, at the last minute, a royal edict is delivered by an army captain. Don Pedro, Emperor of the Brazils, 'feeling compassion for His coloured subjects' has abolished slavery for ever.[96] All are free. So, at the last, even Gus is included. Overt jubilation, however, is confined to some general shouting by the (undifferentiated) slaves and Tom's plans to sail back to England with Namettah and Palmedo, who, having smuggled out a stack of diamonds from the mines, is now a very rich man indeed. Riches, though, are not what it is really all about, for, in Tom's creed, expressed earlier at a time of peril:

Tom: My flag's the Union Jack, and whenever that floats whether on land or ocean, beneath its folds you find courage, justice, and humanity. Every man who claims Old England as the land of his birth has greater reason to be proud – poor though he be – than a king like yours, who encourages slavery and reaps a benefit from the sale of his fellow creatures.[97]

Compared with *The Octoroon* or *The Half Caste*, there is something curiously old-fashioned about *The Staff of Diamonds*. What both the former reveal is some perception, however fitful, of the inner emotional turmoil of the former slave; of that mixed-race self as a zone of irreconcilable opposites. In her very being, the octoroon Zoe embodies the conflict between white and black. Hence the mixed-race character has taken us towards a consideration of slavery as a personal, internally experienced tragedy and away from slavery as a social, structural issue. We do not see any of the mixed-race characters actually working as slaves, though Zoe (*The Octoroon*) is condescended to and functions as the poor relation might in a novel of social manners and Jenny (*The Cabin Boy*) stands on the auction block. The issue of slavery as an institution in whose toils individuals are caught, which was reiterated in the drama of an earlier period through the accounts of capture, enslavement and forced labour discussed earlier, has become internalised.

Moreover, that internalisation has reinforced the transition of slavery from a social institution to a private, domestic concern. The way in which slavery could be translated into the domestic arena (domestic in the sense of hearth and family) had been hinted at early on, but not fully developed, by Jerrold in *Descart, the French Buccaneer* (1828). Slavery was most fully realised as a domestic issue, however, under a specific combination of factors; when, in fact, the light-skinned character met the black buffoon in the context of enslavement. To examine how the prism through which slavery was viewed changed, it is necessary to jump back a few years – to 1852, the heyday of the mania for 'Uncle Tom'.

CHAPTER 7

Uncle Tom – moral high ground or low comedy?

In tracing the development of the mulatto character as a replacement for the fearsome black character of an earlier period or as a figure who can evoke the injustice and degradation of slavery, I have left to the last consideration of one of the crucial staging posts on that journey. Harriet Beecher Stowe's novel *Uncle Tom's Cabin* (1852) was a major cultural phenomenon of the mid-nineteenth century; it was used in popular drama as a summation of all that had gone before and as a validation of the role of the light-skinned character in relation to slavery. Yet *Uncle Tom's Cabin* could have led to a different approach, had not the Jim Crow figure so completely colonised the popular imagination. In that sense, 'Uncle Tom' stands at a crossroads. That he, together with Jim Crow and Topsy, are still instantly and generally recognised names, loaded with significance, while the novel's (light-skinned) George and Eliza Harris are not, is suggestive of the continuity of the racialised cultural climate into which they (and we) were born. It is suggestive, too, of the line of development that can be traced from Crow through to Tom. As I have shown, Crow flourished most intensely on the stage from 1836 to the early 1840s, with another resurgence in the mid- to late 1840s – by which time he had escaped into popular entertainment generally, in minstrelsy and blackface. A ubiquitous presence on the streets, at the seaside and the races, and in the music halls, it was not until the early twentieth century that he died a lingering and protracted death. His ghost haunts us still. Uncle Tom's theatrical heyday in England ran only from September 1852 to around the middle of 1853; yet it was, if not as longlasting as that of Crow, almost as intense. While the vogue for Uncle Tom pointed up many of the themes examined in the last two chapters, in particular the move to a dramatic emphasis on light-skinned characters caught up in slavery, it also marked the rejection, by and large, of any meaningful attempt to portray a serious black-skinned character. This tension, between what could have been done with the source material and what was actually done, between potential and execution, is even more observable with Stowe's later anti-slavery novel, *Dred*, published in 1856.

To understand how 'Tom mania' operated culturally, it has to be seen in context. Alongside the mid-nineteenth century vogue for troupes of blackface – and some genuine black – entertainers was another popular enthusiasm, for tales of slavery told by ex-slaves themselves.[1] It was this that provided the context for Uncle Tom's success. Just as the racism of the Jim Crow variety found a market in a race-conscious Britain, so the abolitionist movement now coming to its peak in America and spearheaded by black abolitionists themselves, also found a ready audience. As already noted, in the thirty years before the American Civil War, every major black leader visited Britain, with more coming in the period 1848–52 than at any other time. Frederick Douglass was perhaps the best known but many others, like Sarah Remond and William Wells Brown, carried out lengthy, serious and sustained lecture tours across the whole country. At another level, the lectures of Henry 'Box' Brown, who displayed a panorama depicting the abuses of slavery and who made his appearance on stage in the very box in which he had escaped, veered towards stage performances.[2] As the *New York Express* commented sourly:

The mother country, of late years, has signalized itself particularly in the great delight it has taken to avail itself of every opportunity to foster, and feed, and flatter, runaway American negroes ... Persians, with longbeards [*sic*], – Turks, with long pipes – Chinese, with long tails, and North American Indians, with *not very long* blankets, are constantly succeeding one another in the *salons*, or at the tables of the *haut ton* ... Nothing goes down, now ... so well as the genuine black.[3]

Slave narratives, with their graphic accounts of terrible cruelties and harrowing escapes, sold in thousands. No doubt part of their appeal was their sensationalism, albeit under sober guise. But they also appealed to the powerful abolitionist thrust in English culture and thinking, which emerged at the end of the eighteenth century, continued to be a powerful force through the abolition of the slave trade (1807), of slavery (1833) and of 'apprenticeship' (virtual slavery) in the West Indies (1838), and now received a new boost with the campaign to abolish slavery in America.[4] Abolitionism should not, though, be confused with racial egalitarianism: paternalist philanthropic attitudes to the suffering black slave could easily coexist with, and help to entrench, a particular stereotype of the black as lower in the racial hierarchy.[5]

The climate was therefore ripe for Stowe's dramatic and vivid indictment of the institution of slavery, *Uncle Tom's Cabin*, to become a runaway success on both sides of the Atlantic when it was published in 1852.[6] The theatre, that ready mirror of popular response, quickly caught on to the appeal of 'Uncle Tom'; versions of the novel were first performed in September 1852 only a few months after its English publication, at the London theatres of the Standard, the Olympic and the Victoria. By December 1852, it was being played at eleven theatres across the capital.[7] According to the dramatist E. Fitzball:

> The publication of 'Uncle Tom's Cabin', the deservedly popular production of Mrs. Stowe, set all the managers mad to produce it on the stage. Every theatre nearly produced its version ... I was engaged by three managers to write three distinct pieces, which I did to the best of my abilities: indeed, it did not require any remarkable ability, as it was only to select scenes and join them together.[8]

Part of the appeal of Stowe's novel for dramatists was that much of its racy, naturalistic dialogue could be transferred wholesale to the stage. Hence the same passages of dialogue recur in versions that differed widely as to their overall thrust, plot outline, or which characters were included and which omitted. But, as well as the more 'straightforward' versions of the drama, there was an Astley's version (Astley's had once been a circus), involving much chasing and fighting on horseback and some minor by-play with dogs,[9] several pantomimes, a version at the City of London which featured a trick pony as 'Tom Tip, Topsey's (*sic*) pony',[10] and others which incorporated white 'comic' characters, such as that by G. D. Pitt.[11]

The novel itself abounds in strong melodramatic situations and pictures: notably the escape of the enslaved mother, Eliza, her child in her arms, over the frozen Ohio River; the whipping of Uncle Tom and a female slave by the brutal slaveowner Simon Legree; the almost unmasking of the escaped slave George (Eliza's husband) in a Kentucky tavern while he is on the run; his heroic stand-off across a rocky mountain pass with the slavehunters; the slave auction that separates a mother and her beautiful young daughter; the heavenly tableau of the saintly white child Eva St Clare and the black Christ figure, Tom. (The latter situation, though, appears more as a feature of the American dramatisations than of the English ones.) And thematically, the novel had great dramatic potential; the stark black-and-white struggle of good against evil; the humble oppressed against a tyrannical oppressor; the narrative of bravery against all odds, with the ultimate prize of freedom as the goal.

It is necessary to consider the novel in some detail, since there are crucial aspects of it that were impossible to stage and others, just detailed, which easily lent themselves to drama. This imbalance meant that while there was potential in the novel for a dramatic portrayal of Tom and other black characters that could have restored some element of human dignity to the black figure (dignity that Jim Crow had so unequivocally trampled on), what actually resulted from the dramatisations was the generalisation of the Crow image to the black male character as a whole. The novel allows a dignity and stoicism to Tom that rarely surfaced in the plays and was swamped in the generality of dramatisations, which depicted his simplicity as simple-mindedness and his simple-mindedness as lovably comical.

Stowe is concerned to depict the evil of slavery as an institution; not just its excesses or the abuses it inspired, but its systemic wickedness. *Uncle Tom's Cabin* was hugely influential. According to Jane Tompkins, it was the 'first American novel ever to sell over a million copies' and it functioned 'both as a means of describing the social world and as a means of changing it'.[12] At the very core of *Uncle Tom's Cabin* is a profoundly Christian value system in which all souls are of equal worth before God, from the degraded Prue, a 'breeder' robbed of all children to whom she has given birth, unto the very last, to the brutalised Sambo and Quimbo, Legree's slave slave-drivers, to little Eva. Even Legree, a powerfully drawn character whose immediate impact is that of physical threat, has the potential for redemption, but it is a potential on which he resolutely turns his back. The action of the novel turns on the separate escapes of George Harris (to rid himself of an abusive master and live as a free man) and his wife Eliza (to save their child from being sold), and the refusal of Uncle Tom to act likewise. This leads to Tom's being sold, first to a benevolent but indolent master, St Clare, and then to Legree, at whose hands he dies.

But if all souls are of equal value and the evil of slavery is that it substitutes man's ownership of man for God's relationship with the individual, all the characters in the novel are not of equal weight. A definite race hierarchy operates within it: to each race is assigned its own particular gifts and qualities, which it is incumbent upon it to develop. Thus to the Africans, the humblest and most docile of peoples, is the God-given task of serving God through missionary work and the practice of religion. For the dominant Anglo-Saxon race, on the other hand, it is necessary to show mercy, nobler to 'protect the feeble than to oppress them'.[13] And, in a reversal of the contemporary American stereotype, the mixed-race characters are not amoral and degenerate but patterns of family virtue. Hence, throughout all the dramatic and exciting incident of the novel, the minute material description of daily life, there is a detailed racial schema in operation. This is so despite the subtle and many-sided nature of Stowe's insight into her subject; her awareness, for example, that the anti-slavery stance of many from the northern states could mask a physical repugnance to the black that did not necessarily obtain in the South.

The protagonists of the novel, the husband-and-wife escapees George and Eliza Harris, are both handsome, light-skinned individuals. So emphatic is the stress on their colour that George, as a fugitive whose description has been circulated, disguises himself by *darkening* his complexion with a little walnut juice, so as to look Spanish. He also dyes his hair. George and Eliza are resourceful and determined, George's strength deriving from his knowledge that he is his 'master's' equal, if not superior, and his burning desire to live in freedom, Eliza's from her Christian belief and maternal love. George is the embodiment of manliness, Eliza of womanliness. George's passion is counterbalanced by Eliza's counselling of patience and submission to God's will. The apogee of Christian fortitude, however, is Tom himself, the icon of the abolitionist medallion 'Am I not a man and a brother?' set in motion. He is the exemplar of divine forgiveness, put on earth to suffer and resign his spirit to God's will. A purely moral emblem, he plays scarcely any structural role in forwarding the action of the novel that bears his name; his resistance, while of the highest moral order, consisting as it does of refusing to obey the will of his owner over that of God, is passive, spiritual and results in his transcendence into a Christ-like figure. In dying an agonising death he is the instrument of saving the souls of others, Legree's brutalised slaves. His spirituality, won through pain, is of the profoundest, but he has also a white counterpart, the natural saint, little Eva, daughter of St Clare. Both are children in God, both travel part of their spiritual journey together. Eva is too good to live, Tom too good not to suffer and die. Against little Eva is set another child, Topsy, the black embodiment of heathen ignorance and mischief, quick and cunning, yet, under the influence of Eva, capable of good.

The hierarchy of colour that operates in the novel is demonstrated by the fact that black-skinned Tom, his wife Chloe, Topsy and even more the 'comic' characters of Sam and Andy all speak in a pronounced 'slave' dialect. However, George, Eliza and the other light-skinned slaves speak in a dialect that is much closer to that of the white characters. The slight, but observable, distinction that Stowe draws between the speech of the light-skinned characters and that of the white characters is almost completely eroded in the dramatisations, in which George and Eliza speak like the white characters and unlike Tom and his fellows.

'WESLEYAN TALKEE TALKEE'

The action and the vivid colloquial speech, not only of the slaves but also of the slavetraders and 'men of business', could all be and were, with varying degrees of success, translated on to the stage. The spiritual heart of the novel, though, was incapable of embodiment within the confines of melodrama. This was not only because of the reluctance to represent on the stage a Christian iconography that might draw the attention of the Lord Chamberlain as censor.[14] Tom's journey is an inner one; it cannot be expressed in the powerful, declamatory and expository style of melodrama, which is suited to strong emotion and exciting physical action, but not to the quieter depths of the metaphysical. Even at the time, for all Stowe's achievement in bringing home the anti-slavery message to a wider audience (she was the 'little woman' who 'started this great [i.e., civil] war'[15]), black abolitionists like Douglass were attempting to counter the message of passive resignation that her principal character expressed. For black activists since, 'Uncle Tom' has become a term of derision, a curse.

The impossibility of representing Uncle Tom faithfully on stage was recognised in a lengthy review by the *Spectator* of the version written by Mark Lemon and Tom Taylor, entitled *Slave Life; or, Uncle Tom's Cabin*, played at the Adelphi, a theatre more usually known for its comedy.[16] It was a relative latecomer to the field, being first performed on 29 November 1852. Not surprisingly, given the abilities of its co-authors,[17] it is, dramatically, one of the most coherent versions and was described by the *Spectator* as 'a perfectly inoffensive drama, of considerable constructive merit'.[18] However, it differed drastically from the novel:

If in the whole compass of literature there is a work of fiction bearing intrinsic evidence that it was not designed ... for stage-adaptation ... that book is *Uncle Tom's Cabin* ... The piety of the book is no mere accident ... but is the moral basis on which the whole superstructure is raised ... Not one of the qualities which strike the heart in Mrs. Stowe's novel is preserved in the play; but then ... not one of those qualities was capable of stage representation. The soul of Uncle Tom floats far above playhouses, and in Wesleyan talkee-talkee repudiates their alliance: so we must not only be satisfied with obtaining a slice of his mortal frame, but must commend the authors for the admirable craftsmanship with which they have subdued a stubborn material.[19]

Indeed, the 'characterisation' of Uncle Tom varies wildly in all the plays, linked only by its unlikeness to Stowe's conception. In the novel his strength and saintliness, because of Stowe's utter sincerity, do carry conviction but as soon as he steps out of that intense atmosphere, he crumbles into dust. His struggle is inward and spiritual, incapable of representation within the bounds of melodrama. Nor does he advance the plot, as far as action and incident go. He does not run, he does not hide, he does not fight. Rather, he is the means through which Stowe intends us to access the deepest truths about slavery and its effect on the human soul. Therefore, because the novel itself cannot offer a credible persona on which to build a stage version of Tom, since what a melodrama demands above all is action, what is suggested about Tom in the plays is all the more revealing of the matrix of racialised beliefs, attitudes and stereotypes that were com- pounded by this latest interpretation of black-white relations. In other words, the Tom of the novel, an unlikely character except when interpreted through a deeply Christian value system, becomes, for the dramatist, a *tabula rasa*. Hence what dramatists did for the most part was to use ideas and images that were already familiar from the representation of the black character.

The very first version to be staged, *Uncle Tom's Cabin; or, the Negro Slave* (at the Standard, a large East End theatre), on 8 September 1852[20] was judged by the *Era* to have been 'produced with the greatest possible success, and really merited very considerable praise for the interesting nature of its plot, and the admirable manner in which it is produced'.[21] It contains what were to become the standard elements of the separate escapes of George and Eliza, Tom's refusal to escape, the assistance given by the Quakers to the fugitives and Tom's sale to Legree. However, it differs from other later versions in that the saviour of all at crucial points in the narrative is the good-hearted, brave, down-to-earth white character Van Tromp, who scarcely features in the original novel. A former slaveowner who has seen the light, it is Van Tromp who fights off the slavehunters Marks and Loker; Van Tromp who tells George how to escape by riding a log down the rapids of the Ohio River; Van Tromp who is almost killed by bloodhounds when assisting George; Van Tromp into whose hands fall all Legree's estate, and slaves; Van Tromp who, in the end, makes all right.

In this can be seen refracted the paternalistic prejudices formed through- out the course of abolitionism. Douglas Lorimer has argued that aboli- tionism, in the persistence with which it pursued its case and under the necessity of pleading its cause, also served to entrench a simplified racial stereotype of the black as a noble but suffering supplicant who appealed to anti-slavery sentiment.[22] The Standard's version of *Uncle Tom* (a confusing potboiler in terms of its action) reflects that vision. Thus Tom himself displays almost nothing of the exaggerated 'black' dialogue that subsequent versions assigned to him. Instead, he retains more than a little of the noble

African, wrenched from his homeland, who had long been a familiar figure on the English stage. This Tom is dignified with the slavehunter Loker:

Loker: Fine Times when freedom of speech is granted to a Black face . . .
Tom: Chance may have given a power over the limb but Heaven gives power to that and freedom to that which they can never fetter, the mind.[23]

And, when Van Tromp shakes his hand, Tom is moved to reflect:

Tom: Tisn't everyone would give his hand to a Man of Colour, many have an antipithy [*sic*] to Black . . . If all were as liberal minded as he, he who has left the dusty sons of Africa would never feel the Racking Chain that binds them. Alas, there are but few, but those few, like the distant storm that gathers in strength and power as it comes, may work the good they labour for – and, rushing as the Tempest, sweep from the earth's fair surface the name of slaves.[24]

This could have come straight from the abolitionist literature of the previous century. The dramatist has reached for the old language, long familiar from the slave trade, to evoke the experience of contemporary domestic slavery. It is not the language of the American experience or of Tom in Stowe's novel; rather, it is closest to Thomas Morton's high-flown style in *The Slave* (1816).

   This image of Tom, as the suffering and noble slave of abolitionist literature, is still extant in the curious version produced one week later by Eliza Vincent at the Victoria (the former Coburg) on 15 September 1852 under the title *Uncle Tom's Cabin; or, the Fugitive Slave!*.[25] But here the image is already showing signs of its future development. Tom's language veers crazily in register and tone. When Eliza comes to his cabin to warn of the impending sale, he greets her in the language of pure melodrama: 'Ha – that haggard face – and wild dark eye tell a tale of suffering – I wish to ask but dread to know the cause.'[26] On the other hand, when Tom, George and Eliza are all on board a slave ship, Tom lapses into the staple phonetic of minstrelsy: 'I tell you George dar is hope . . . on de oder side of de riber you would be safe . . . if you can get into de boat wid your Lizy.'[27] In this version Tom has little scope for developing his persona, his role being largely limited to one or two speeches expressing moral defiance of Legree, for which he is whipped to death, off stage.

   However, the first of Fitzball's versions, written for the more upmarket Olympic, is another matter (*Uncle Tom's Cabin*, 20 September 1852).[28] No longer is it for Tom to give vent to the injustice of slavery – that is now the sole province of the light-skinned George. Instead, our first encounter with him, in the snug, almost fairytale, confines of his cabin, snow falling thickly outside, is this:

SCENE FROM THE NEW DRAMA OF "UNCLE TOM'S CABIN," AT THE OLYMPIC THEATRE.

10 *Uncle Tom's Cabin* at the Olympic *Illustrated London News* (2 October 1852), courtesy
of Senate House Library, University of London

Tom: He! he! he! Well m' do lub massa: Him nebber tink to part Tom from him
childers: Tom lay down him life for good kind massa ... dere nebber wur
sich massa an sich missis: I do tink dem nabber sell mself ... *dear* massa.[29]

His reaction, when he finds out he is to be sold, is in similar vein:

Tom: No: no: I ain't going: Let Lizy go ... tant in natur for her to stay ... I must
be sold to pay masser's debt, or all tings, maybe, go to rack an ruin: Poor
Massar and Missis, turn'd out o' their comforble home ... Masser ant to
blame Chloe; he'll take care o' you an the childer when Tom's gone: and if
Masser's in trouble Tom's willin to go – to *die* for m (*Dashing away tears*).[30]

This is Tom in all his unreasoning docility, and is the image of Tom
which, by and large, pertains henceforth, though laid on more thickly here
than in some versions. ('Uncle Tom, a quiet, low comedy part, with more
than a dash of sentiment' was the way the *Era* characterised it in one
notice.)[31] Nothing could be more expressive of racial inferiority than this

unctuous dependence on the very institution to which the slave's life was forfeit. Here the black is rendered sentimental and pathetic to an unprecedented degree and we can perhaps see in Tom's speeches the conjunction of two projections of racialised belief. On the one hand, the sentimental pathos of Tom is on a continuum with the kneeling, manacled slave begging to be recognised as a man; the object of white pity and paternalism. But, at the same time, in his use of language – the childlike self-referral in the third person, the use of the all-purpose 'm' as a pronoun, and especially in his occasional more comic moments – he is a re-presentation of the grotesque Jim Crow.

His by-play with his garrulous wife Chloe, for example, depends on the familiar notion of the bathetic nature of black love and the black family: their children, tucked up asleep, are, in Chloe's words, 'like so many innocent black coopids atop o' white clouds: Only listen how beauty em's a snorin.'[32] The image of domestic happiness which is about to be sundered by the sale of Tom is presented like this:

Tom: ... massa an missy won [*sic*] flesh, in blood: An arn't you an I same metal. Only 'm do think, you most beautifulest and lobberly woman, eber lib'd out o' paradise (*kisses her*) He! he!

Chloe: Oh Tom! you're a duck, dat's what m' is ... (*Tom hugging her, the candle in her hand*)

Tom: Oh Cloe! Chloe! m's Wenus an ... al de greases [graces].[33]

The pun on grace/grease, made at Chloe's expense, refers not only to her presumably spilling candle wax as she is hugged, but also to the common stereotype of black skin, expressing repugnance to it. It is worth remembering that, about a decade and a half earlier, at the height of the Crow craze, the same playwright, Fitzball, had portrayed a demonic black villain in *The Negro of Wapping* (1838). That play owed virtually nothing to the mania for Crow and harked back to the much older tradition of black representation, with its black villain, Sam, set firmly in the mould of the vengeful African cast into slavery. Of course, Tom is not a villain and so cannot be compared directly with Sam, but nothing of the earlier play's concluding acknowledgement, however cursory, of slavery as a structural issue, involving deracination and enforced labour, now remains. Nor does Sam's melodramatic but relatively straightforward language, though at the very last Tom (who in this version does not die) is allowed a moment of dignity. As Tom, his wife and children sink to their knees together with cries of joy and George, Eliza, their child and Mr Shelby enter, forming a picture, Tom speaks thus:

Tom: Merciful power! You have not forgotten, look down and witness the mingled gratitude of the poor slave. (*Moment of devotion in which the picture is contemplated in silence: all the men take off their hats*).[34]

In the Lemon and Taylor version, Tom is at least treated with consistent seriousness, and is allowed to speak in a fairly mild version of 'black' dialect, but then he hardly appears in the play at all. His Christian devotion, the main aspect of Tom as a serious character, is almost elided, as the *Spectator* pointed out.[35] His primary function here, apart from a short scene with his family, is to be beaten up (off stage) by Legree's henchmen for assisting Eliza (also Legree's captive) with cotton-picking and for refusing to whip her. For this he is briefly and brutally dispatched by Legree with a bowie knife. In the words of the *Era*'s reviewer, this Tom is 'a passive black, always sinned against and never sinning'.[36] Only, it seems, in those plays in which Tom is a semi-comic turn is he allowed to flourish; there is now so little scope for a black-skinned character to take centre stage as a major protagonist against slavery.

'WHY NOT DIS NIGGER?'

Tom, though, is not the only representation of the black in these plays. The version for the Standard opens – as do a number of others – with another picture, familiar from *Obi* (1800) onwards, of the happy plantation scene. Here attention is focused on the minor comic characters of Sam and Andy. Sam is the stereotype of minstrelsy, his stupidity matched by his self-importance, his inability to use language matched by his pride in his 'speechifying'; Andy is his more clued-up sidekick. It is they who locate the audience in this other world of the plantation, they who confirm the audience's preconceived expectations of slave life and mores. Sam is all for defending the slaves' rights:

Sam: You see fellow countrymen, you see what's this Chile up to, it's for fending yer all, yes all of yer, I'll stand up for your rights, I'll fend em to my last breath … boys like you Andy means well but they can't be spected to collusitate the great principal [*sic*] of action.[37]

Despite such a declaration of slave solidarity, Sam is quite prepared to make a genuine search for the missing Eliza, in this version as in all others, to recapture her for her new master. That he is happy to enhance his own standing by finding her and bringing her back exposes the hollowness of his boasts about 'rights': 'Well it's an ill wind that blows nowise, dat are a fact, well of course dere is room for some nigger to be up, and why not dis Nigger?'[38] Only when Andy points out that 'Missee don't want her catched' does Sam change his tune.[39] Then, in the manner of comic servants every-where, he manages to thwart Eliza's recapture while pretending to aid it.

All this is in Stowe's novel, detailed at great length, and she makes it clear that part of Sam's 'front' is just that, a face to meet the faces that he meets. He is unctuous with his deeply religious mistress, bragging before his fellow slaves, and, by playing the part of the deferential, stupid slave, per-forms a classic doubletake on the slavetrader Haley in the search for Eliza that enables Eliza to gain enough time to make her escape. When Haley, accompanied by Andy and Sam, finally arrives at the ferryhouse where Eliza is vainly awaiting a chance to cross the ice-bound river, it is Sam who spots her and manages to draw her attention while distracting Haley so that she can flee. While Stowe looks askance at her creation for his fundamental dishonesty, it is possible for a later generation to recognise Sam's ability for 'puttin' on massa' as a viable slave strategy, even though he is cast within the bounds of stereotype. But to develop too far the notion of a subtle, mani-pulative Sam, working white society for his own purposes, would weaken the concept of a racialised hierarchy (albeit inverted by what Jean Fagan Yellin terms a 'Christian transvaluation'[40]) on which the novel depends. Sam, in other words, would be stepping outside his allotted role in the moral order, using dishonesty and subterfuge in the service of his own conception of justice. At that point, his struggle against slavery becomes political, rather than moral. In Stowe's ordering the political is always subsumed to the moral. Even if this were not so, such a reevaluation of Sam's character and strategy would run counter to the rigid racialism expressed in the plays.

On stage, Sam and Andy remain black buffoons to a greater extent than in the novel. Generally, their function in the overall action is greater and Sam's use of language, evidenced above, is given ample scope. In the version by Vincent for the Victoria, Sam, as well as taking the limelight in the scene in which 'Lizzy' (as she is in this version) is discovered to have gone missing, is also shown having a quarrel with MilkWhite (a very minor figure in the novel) over her infatuation with the white comic figure, Tom Tickler. Tickler has no parallel in the novel. The dialogue between Sam and MilkWhite makes the usual obvious pun and has the characteristics of 'minstrel'-type speech:

Sam: So Miss MilkWhite, you may turn black if you please – and you may turn de corner an I care a button – you no get ober me dat way howsomdever.
MilkWhite: Massa Tickler am got a wife – but if she dies, him says – I shall be Mrs. Tickler.
Sam: Hold your tongue MilkWhite and go and do um work.[41]

There is an echo here of the type of 'Ethiopian opera' that was so popular from the days of Crow onwards, its humour lying in the premises that a) romance between blacks was funny and b) their pretensions were even funnier. Often such 'romances' revolved around the rivalry between a grotesque black (like Crow) and a 'dandy' type, aping his betters, for the affections of their beloved, who just wants to do as well for herself as possible. Indeed, while *Uncle Tom* was playing to packed houses, just such a piece, G. H. George's rhyming doggerel with songs attached, *A Colour'd Commotion*, was playing at the Strand.[42] A somewhat similar attempt at exaggerated buffoonery can be seen in Pitt's *Uncle Tom's Cabin* (1852), involving the white character Billy Bombast, the object in this case of the female slave Snowball's affections.[43] The giving of absurd names that alluded to whiteness was a common tactic of minstrel comedy. On the grounds that you cannot have too much of a good thing, Billy too, though 'white', is in blackface – and ethnic Pelion is piled on racial Ossa:

Sam: Is that the natural colour of your cheeks Massa [?]
Billy: No, not exactly, my wife was a black nigger taken away by the Chicktaws . . .
       She didn't like my colour so she rubbed my face over with charcoal and
       grease, and then scrubbed me till at last I bolted . . . shew me the way to the
       kitchen, and I'll soon Clar de kitchen. (*Sings ad lib.*)[44]

('Clar de kitchen' was a popular minstrel song.) Billy is later captured as a rebel Indian chief who can be sold as a slave, and Snowball consequently loses all interest in him.

The versions of Uncle Tom and their peculiarities of emphasis have to be seen in the context of a public taste by now familiarised to, and expectant of, a particular grotesque image of the American black. Hence much material of this nature has less to do with forwarding the action than with perpetrating more 'comic' black dialogue. While in Pitt's version the comic stupidity of Sam and Andy serves more as a feeder to Billy Bombast, in others it is Sam's buffoonery that is emphasised. In the first of Fitzball's versions (for the Olympic), for example, Sam makes a lengthy, would-be comical speech to the ferryman's wife, Mrs Budd, establishing Haley's credentials – 'Masser quite a gemplem: only look at m: Why dere am his match in Queen Victorys drawin room.'[45] – then, after holding open the window and urging Eliza to escape, he manages successfully to fall down in front of Haley while Haley is pursuing Eliza up the rocks.

Topsy is the other character type who falls into the category of the grotesque. For the most part she is put on stage for her comic shock value as an expression of complete amorality. Most versions are content to reproduce extracts of dialogue, sometimes rather garbled, straight from the novel, in which Topsy steals ribbons from under her mistress's nose, is told to confess and so confesses to what she *has not* done. Topsy has no concept either of right or of wrong, or of mother or father, having been raised by a 'speculator'. In the novel her state of brutalised, heathen ignorance is a foil to the naturally profound moral sense of Eva and a comment on the evil of slavery's destruction of family life. In the plays she is a brief black comic turn, much in the manner of Sam and Andy, but, by and large, she plays no part in forwarding the plot. She afforded a certain scope for effect to the actresses who played her, usually in a turban and freakish dress suggestive of the black child slave-servant that one sometimes sees in eighteenth-century portraits of the aristocracy.[46] Topsy's comic strangeness was popular, for she could be comfortably laughed at, sealed off as she was from the rest of the moral universe. Only in Lemon and Taylor's version does she become a major figure: a sentimentalised and docile version of the character whose sharpness as a type stood out in the novel, she is here smoothed off into the comic servant, who, disguised as a boy, aids George's escape, helps to reunite George and Eliza and thwarts Legree's plans. Her constant catchphrase, 'I's so wicked', is belied by her actions, but also serves to establish her inferior status. It was a change that was not altogether to the taste of the *Spectator*'s reviewer:

We only wish they had abstained from making *Topsey* [*sic*] assume the disguise of a pert 'tiger' [i.e., a showily dressed boy servant]. The other personages of the piece exhibit the various actors in positions which we have seen over and over again; but *Topsey* as represented by Mrs. Keeley is one of those bold though highly-finished pictures of character which, however small, stand out from the general mass, and we regret to see it toned down into mere stage-conventionality.[47]

The *Era* was more wholehearted, praising 'the surprising manner in which [Mrs Keeley] more than realized the conception of the author . . . As the negro girl, believing herself to be "wicked", and yet capable of doing good, she was inimitable. Everybody seemed delighted with the portraiture she afforded.'[48] Topsy has become not too unfamiliar, is now held within the moral universe, albeit as an inferior.

THE SLAVE DRAMA AS DOMESTIC MELODRAMA

Uncle Tom and Topsy have survived in the popular imagination because, for the most part, they fitted so well into the minstrelised vision of the black. This, however, is not the only legacy that the *Uncle Tom* plays passed on. They also marked a change in the way that slavery was approached in English drama. From *Oroonoko* (1695) onwards slavery had been denounced on the stage, passionately if intermittently, for its assault on the individual in terms of universal values of liberty and human equality. In play after play the structural context of slavery is, however glancingly, alluded to in speeches referring to seizure, capture and enforced labour away from the homeland; a brief recapitulation, in fact, of the triangular trade. Such set pieces would, in many ways, be anachronistic by the mid-nineteenth century. But in losing them, a wider perspective on the issue is lost that connects continents; connects cause and effect. With the *Uncle Tom* plays, however, as with the original novel, the condemnation of slavery is expressed dramatically not so much as an assault on the universal human right to liberty as an assault on the family and family life. Or, rather, two families. First, there is the comical family of Uncle Tom; nearly every play has a scene in Tom's cabin, with black children huggermugger, sometimes even being thrown food by their mother Chloe who, however, hands it to the white son of the plantation owner, George Shelby. Tom, childlike himself, is nearly always shown being instructed in the art of writing by George. His admiration of George flatters the audience directly. 'How easy white folks always does things!' he exclaims.[49] No doubt many of those who flocked to see *Uncle Tom* could not read or write either – but Tom assured them that they could, if they would. In contrast to the many incidents of the novel that were only occasionally dramatised, this is a constant, some form of it appearing in virtually every version. Most reflect, with comfortable, patronising warmth, the basic inferiority of Tom's family. Only in the complete reworking of the novel by Lemon and Taylor is the scene altered to show Tom's children learning to write. In fact, their depiction of Uncle Tom's family life is more tender and natural than most. But Tom, as I have said, has a certain dignity accorded him by Lemon and Taylor which is elsewhere denied him. The version by Richard Shepherd and William Creswick (see below), performed at that home for melodrama, the Surrey, also insists on Tom's tears for his children, but the basic unreality of their Tom renders his emotion less affecting.

Second, there is the almost white family of George and Eliza and their son Harry. George and Eliza are married but unable to live together as man and wife, and George, from being a skilled worker in a factory, is to be sent back to the plantation and forced to take another 'wife'. Hence he is determined to escape to Canada. Then, when Harry is sold away from Eliza, she, too, is forced to flee. Stowe's novel, with its emphasis on the family – from the central situation of George and Eliza, to the separation of

Tom, Chloe and their children, to the story of the motherless and fatherless Topsy, to the sexual degradation of young women sold away from their mothers at auction – obviously lends itself to domestic melodrama of the most powerful nature. Indeed, the characterisation falls neatly into place: there is Uncle Tom, a variant of the good old man; Eliza the virtuous heroine and mother, pursued by the slavetrader villain Haley, who is intent on breaking up the family unit for his own ends; George, the hero husband, defying death for his wife and child; Sam, Andy and Topsy, all, variously, comic servants. The good child who dies young might also, in the person of Little Eva, have found a place in this scenario, but she features only rarely in the English dramatisations of the novel. Where she does shine is in the full American version, by George Aiken – six acts long, and taking, according to Birdoff, some five hours in the performance.[50]

Thus, in all the plays, Eliza's love for her child, that most sacred of domestic ties, is insisted on at every turn – to Mrs Budd (the ferryman's wife who, in some versions, helps Eliza to escape), to Mrs Bird (the kind-hearted senator's wife who takes her in), and in appeals to Legree or Haley. It is emphasised in the Lemon and Taylor adaptation, for example, which interpolates a scene in which Eliza reads Harry a goodnight story as he falls asleep. Then, as she prepares to take him away, a lengthy passage details the small, domestic preparations she makes:

Eliza: Poor boy! poor boy! they have sold us, but your mother will save you yet. (*she places a toy upon the table*) That toy may keep him quiet should he be alarmed when I wake him. (*she goes to a cupboard, L., and opens it, then spreads out a handkerchief as though to form a bundle; she places cakes and fruit in it, listening every now and then*) He will need something before I shall dare to seek for shelter or refreshment. Where is his mantle? (*takes out a mantle and places it on the bed*) The night is frosty; poor fellow he may have far to travel. (*she takes out some articles of infant clothing, a lace cap and small frock*) Ah, this! (*from a box, R., she presses it to her lips*) Time was when I should have wept to have parted with this relic. They are too happy to be mourned for – all is ready. (*She rouses* HARRY.)[51]

Of course, the charm of this passage is that it is so simple and unaffected. The collection of small domestic articles that she prepares for the journey summons up her past life; such a physical evocation was a familiar locus of domestic melodrama. Here it is tenderly and sensitively achieved. Most of the plays are far more declamatory in style, more overtly melodramatic when Eliza is contemplating her and Harry's fate if she does not escape. This, for example, is Eliza ('Lizzy') in Vincent's version (Vincent was known for heavy melodrama):

Lizzy: . . . No it was not a dream. I heard the words plainly – my boy is sold – my
heart beats as if it would burst – ah. I see a chance to free my boy, oh be firm
my nerve – be bold my woman's heart . . . (*takes up child and exits thro'
window.*)[52]

Fitzball, a master of blood, thunder and 'blue fire' in some of his other
work, is also true to form. He takes things even further, for his Eliza
contemplates murder:

Eliza: What have I overheard? *My* child *sold*: the only comfort of my existence to
be torn from me! . . . Yonder he lies, fast asleep; little dreaming of our
separation: a separation, perhaps, for ever, in this world. (*Grasping a knife
on the table*) What if, at once, while he is asleep, I end at once his miseries, as
my poor husband said (*Dropping the knife*) Oh! heaven forgive me![53]

Whether portrayed through the histrionics of melodrama, or the naturalism introduced by Taylor, it is slavery's destruction of the mother's tie to
the child that is the strongest and most emotional indictment of the
institution. Rights of property in another human being are less the issue
here, though, as I show below, this argument is raised by George, in a
manner that sometimes evokes the discourse of the past.

Some versions also allude to Tom's distress at his separation from his
children. However, in a major departure from the novel, virtually nothing
is made of what Stowe terms his 'stubborn preference' for freedom. The
Tom we see in almost all the plays is only too happy to serve a good master,
and willing to serve a bad. His black skin denotes the utmost servility. It
is from George that the bitterest denunciations of slavery emanate, often
taken almost verbatim from the novel, but varying in their length and
emphasis. Those denunciations focus either on the devastation that slavery
wreaks on the right to family life, thus emphasising the domestic, or, in an
echo of earlier dramas, on the nature of man and liberty. Nearly all have
some version of the following:

Eliza: Oh George, your master
George: My Master! Master in what, am I not in form and strength his more than
equal, in heart and intellect his superior? Although chance and an unjust
law, a law that every nation but our own despise, deny, gave power over
me, 'tis but the Law of Man; the Law of Heaven, I feel, gives freedom to
my soul and bids me burst the trammels that corrupt justice and despite
power would bind me in, bids me be as Heaven ordained I should be –
free as the air.[54]

This is still redolent of the language of universalism, of earlier expressions
of anti-slavery sentiment. Like other mixed-race protagonists, it is George
who comes closest to expressing sentiments of vengeance. Here, too – and

in a drama founded at bottom on the iniquity of slavery based on race – the black avenger has become the almost white one.[55] This is Fitzball vehemently reworking the same theme, after a passage in which even Eliza has expressed the view that the Almighty 'ordains for some great end, that the African *should be* a slave':[56]

George: Master! Who made him my master? What right has he to me? . . . In strength: in intellect I am infinitely his superior: yet, I am driven about by the command of such a thing . . . when I ventured to ask to come hither: I was tied to a tree, and the lash of his accursed whip, still writes the word *vengeance* across my shoulders . . . I'll *kill him*.[57]

The attack on slavery is particularly pronounced in the version by Shepherd and Creswick, simply entitled *Uncle Tom's Cabin* and performed at the Surrey on 27 October 1852. This version, which initially is fairly faithful to the novel, was well received by the reviewers. To the *Era* it was 'the best adaptation as yet' and 'a decided "hit"'[58] and, according to the *Illustrated London News*, it 'achieved extraordinary success'.[59] Much of its dialogue was drawn from the novel; for example, none of the other adaptations gives at such length the scene between George, on the run, and his former factory boss (not his owner), Mr Wilson. Wilson is a kindhearted man, torn between his distress at George's plight and his anxiety that George is 'setting [himself] in opposition to the laws of [his] country' and 'running such a dreadful risk'.[60] In this version, as nowhere else in the English versions, to my knowledge, George details at length how his mother, sisters and brothers were all put up for sale:

George: . . . She knelt down before this, my present master and begged him to buy her with me, that she might have at least one child with her, and he kicked her away with his heavy boot. I saw him do it, and the last I ever heard of my mother was her moans and screams, when I was tied to his horse's neck, to be carried off to his place.
Wilson: I own these things are very bad, but –[61]

George's refrain, that he owes no duty to laws that separate husband and wife and child, that 'crush and keep us down'[62] echoes the novel's constant domestic theme and entrenches slavery as a domestic issue.

That the continual reiteration of the attack on slavery is not accidental is evidenced by the way in which Shepherd and Creswick depart from the novel. They conclude their adaptation with an out and out slave revolt on the Legree plantation, even as George is grappling with Legree:

Quimbo: Oh Massa – The slaves are up, at the fall of whip on Uncle Tom – dey all now in mutiny 'cos they say he read 'em words of comfort. (*Loud shout*)

George: That voice, perhaps hers! (*Unconsciously leaves Legree – the fire increases.*)
Quimbo: They have set fire to the buildings!
        ...

Legree: My pistols! Sword. your gun! (*Exit Quimbo*) I'll teach 'em yet. (*Re-enter Quimbo with others*)
Quimbo: Massa! Massa! They come this way (*Enter slaves with lighted brands.*)
Omnes: Down with the oppressor. (*General fight – Legree desperate – he is beaten off.*)[63]

A satisfying conflagration and the (unlikely) arrest of Legree by Tom conclude the riot, though not before Tom has really acted the part of an Uncle Tom:

Tom: ... The mutiny no fault o' mine, no fault o' this poor chile's [Harry] ... Oh don't hurt poor child – I won't run massa – I'll go back to the slaves, tell how bad to disobey the massa and rise agin 'em – told 'em so afore – when they wouldn't let me be flogged.[64]

Just as George's violent insistence on freedom is contained within his status as being of white and, in this version, aristocratic, parentage, so the satisfying spectacle of revolt is held in check by Tom's nauseating obedience. At the very end, the play harks back to the type of resolution familiar from *The Slave* onwards, in which Britain prided itself on having abolished the slave trade, but with an emphasis on the domestic that marks the incorporation of the slavery play into domestic melodrama:

St. Clair: George, brother – my hand and all are yours! What is your purpose?
George: To breathe the air of Freedom's land, Canada! Where the roof that covers, however humble, shall protect me ... where wife – children, by sacred tie shall still be mine ... where waves the flag, nation's flag upon which the sun sets not, and wherever it waves man's right is held as sacred as his life.[65]

CASSY – THE FEMALE AVENGER

If George can be seen in a number of the plays as retaining some of the characteristics, in heroic rather than villainous mode, of the avenging black figure, Lemon and Taylor have, in their adaptation, gone some way further by recasting that figure as a woman. Here Cassy, the enslaved mistress of Legree in the novel, who is determined to revenge herself on him for her degradation but is a figure often dropped from the English stage versions, is given a central role. It is she who warns Eliza of the sale of both her and her child to Legree; who threatens and defies Legree; who attempts to protect

Tom; who is only stopped from stabbing Legree by Tom and who, at the last, fires the fatal shot that kills him. Legree and his henchmen are pursuing George, Eliza, Cassy and Topsy up a rocky pass:

George: ... Now, Topsy, mind I take the first man; you take the second ...
Eliza: But if you don't hit?
George: I *shall* hit.
Cassy: Stop; mind, George, Simon Legree's life is mine. It was his hand crushed me to what I am. It must be my hand that shall avenge me![66]

But before all this, Cassy has unflinchingly outlined her descent into degradation at Legree's hands to Eliza in a way that must have had the power to shock a contemporary audience. The sexual nature of Legree's transactions is quite explicit. Here he is talking about Eliza, his latest purchase, to Loker, in Cassy's presence:

Legree: ... that yellar gal – oh, brandy. Come, I'll wet the bargain. (*CASSY motions TOM to leave – he does so*) She's a beauty she is; quiet as a pigeon. Clar skin; eye – bright as lightnin', and teeth white as new dominers ... (*sees CASSY*) ... Cass yer! what do you look that way for?
Cassy: (*placing her foot on the chair and resting her head upon her hand*) So you have bought some new hand, Simon Legree?
Legree: Yes. What's that to you? I buy what I like; *sell* what I like ... I'll bring home one as shall break your heart with jealousy, that's fact.[67]

His clumsy attempt to 'be friends' with Cassy and pull her on to his knee simply emphasises the crudity of his sexual use of her.

The detail of Cassy's stance – one foot on the chair, hand under her chin – suggests her power over him and is emblematic of her positioning outside the boundaries of respectable female society. That she is not white, that she is enslaved, but that she is, nonetheless, contained within the strict overall confines of the melodramatic form made it, perhaps, more possible for the dramatists to push at the boundaries of what it was acceptable for a woman to express:

Eliza: And the child! What of him?
Cassy: They told me that he had slept to death upon my bosom. I knew that he was dead, and I am glad of it now ... Again I was sold. I passed from hand to hand until at last I became what I am now – utterly lost – utterly degraded ... For six years I have been the companion of a man – brutal, drunken, and inhuman ... and now my tyrant has grown weary of me and has bought another mistress.[68]

Satisfyingly, Cassy does succeed in killing her man and, even more satisfyingly, is not punished by an early death either for her life of degradation or for the murder – surely a stretching of convention. She was not without peers on the stage: the month before Lemon and Taylor's drama was performed, *Sarah Blangi* (adapted from a French original) was playing at the Olympic in Drury Lane. 'The conception of a creole having a slain father to avenge on a whole family, and pursuing her work in the spirit of *Zanga* and *Iago* forms the basis of a very powerful and exceedingly well-acted *drame*', declared the *Illustrated London News*.[69] Perhaps, though, the fact that Sarah was acting out of duty to her father made her crimes more palatable, for there was no suggestion in the above review that Sarah was too strong a figure to take, as was, perhaps, implied in the *Era*'s mention of Cassy: 'Madame Celeste as Cassy, was, we cannot help saying, more melodramatic than natural.'[70]

UNCLE TOM, OLD TOM AND ANTI-TOMISM

Cassy apart, the thickly laid-on piety of the various *Uncle Tom*s soon met with a reaction. Some of this was simply due to the excess of plays which continued to crowd the stage, alongside all the books, pamphlets and novelties that were produced. The Sadler's Wells pantomime, for instance, moved swiftly from Uncle Tom to end 'with the exhibition of the greatest slave-master of all – "Old Tom" [i.e., gin]'.[71] Fitzball's second version of *Uncle Tom*, at Drury Lane in January 1853, which introduced the character of a pedlar, specially devised for George Wild of Wild's travelling theatre, was pronounced a critical failure, though it temporarily redeemed Drury Lane's perilous financial fortunes.[72] According to the *Era*, 'The subject is growing thin to barrenness, and the national sentiment is in a state of reaction from the tension [in] which it has been much too long kept.' Uncle Tom's sermonising 'might have been supplanted to advantage by the bones and banjo', which shows how closely the *Uncle Tom* plays – despite their overt message – fitted into a conception that 'black' equalled minstrelsy.[73]

The same mix was part of *Uncle Tom and Lucy Neal; or, Harlequin Liberty and Slavery*, the pantomime at the Pavilion, an East End theatre.[74] This 'depicted the evil powers of slavery' (allied with 'Old Monopoly' and 'Cruelty') but also included 'Mr. Cave … the celebrated delineator of nigger character, as Dandy Jim' winning 'immense applause in two very well executed negro ditties'.[75] 'Lucy Neal', a popular minstrel song, is here embodied as the niece of Uncle Tom and the sweetheart of Herman, whose 'cruel dad' forbids their love.[76] Slavery, ably assisted by Old Monopoly and Cruelty, aims to capture Tom and Lucy. The Pavilion, which was a home for nautical drama, deftly combined in this offering the condemnation of slavery and the appeal of minstrelsy with the celebration of a very English freedom:

> Happy England, glorious nation
> Where freedom dwells in every station
> Thy wealth and ships that plough the wave
> Are freely given to free the slave
> A refuge for all who in distress
> Seek thy shores of happiness . . .
> True liberty in its purity there is seen
> A glorious people, a beloved queen.[77]

By the Easter of 1853, J. R. Planché's one-act extravaganza *Mr Buckstone's Ascent of Parnassus* was winning favourable reviews. A parody of Albert Smith's *Ascent of Mont Blanc* (1852), it portrayed Buckstone as an actor-manager, invoking the aid of Fashion and Fortune to discover what appealed to the public taste. Along with the Corsican Brothers and other popular novelties, no less than six Uncle Toms make an appearance:

> *Mr. B*: 'Oh! my prophetic soul! my Uncle' – Tom!
> But here are half a dozen uncles more!
> . . . Mercy on us, with what fury
> Has this black fever raged! – The Olympic, Drury,
> Adelphi, Marylebone, Victoria, Surrey!
> Against each other running hurry-scurry.
> Whipping their Topseys [*sic*] up in ways most scurvy,
> And turning the poor drama topsy-turvy![78]

'A clever little song' was then sung by Mrs Fitzwilliam, 'winding up by the expression of a wish, most heartily responded to by the audience, that [Uncle Tom] would go "where the other nigger'd gone"'.[79]

> Wherever you travel, wherever you stop,
> Uncle Tom his black pole's [*sic*] sure to show;
> With his songs, polkas, waltzes, they fill every shop,
> Till like Topsy, 'I 'specs they must grow!'
> The stage had enough of Jim Crow,
> A jumping and a 'doing just so',
> And 'twould be quite a blessing if poor old Tom
> Would after that good nigger go.[80]

Some of the anti-Tom material, though, was far less good-humoured, cruder and more overtly racist than this. At the height of Tom mania, for example, William Brough was responsible for two such burlesques, *Uncle Tom's Crib*, performed at the Strand, and *Those Dear Blacks!*. The first piece, in which Uncle Tom is the landlord of a public house, revolves around the threadbare, Jim Crow-type situation of a romantic triangle in which Dandy Jim and Squashtop vie for the affections of Dinah. 'Meagre' was the epithet bestowed on it by the *Era*. Interestingly, however, its attack on Uncle Tom did not, at this stage, seem to go down well with the audience: 'The attempts at some clap trap allusion to the prevailing mania about "niggers" [presumably Tom mania] were by no means cordially received.'[81] This would imply that Tom had become dissociated from any serious anti-slavery sentiment, for, the review continued, 'some hints at the humbug sentimentalism of the oldwomanry of Exeter Hall were smart, and even warmly caught up'.[82] Exeter Hall symbolised the earnest Evangelicalism of a large section of the abolitionist movement. An alternative reading would be that the 'clap trap allusion' refers to anti-slavery rather than anti-Tom sentiments, in which case the audience are showing their disgust with abolitionist sentiment *per se*.

Those Dear Blacks!, apparently based on 'French materials', sounds even more unpleasant. Played at the Lyceum in November 1852, it is the story of a 'Yankee Nigger, "ignorant as dirt", and proud as Lucifer' who, coming into an inheritance and travelling to England to find a white wife and white servant, is imposed upon by a penniless English clerk, Featheredge, played by Charles Mathews, son of the famous comic impersonator. As might be expected, the black, Lillywhite, ends up in his rightful place as the servant and Featheredge, whom he has hired, as his master. 'Mr. Suter makes a capital "darky", and is preposterous as can be, and ridiculous in the extreme,' the *Era* noted.[83]

When the liberal and progressively inclined *Westminster Review*, commenting on recent American literary production and on a spate of pro-slavery novels, declared that 'Uncle-Tomism has had its day', it was both right and wrong.[84] The craze for Uncle Tom burnt out fairly quickly, though performances of *Uncle Tom* plays continued sporadically for a number of years.[85] Yet his legacy lingered on. He had added his unresisting docility, piety and simple-mindedness to the bizarre amalgam that was, by now, ready to be drawn upon for the representation of the black character on the English stage. He had confirmed that it was not he, but the light-skinned mulatto character who could contest slavery. The *Uncle Tom* plays had validated the status of the black as a comic, even grotesque figure or, at best, as a nonentity, from whom all threat had gone. The plays had anchored consideration of slavery within the domestic framework. The slight opportunity that Tom's dignified and freedom-loving but submissive stance offered for a fuller and more respectful presentation of the black character in popular culture had been largely ignored. Lemon and Taylor came closest to this, but their Tom is scarcely present. Even his savage murder is over in the blink of an eye.

Nor would Tom's legacy be substantially altered by the next (and even briefer) fad for Stowe's far more militant work, *Dred: the tale of the Great Dismal Swamp*.

DRED – A NEW DIRECTION?

Uncle Tom's Cabin had been Stowe's response to the passage of the Fugitive Slave Act of 1850, which made assisting runaways to escape to the North a criminal act, and made it possible to seize and reclaim them even when they were there. Similarly, *Dred*, published in August 1856, was a response to 'legal' and extralegal attempts to extend slavery to Kansas and, by implication, to the rest of America. 'In retrospect,' claims Judie Newman in her introduction to a modern edition of *Dred*, 'the Kansas conflict suggests a dress rehearsal for the Civil War.'[86] The novel, largely unknown to the general reader today, had an immediate impact; in its first year it sold 150,000 copies in America and 165,000 in Britain. Like *Uncle Tom's Cabin* before it, it was swiftly seized on as dramatic fodder and by October/ November 1856 was being performed in London at the Queen's, the Victoria, the Surrey, the Britannia and the Standard. 'Never has there been so glorious a success,' trumpeted the Victoria; 'Dred, the most surpassing of all the Surrey successes,' claimed the Surrey; for the Britannia, it was 'triumphant'; and for the Standard, 'the most brilliant hit ever achieved'.[87]

The novel itself – almost 700 pages long – is too complex to be properly summarised here, but deals with the social structures of plantation society, including the situation of poor whites or 'white trash', the need for whose labour is completely undercut by the presence of skilled, cost-free labour in the form of slaves; the corruption (affecting both black and white) and waste endemic in slavery; the impossibility of its reform by gradualist measures; the collusion of the churches in sanctifying and justifying it; the struggle for abolition; the violence and lynchings that keep it in place (all legally justified, since a slave was the absolute property of the master and not a person in the eyes of the law); and the presence of self-liberated, independent Maroon communities of former slaves, eking out a precarious existence in the inaccessible reaches of the swamps of the South.[88]

Among the characters whose fates we follow are Nina Gordon, an initially frivolous but immensely loving young woman who has inherited the plantation from her father, Colonel Gordon; her brother Tom, a violent ne'er do well, who takes control of the plantation after Nina's death from cholera; and Harry, a highly educated and cultured slave whom Colonel Gordon had refused to manumit so as to ensure that he would always be there to manage the plantation for Nina. Harry is the half-brother of Tom and Nina (though only Harry knows this), but is violently hated by Tom and forced into escape and outlawry. Harry is married to the beautiful Lisette, a slave. He also has another sister, Cora, fathered by Colonel Gordon. She lived in freedom until the death of her husband but was then forced back into slavery. There is the older slave woman Milly, whose life story and philosophy are closely modelled on those of the black abolitionist Sojourner Truth; the poor white family of the Cripps who are tended by the immensely faithful and devoted slave Uncle Tiff; the idealistic plantation owner and would-be reformer Clayton, who loves Nina; and the eponymous Dred.

It is Dred who lives as a Maroon; Dred who rescues escapees hunted down in the swamps by dogs; Dred who, armed with his rifle, knows, as later generations would come to know, that political power comes out of the barrel of a gun. He attempts to organise an uprising among the slaves, though in the novel this is aborted before it takes place. The character of Dred, who frequently speaks in a strain of exalted, biblical prophecy, combined with a shrewd judgement of the current situation, is closely modelled on that of Nat Turner, a mystic and leader of a revolt in Virginia in 1831, who was ultimately hanged. Moreover, a slave named Dred was one of those involved in the planned 1822 revolt, under Denmark Vesey. In the novel Dred describes himself as the son of Vesey, thus illustrating, as Newman argues, Stowe's awareness of the continuity of black resistance.[89] Even the gentle and humble Uncle Tiff, motivated as he is by his concern for the Cripps children, is able – unlike Uncle Tom – to flee to the community in the swamps and is known to Dred for his assistance to fugitives.

It is obvious from the above summary that *Dred* is far more emphatic in its concept of black resistance – up to the level of armed insurrection – than *Uncle Tom's Cabin*. As has been noted, black abolitionists at the time had criticised the model of passivity and submission that Tom embodied. One might therefore surmise that dramatisations based on *Dred* would counter the myth of the grotesque black buffoon and incompetent. To a certain extent, this is true. The one for the Surrey seems to exemplify Fitzball's approach, in that scenes have been selected and sutured together, and much dialogue has been lifted straight from the novel.[90] The exception to this is

Dred himself. As *The Times* rather cattily put it, the Dred of the novel 'with his mouth perpetually overflowing with Scriptural phraseology, scarcely utters six lines that would be ... tolerable if spoken within the walls of a theatre'.[91] Although some of the manuscript is missing, and evidently huge jumps have sometimes been made to cut from one situation to the next, it is obvious that Dred is, above all, a man of decisive action. Take this passage, in which Dred confronts Tom and his henchmen while shielding an injured fugitive from them:

Dred: ... Who takes him will take this [i.e, a shot from his rifle], and one is quite enough to carry at a time – you like sport you say Tom Gordon – do you – ... whose [*sic*] man enough to take him – come.
Omnes: Tis Dred –
Dred: Aye Dred – Dred the free man – protecting the poor slave. Come (*They* [Tom Gordon's men] *rush on him*) He [Dred] *fires – a man falls – he knocks two other's* [*sic*] *down with his clubbed rifle – seizes Tom Gordon – throws him in the air – he falls heavily and lays stunned while doing this the others rise and are about to stab him as he* [illeg.] *– stands pistol in hand adroitly over the slave's body – they recoil – he laughs – act falls.*[92]

The *Era*, which considered that there was 'a good deal too much of the horrible' and 'a trifle too much of the startling' in the drama, went on: 'The "startling" ... consists always in the sudden appearance of Dred whenever he is wanted, armed with a rifle and revolvers, and who never has less than six ruffians accompanied with we know not how many bloodhounds opposed to him, and who always succeeds in killing some and keeping them all at bay.'[93]

Dred – a 'stubborn "nigger"' *The Times* called him – is, then, no Uncle Tom in either his submissive or his minstrel guise; in Dred's hands 'the delivery of the oppressed comes as a matter of course'.[94] Yet despite this, the overall effect is not that different from the *Uncle Tom* plays. Harry is the light-skinned character (*vide* George in *Uncle Tom's Cabin*), caught up in the toils of slavery and submission to an overweeningly cruel master; he and his sister Cora 'represent those unhappy slaves whose misfortunes are doubly enhanced by the fact of their being *white* ... and having aspirations which are rarely known save in the breasts of freemen'.[95] Dred, though he does have the avenging status of the black character pre-minstrelsy and does, in this version, lead an uprising in which he kills Tom (and dies himself), is turned almost into a kind of *deus ex machina*. He is able to intervene more or less as required and his actions enable Harry, Lisette and Cora to make their way to freedom in Canada. Whereas Karfa in *Three-fingered Jack* dominates and determines the action, and is a more formidable figure for that, Dred does not; his is one story among others. Given, too, that the *Era* described him as a 'freed man' (see also Dred's self-description quoted above) and claimed that the drama depicted the 'atrocities of the slave trade', one wonders how far Dred's status, as an escaped slave fighting slavery, would actually have been understood by the audience.[96]

Moreover, Dred is flanked by black characters who are presented in much more familiar terms. There is the child, Tomtit, a minor figure in the novel, and Pompey, also minor, both 'amusing specimens of the Jim Crow style of nigger'.[97] The passage quoted above, in which Dred fights off a phalanx of villains, is immediately followed by a scene (taken from the novel, but presented there with a certain irony and distancing effect) in which the slaves owned by the philanthropic Claytons put on a sentimental minstrel song and dance entertainment for them. In the play this is presented absolutely straight, and the scene opens with the following chorus:

> Happy nigger, Massa kind
> Grateful darkies Massa good
> Here him shackles neber find
> Nor lash to spill der nigger's blood
> Happy nigger, long him pray
> Massa's life be holiday.[98]

Such scenes of plantation rejoicing can be traced back at least as far as John Fawcett's serio-pantomime of 1800, *Obi*.

Finally, there is Uncle Tiff, 'nurse, tailor, cook, gardener, and tutor to the Cribbs [*sic*] family'.[99] Although he is presented in the novel as in part a comic character – in his exaggerated respect for the blood of the Peytons that runs in Mrs Cripps's veins, for example – he is also taken seriously as a practical, resourceful and loving man who would go to great lengths to protect and care for the Cripps children, and as an exemplar of true Christian faith. He is highly feminised both in the novel and in the plays, that being a prominent aspect of his goodness. We first meet him, before Dred has come on the scene, mending clothes and attempting to comfort the dying Mrs Cripps in the rundown hovel that is the Crippses's cabin:

Tiff rises, puts down stocking – holds child in his arms and smooths [sic] down bed.
Bress der lord – no use in giving up – bless you missis, we'll be all right again in a few days . . .

Mrs Cripps: Tiff, you're a good creature but you don't know how I've been lying alone . . . worrying – watching – weary – and all for nothing for I am worn out and I shall die.

At this, Tiff puts on the kettle, takes the baby out of his cradle and puts him on Mrs Cripps's bed beside her, mends the fire, puts his sewing away and makes the tea, all the while attempting to comfort her: 'Poor ting – poor ting – Tiff known her from her childhood – loved – honor'd – serv'd her faithfully.'[100]

In effect, Tiff is Mrs Cripps's wife. Although his speeches are close to the words that Stowe puts in his mouth, passages such as the above, when presented on stage with Tiff's ragged and absurd clothing in full view as well as the grotesque cart in which he pushes the baby around, would assimilate him more closely to the nonthreatening, docile and ultimately ridiculous stage Uncle Tom. In the Surrey production the part of Tiff was played by Henry Widdicomb, known for his 'comicalities' and 'exaggerations', though in addition he here displayed 'tender pathos and sterling legitimate ability ... in this very difficult part'.[101] *The Times* concurred:

Old 'Tiff', who is the most entertaining personage in the novel is transferred to the stage with but little alteration, save that towards the conclusion he is armed with a brace of pistols to assist in the overthrow of Tom Gordon. That Mr Widdicomb in this part would elicit the frequent roars of his audience might be expected, but his occasional touches of pathos deserve especial commendation.[102]

Even armed, this creature is funny, not dangerous. When to this image is added Tomtit's childishness and sense of fun and the doings of the other minor slave characters, Dred's potential for expressing an alternative view of black capacities is effectively undermined. Moreover, his pseudo-biblical language, even when modified for the stage, marks him out as not quite of this world and as a creature apart from his fellows. As Topsy is sealed off from the accepted moral code, so Dred is sealed into his own highly idiosyncratic moral code. Hence his views cannot be generalised beyond himself; he is not a recognisable 'type' as are Tiff, Tomtit and Pompey.

Many of the same points could be made about W. E. Suter's version, performed at the small and somewhat shabby Queen's in October 1856. It is, however, dramatically more coherent and the necessity of liberty is asserted not only by Harry and Dred, but also by one of Tom's own slaves, Hark. To a certain extent, this broadens the aspiration to freedom beyond just Harry and Dred, both of whom, as has been seen, are atypical of the black slave; Harry because of his white parentage, Dred because of his unique status and moral stance. When the story opens, Nina is already dead and Harry and Lisette are awaiting the advent of Tom as the plantation's new owner. Harry's mixed-race status is firmly established at the outset, with echoes not only of George in the *Uncle Tom* plays but also of some of the mixed-race characters discussed previously:

Harry: ... Oh! how often I have wished that I were a good honest black nigger, then I should know what I was; now I am neither one thing nor the other, I come just near enough to the condition of the white man to look into it, and to appreciate it. I have been educated as a gentleman, and am left a slave.[103]

Tom, who never appears without using his whip on one or other of the slaves, decides, on seeing Lisette, to take 'this pretty quadroon' for himself.[104] A fight ensues when he strikes Harry with his whip for attempting to interfere, and Harry and Lisette flee to join Dred. In this version Dred's role as a *deus ex machina* is even more obvious. The other characters – Harry and Lisette, Tiff and the Cripps children, Tom and Cripps himself – carry forward the action (often physical and highly violent), at crucial points of which Dred suddenly appears and intervenes decisively. Just as rapidly, he then vanishes. He flogs Cripps and throws him out of the window after Cripps has attacked Tiff and the Cripps children in the hovel that is their home, then, having prophesied vengeance for the 'poor slaves ...[who] raise their manacled hands to Heaven', exits.[105] When, in the same scene, Tom and his slaves pursue Harry and Lisette to the cabin, seize Tiff and attempt to seize Harry and Lisette, 'DRED *appears at the window, with his rifle levelled* – ALL *start.*'

All: Dred!
        Enter DRED, at window.
Dred: Ay, Dred, the Avenger![106]

Dred fires at Tom, wounding him, knocks down two men with his riflebutt, throws it down, pulls out a brace of pistols and escapes.

The denouement, in the Great Dismal Swamp, is similar, but far more extended. Tom, with his men, has made his way to Dred's hideout, where he discovers Harry and Lisette and taunts them with his discovery of the document that confers Harry's freedom. As he threatens to destroy it, Dred '*emerges suddenly from bush, snatches the paper from Tom's hand, hurls him round ... and presenting rifle at him with one hand, with the other holds aloft the paper*'.[107] At the last, Tom and Dred die by each other's hand. Dred's final words are unequivocal: 'I can see far into the future – can behold the time when white and black shall be of equal worth. Grieve not for me; I go where all are free; go where my colour is no crime, there – to the abode of bliss – and – liberty – liberty!'[108]

No wonder that when Ira Aldridge played Dred in Belfast, the reviewer commented on his 'uncommon enthusiasm'. Yet this powerful statement has already been partly contradicted in the pattern of action that the play has followed. Scenes of violence and stirring expressions about liberty and slavery are set against more typical stage depictions of slave life. The play's very opening presents that familiar, happy plantation world, characterised in the preliminary description as 'The Slaves' enjoyment interrupted – A black sprite fond of dancing – A Negro's idea of fun' before it gets properly into its stride with 'A tale of sorrow – Woman, man's best comforter ... Sudden arrival of Tom Gordon, the slaves' new master', and so on.[109] Or there is the depiction of the courtship between Jim, one of Tom's slaves, and Katy, formerly Nina's, which is full of malapropisms like 'infection' for affection, 'detachment' for attachment, 'indisposition' for disposition, 'funnyment' for firmament, etc. This scene concludes, after all the violence involving Cripps, Tiff and Dred described above, with Jim and Katy singing a duet to the tunes of 'Lucy Neal' and 'Buffalo Girls'. One verse, sung by Jim, goes:

> Him is black, oo is brown,
> Both am nobby figure,
> And, no doubt, our first born,
> Will be a piebald nigger.[110]

Thus the struggle for freedom and the aspiration to liberty, dramatically expressed by Dred's, Harry's and even Tiff's actions, are framed by the familiar and dominant clichés of minstrelsy. A clear linguistic distinction is drawn between those who are willing to fight openly and die for liberty, such as Dred, Harry and Hark, who all speak the standard English of melodrama, and those who speak in 'slave' dialect. The latter are the focus of the comedy; even when attempting to thwart Tom, they do so in comic fashion. For example, when Jim is ordered by Tom to 'stop that girl [Lisette] – run', Jim simply runs around the room, 'hard as eber him can, massa'.[111] In the event, as with the Surrey's version, the attention focused on slaves like Jim and the doughty but comical Tiff, belies the more serious note struck by Dred.

The dramatisation presented at the Victoria departs much further from the novel than either Suter's or the Surrey's. In this version Nina and Harry are married with a child; Harry is his half-brother Tom's escaped slave. Tom discovers Harry at home with Nina and lashes out at him with a whip. Harry returns the blow and flees to 'join Dred in the great dismal swamp [–] aid the slaves' great cause – fight under the banner of liberty'.[112] He is recaptured by Tom but rescued by Dred, disguised as a dealer in slaves who breaks in those too difficult to handle. (One wonders how this deception was achieved, given the emphasis, in the novel at least, on the 'ebony' of

Dred's skin. No comment is made on it in the *Era*'s review.) The two
escape, Tom pursues, and a battle in the swamp follows in which Tom and
his henchmen are successful. Harry is taken away to be tried and sentenced
to death for having fired on his master.

Once again, Dred is the prophetic and vengeful righter of all wrongs,
who dies at the last for Harry's sake, saving him from being fatally stabbed
by the treacherous Tom. In a twist which owes nothing to Stowe and
everything to the history of melodrama, it is dramatically revealed in court
that Harry and Tom were switched at birth. It is Tom who is the son of the
female slave, Milly; Tom who is therefore the slave and Harry the owner.
That Harry frees Tom on the spot does nothing to mitigate Tom's hatred
of him. Though this is not openly stated, the implication is that Tom's evil
and feckless nature stems from his parentage, as does Harry's natural
nobility – the evil of the mulatto will out.[113]

In this version Dred combines a fervent commitment to liberty with
approval of the restoration of the status quo. His dying words to Harry
close the play:

Dred: Harry – I've had a dreadful struggle to reach you – they caught me at last –
hunted me down with dogs – wounded and bleeding as I was – I thought I
would see you once more and hail you as Colonel Gordon's heir – bless you
all – there's a storm rising in the South – a dreadful struggle will take place
in this great nation . . . I die Harry – in your happiness don't forget poor
Dred or the night you passed in the Great Dismal Swamp.[114]

The 'storm arising in the South' refers to an expected mass uprising of
the enslaved in which Dred, given his history and his sentiments, would
have expected to take part. Yet in hailing Harry as the rightful owner of the
plantation ('Colonel Gordon's heir') and commending his happiness, he is
also, with his dying breath, validating Harry's ownership of the plantation
and its human property. The backwash of all the play's fast-paced action
and incident would easily have masked such a basic inconsistency, but this
conclusion also demonstrates that there was, by this time, little to fear from
even the most determined of black rebels.

Afterword

Ultimately, both Uncle Tom and Dred flattered but failed to change substantially the nature of the black image presented for popular consumption. The nobility of Oroonoko had been eroded by the continuing pressure of a culture still steeped in slavery until, a shadow of his former self and an anachronism from an earlier age, he survived only as parody. Othello towered over all, yet, despite his iconic status, he could do nothing to change the contours of a dramatic stereotype that, essentially, was set by Charles Mathews and T. D. Rice and became burnt into popular consciousness. Throughout it all, for over a quarter of a century, during this time of rapid social and political change, Ira Aldridge toiled up and down the country resurrecting the dramas of the past with their wider perspective on the black; choosing those serious melodramas that could offer scope for a fuller depiction of black potential ; playing in whiteface the despised Jew, Shylock; and even attempting to turn the old, old stereotype of the villainous Moor into a thoroughly Victorian hero. It was all to little avail.

In 1857, the year following Dred's advent, came a major rebellion against British colonial rule in India, and the language that was used of those rebellious natives echoed the language used against rebellious blacks.[1] A continent whose culture had once been respected, in some circles at least, for its antiquity and subtlety became the home of 'niggers' whose barbarities knew no bounds.[2] In 1865 came the Morant Bay rebellion in Jamaica, savagely put down by Governor Eyre. It reawakened the still fresh memories of 1857, reinforcing belief in the untrustworthiness of the lesser breeds. Its aftermath exposed the vitriolic racialism that had become entrenched through slavery and colonial rule and that was embedded in both scientific thinking and popular culture.[3] Eyre was supported by some of the most prestigious writers and thinkers in the land, including Thomas Carlyle, John Ruskin, Alfred, Lord Tennyson and Charles Dickens.[4]

It was a stark demonstration of how racialised had become the continuum of response to any threat to British power; such responses were emphatic of a white racial superiority that had long been in the making. What I have explored here is a small part of that process, showing how images and conceptions of the black dramatic character, part of the mental furniture of succeeding generations of British people, grew out of earlier notions, changing and degrading in response to political, economic and cultural pressures. In this sense, nineteenth-century popular theatre, with its protean appetite for all kinds of material, its recall of the past and its persistence and ubiquity within the cultural landscape, serves as a massive repository of ideas and images. But in its transformation of that material it also exposes, albeit obliquely, some of the conceptual, even ideological, currents that flow through society. Racism, says Nancy Stepan following George Mosse, is a '"scavenger ideology" capable of feeding on whatever materials [lie] at hand'; an examination of popular theatre, which, too, could feed 'on whatever ... lay at hand', can reveal that ideology in the process of formation, not so much at the level of 'scientific' argument as at the level of popular belief.[5]

In saying this, I am not claiming to know precisely how such images were received, rejected or accepted by their audiences. There would, no doubt, have been a great range of response that is, at this historical remove, simply unknowable. But they must have fed the imaginations and stocked the minds of their publics; provided a context for conceptualising and comprehending the issues they invoked. And the changing dramatic presentation of the black both reflected and contributed to a climate of opinion which became less and less favourable to conceptions of black equality, black freedom or black capacity. In short, the changes over time in the stereotype of the black, with whom there had been a long, involved and bloody history of subjugation and enslavement, are the outward and visible signs of the growth and development of racism as a coherent, structured ideology; a way of ordering, not just understanding, the world. The process of development, as evidenced in the daily, weekly, monthly, transmissions of popular theatre, was often uneven, with eddies that sometimes ran counter to the main current, or tributaries that ran vigorously for a while then petered out, yet it can be seen, when observed over time, to flow onwards to a future defined increasingly in the terms of racial hierarchy.

Above all, the image of the black, as presented on the stage, was largely drawn from his and her positioning in the structures of slavery. It was an image that used as its basic material the beliefs and folklore derived from centuries of contact, of exploration and attempted exploitation; in terms of the drama, elements of that image can be traced back to the 'evil blackamoors' of the sixteenth century. It was an image that changed not only as the climate of opinion over slavery changed but as attitudes towards the emancipated blacks of the West Indies changed and as biological-cum-cultural explanations for white economic and colonial dominance began to take root. In the process the black image became shorn, first of noble, then of fearsome and, finally, almost of human qualities – all that was left was its incarnation as a figure as artificial as the pantomime clown. But there are no real clowns to reflect ruefully on how they are viewed in the larger society. The artifice of the 'nigger minstrel' existed in the same universe as the struggle for black freedom in America, the lives of the black poor in England and the struggle for the reality of emancipation in the West Indies.

The extent to which this changing conception of the black, intimately connected with slavery as it was, was reflected not only in the published commentary and analysis, in the journals and newspapers of the middle and upper classes, but also in a popular culture that, for most of the period under discussion, continued to be accessed by all sectors of society, has been scarcely recognised. The cultural influence of slavery, as opposed to its political and economic influence, has been little explored. Slavery not only underdeveloped Africa, as the Guyanese historian and revolutionary Walter Rodney has shown in *How Europe Underdeveloped Africa*; it also underdeveloped or, rather, distorted the tendency of much English popular culture and in some ways stunted the popular imagination. That a few decades after the period of which I write, large swathes of the population showed themselves ready to embrace the overt cultural/racial superiority of the classic phase of imperialism;[6] that we are living today in an era when 'race' is as pressing an issue and as subject to prejudicial interpretation as ever shows how powerfully the cultural effects of slavery, together with the colonial domination that accompanied and eventually outstripped it, have outlasted the material fact itself.

At the outset of the period under discussion, it is true that, for all his slave status, the black was accorded a certain fear and respect. As Oroonoko, he was even to be lauded. At a time when arguments in favour of natural human rights were in the ascendant and the abolition of the slave trade was almost won, he was, as Zanga, as Hassan, as Three-fingered Jack, endowed with powerful justification for his evil nature. He was dangerous. But his vengeful threat began to diminish as, under the pressure of slavery's continuance, the polarisation of views and the insistence of pro-slavery propaganda, he was equated more with the brute creation and less with the human. Couri is still a man, but a lesser man; Muley is defeated by a monkey. And on the cusp between the abolition of the slave trade and the perceived necessity of continuing plantation slavery is Gambia, that most unlikely of heroes: more noble than Oroonoko; a black avenger on his *master's* behalf; accepting of his enslaved status; a celebrant of English freedom. Only at a particular period, very briefly and at the height of abolitionism, could love between black and white be celebrated, as in George Colman's *Inkle and Yarico* (1787), or a worthy attempt be made to validate African culture, as in *The Africans* (1809).

The black might have continued to dwindle and decline as a feature of theatrical life, were it not for the devastation wrought by another and different racism, derived from the American practice of slavery. This was not mediated or glossed by distance, as had been Britain's implementation of slavery in the West Indies. Harsh in its instrumentality, this new racism attempted to mark out and control, through ridicule, a terrain in which a threatening and frequently rebellious enslaved black population lived cheek by jowl with their white 'owners'. This racism saw the black as a complete grotesque, a laughable buffoon; for, if he was not comic, then *what was he*? Was he the figure who, with his fellows, could find entry into your household 'with hatchets and axes ... [sparing] no life ... storming house after house'?[7] The antidote to such fear was supplied most notably by the American entertainer Rice. If his comic black was not so completely devoid of humanity as those that came after, Rice nonetheless set a template that was not only copied but developed to even more ridiculous extremes. English audiences lapped it up. Oroonoko, in effect, became Jim Crow.

In fact, Jim Crow and his like no longer had any real purchase on the serious issue of slavery. Yet the strength of abolitionist culture in Britain meant that there was still widespread interest in and debate over it. Such debate was not reflected directly in the theatre, but dramatists continued to explore the issue through the medium, increasingly, of the mixed-race character. He and she took on many of the dramatic functions that had previously been the prerogative of the black. At the same time, once slavery had been abolished by Britain and the focus of interest shifted to the American situation with its greater emphasis on slavery as a domestic matter, the consideration of slavery as a structural economic phenomenon, reflected in the earlier dramas, changed to a consideration of it as a domestic issue, involving the family.

The one common feature throughout the late eighteenth-century dramas and those of the nineteenth century, from those concerned with abolitionist sentiment and those featuring the degraded and vengeful black, to those fixed on Jim Crow, and in the tar dramas from first to last, is the Englishness of liberty, the peculiarly English nature of freedom. A celebration of freedom for 'Afric's sable sons' is sung to the tune of 'Rule Britannia' at the end of Bellamy's *The Benevolent Planters* in 1789; 'Rule Britannia' is sung in the minstrel-type entertainment *More Ethiopians!!* in 1847 and, in 1852, Britannia in person concluded *Uncle Tom and Lucy Neal*.

Of course, there are always alternative possibilities, the road not taken, the unregarded opportunities for a new and more humane exploration of the dramatic potential of the black character. The broad comedy of Mungo remained, but not his assertion of himself or his disrespect for authority. The love between Trudge and Wowski was not reworked for a later age. Uncle Tom could have offered a path back to a fuller vision; Mark Lemon and Tom Taylor went as far as they felt able with a dignified interpretation of this character, but he remained little more than a cipher. Fabian was another answer, but swiftly became dated; the dynamic Karfa yet another. The militant Dred issued a brief challenge that was forgotten as soon as it was over. Othello stayed loftily on his pedestal or was mercilessly guyed in burlesque. In an age where everything was material for the stage, that great hero, Toussaint, was almost completely overlooked. I have discovered only one play that features him; an uneasy mix of comedy and melodrama that depicts his main concern as saving his owner's family from the black revolution.

This is a story that has no ending; no final closure or neat resolution. Yet if we take those few short months towards the end of 1856, some of its major strands can be seen to present themselves. There was Dred – who might have represented a different approach but did not – appearing to applause before audiences in London. There was the 'tedious' black doctor Fabian,[8] who had represented a different approach, but had not got very far. Meanwhile, the murderous hero of *The Half Caste*, had, with his fellows, struck out in a new and fruitful, though equally stereotyped, direction.[9] No doubt somewhere some 'Ethiopian' melodists were performing the rituals of minstrelsy, while Aldridge, hurtling from Hull to Guernsey to Oldham,[10] still performing the drama of the past and playing his own version of the black hero in *Titus Andronicus*, must have wondered when the London breakthrough that he desired and deserved would ever come.

Notes

INTRODUCTION

1. *Gentleman's Magazine* 19 (1749), pp. 89–90; see also David Brion Davis, *The Problem of Slavery in Western Culture* (Oxford: Oxford University Press, 1988, first publ. 1967), p. 477.
2. See Joseph Inikori, *Africans and the Industrial Revolution in England: a study in international trade and economic development* (Cambridge: Cambridge University Press, 2002).
3. The exception is Douglas Lorimer, *Colour, Class and the Victorians: English attitudes to the Negro in the mid-nineteenth century* (Leicester: Leicester University Press, 1978). Christine Bolt's *Victorian Attitudes to Race* (London: Routledge, 1971) focuses on particular political race issues and on scientific racism. Nancy Stepan's *The Idea of Race in Science: Great Britain, 1800–1960* (London: Macmillan, 1982) illustrates the continuity of scientific race theorising.
4. I am not here arguing that this is the only way in which racism develops and is sustained, but my focus is on the transmission and transmutation of racial images, not on the acting out of that racism at material, economic and political levels. Rather, I show that such images have their genesis in a changing material reality.
5. Jim Davis and Victor Emeljanow, *Reflecting the Audience: London theatregoing, 1840–1880* (Hatfield: University of Hertfordshire Press, 2001). Excellent introductions to nineteenth-century theatre generally are Joseph Donohue's 'The theatre from 1800 to 1895', in J. Donohue (ed.), *The Cambridge History of the British Theatre, Volume 2, 1660–1895* (Cambridge: Cambridge University Press, 2004), and Michael Booth's *Theatre in the Victorian Age* (Cambridge: Cambridge University Press, 1991).
6. It is inevitable, given the history of theatrical development in England, that such source materials relate largely to what was performed in London, but basic dramatic fare swiftly became circulated throughout the country, though often adapted to local circumstances.
7. A. Sivanandan, 'Challenging racism: strategies for the 1980s' in his *Communities of Resistance: writings on black struggles for socialism* (London: Verso, 1990), p. 64.

8. Quoted in Michael Craton, *Testing the Chains: resistance to slavery in the British West Indies* (Ithaca: Cornell University Press, 1982), p. 321.

9. Quoted in *ibid.*, p. 323.

CHAPTER I

1. See A. G. Barthelemy, *Black Face, Maligned Race: the representation of blacks in English drama from Shakespeare to Southerne* (Baton Rouge: Louisiana State University Press, 1987).

2. *Ibid.*, p. 161.

3. *Ibid.*, pp. 154, 161.

4. *Ibid.*, p. 162.

5. Jan Carew, 'The end of Moorish enlightenment and the beginning of the Columbian era', *Race & Class* 33:3 (1992), pp. 6–7.

6. Basil Davidson, 'Columbus: the bones and blood of racism', *Race & Class* 33:3 (1992), p. 18.

7. See Eric Williams, *Capitalism and Slavery* (London: Deutsch, 1964); Walter Rodney, *How Europe Underdeveloped Africa* (London: Bogle-L'Ouverture, 1972); and Inikori, *Africans and the Industrial Revolution in England*.

8. There is a huge literature on this subject, but of seminal importance are the works of David Brion Davis, *The Problem of Slavery in Western Culture* and *The Problem of Slavery in the Age of Revolution, 1770–1823* (Oxford: Oxford University Press, 1999, first publ. 1975), and Winthrop Jordan, *White Over Black: American attitudes toward the Negro, 1550–1812* (Baltimore: Penguin, 1969).

9. Aphra Behn, *Oroonoko, or the Royal Slave*, in *Oroonoko and Other Writings* (Oxford: Oxford University Press, 1994, first publ. 1688).

10. Aphra Behn, *Abdelazer, or the Moor's Revenge*, reprinted in Janet Todd (ed.), *The Works of Aphra Behn, Volume 5. The Plays, 1671–1677* (London: Pickering and Chatto, 1996).

11. Thomas Southerne, *Oroonoko*, ed. M. E. Novak and D. S. Rodes (London: Edward Arnold, 1977). All quotations in this chapter are taken from this edition.

12. At the time of the novel's composition, Surinam was a British possession, but by the time of publication (1688) it had been ceded to the Dutch.

13. From *Comparison Between the Two Stages* (1702), quoted in R. Jordan and H. Love (eds.), *The Works of Thomas Southerne* (Oxford: Clarendon, 1988), vol. 1, p. 89, and J. W. Dodds, *Thomas Southerne, Dramatist* (New Haven and London: Humphrey Milford, 1933), p. 128.

14. D. E. Baker, *Biographia Dramatica or, a Companion to the Playhouse* (London: Rivingtons, 1782), pp. 20, 426–7.

15. D. E. Baker, Isaac Reed and Stephen Jones, *Biographia Dramatica, or a Companion to the Playhouse, Volume 3* (London: Longman Hurst, 1812), p. 103.

16. R. L. Root, *Thomas Southerne* (Boston: Twayne, 1981), p. 87.

17. Anon., 'The Tryall of Skill' in Frank H. Ellis (ed.), *Poems on Affairs of State: Augustan satirical verse 1660–1714, Volume 6, 1697–1704* (New Haven: Yale University Press, 1970), p. 708.

18. Roxann Wheeler, *The Complexion of Race: categories of difference in eighteenth-century British culture* (Philadelphia: University of Pennsylvania Press, 2000).

19. See Basil Davidson, *The African Slave Trade* (Boston: Little Brown, 1980), p. 64.

20. Southerne, *Oroonoko*, Act 3, scene 2.

21. *Ibid.*, Act 1, scene 2.

22. Behn, *Oroonoko*, p. 58.

23. Jordan and Love (eds.), *The Works of Thomas Southerne*, vol. 2, p. 95.

24. Southerne, *Oroonoko*, Act 3, scene 2. See 'Remarks by D. G.', in *Oroonoko: a tragedy in five acts . . .* Cumberland, vol. 25/6.

25. Southerne, *Oroonoko*, Act 3, scene 2.

26. *Ibid.*, Act 5, scene 5.

27. *Ibid.*, Act 2, scene 2.

28. *Ibid.*, Act 1, scene 2.

29. *Ibid.*, Act 1, scene 2.

30. *Ibid.*, Act 1, scene 1.

31. Baker, *Biographia Dramatica* (1782), p. 211. Hawkesworth was a friend of Dr Johnson and the editor of Swift's *Works*.

32. Baker, Reed and Jones, *Biographia Dramatica* (1812), vol. 3, pp. 103–4.

33. John Genest, *Some Account of the English Stage from the Restoration in 1660 to 1830* (Bath: Carrington, 1832), vol. 4, p. 478.

34. See the discussion of Hawkesworth in J. R. Oldfield, *Popular Politics and British Anti-Slavery: the mobilisation of public opinion against the slave trade, 1787–1807* (London: Frank Cass, 1998), pp. 23–5.

35. John Ferriar, *The Prince of Angola, a tragedy, altered from the play of Oroonoko and adapted to the circumstances of the present time* (Manchester: J. Harrop, 1788), p. i.

36. Seymour Drescher, *Capitalism and Antislavery: British mobilization in comparative perspective* (Basingstoke: Macmillan, 1986), pp. 69–73.

37. Ferriar, *Prince of Angola*, p. ii.

38. *Ibid.*, p. iii (emphasis in original).

39. Both quotations from *ibid.*, Act 1, scene 1.

40. Quoted in R. J. Broadbent, *Annals of the Liverpool Stage from the Earliest Period to the Present Time* (Liverpool: Edward Howell, 1908), p. 72.

41. *Ibid.*, p. 120. At a stormy performance in Liverpool, Kemble is reported to have 'asked the local public "Shall I tell you what you are like? You are like Captain Driver in Oroonoko."', *ibid.* Inchbald makes the same point about the play's prohibition in her edition of *Oroonoko*. See Southerne, *Oroonoko*, ed. Novak and Rodes, p. xxix.

42. Dodds, *Thomas Southerne, Dramatist*, p. 154.

43. Thomas Bellamy, *The Benevolent Planters* (London: Debrett, 1789). Also in facsimile in Jeffrey N. Cox (ed.), *Slavery, Abolition and Emancipation: writings*

in the British romantic period, Volume 5, Drama (London: Pickering and Chatto, 1999).

44. Bellamy, *Benevolent Planters*, prologue and Act 1, scene 3.
45. Genest, *Some Account of the English Stage*, p. 568.
46. Bellamy, *Benevolent Planters*, Act 1, scene 1.
47. *Ibid.*, Act 1, scene 3.
48. *Ibid.*
49. Edward Young, *The Revenge: a tragedy*, first performed at Drury Lane, 18 April 1721. Frequently reprinted; included in Elizabeth Inchbald's *British Theatre* (London: Longman Hurst, 1806), vol. 4, and *The Acting Drama; containing all the popular plays standard and modern*, revised by J. P. Kemble (London: Mayhew, Isaac and Mayhew, 1834). This version restores some of the cuts made in Inchbald's version – but neither is as full as the text published in 1776 by J. Rivington and Sons.
50. Young, *The Revenge*, 1834 edition, Act 1, scene 1.
51. Preface to Young, *The Revenge*, in Inchbald's *British Theatre*, 1806.
52. *Ibid.*
53. Quoted in 'Theatrical Strictures no.1 Mr. John Kemble', in *Ireland's Mirror, or, a Chronicle of the Theatre* (August 1804), excerpted in Richard John [O] Smith, *A Collection of Materiel [sic] Towards an History of the English Stage* (London: The Author [1825]), vol. 19, unnumbered.
54. Young, *The Revenge*, 1834 edition, Act 1, scene 1.
55. *Ibid.*, Act 5, scene 2.
56. *Ibid.*
57. Quoted in Wylie Sypher, *Guinea's Captive Kings: British anti-slavery literature of the XVIIIth century* (New York: Octagon Books, 1969, first publ. 1942), pp. 57–8.
58. *Ibid.*, p. 61.
59. Simon Schama, *Rough Crossings: Britain, the slaves and the American Revolution* (London: BBC Books, 2005), p. 31.
60. Robin Blackburn, *The Overthrow of Colonial Slavery, 1776–1848* (London: Verso, 1988), pp. 157ff.
61. See James Walvin, *Black and White: the Negro and English society 1555–1945* (London: Allen Lane, 1973), ch. 7; Gretchen Gerzina, *Black England: life before emancipation* (London, John Murray, 1995); Adam Hochschild, *Bury the Chains: the British struggle to abolish slavery* (Basingstoke: Macmillan, 2005); and Schama, *Rough Crossings*, ch. 2.
62. M. G. Lewis, *The Castle Spectre*, first performed at Drury Lane, 14 December 1797, Cumberland, vol. 15. Also in J. N. Cox (ed.), *Seven Gothic Dramas, 1789–1825* (Athens: Ohio University Press, 1992).
63. Lewis's preface to the printed version of *The Castle Spectre*. Quoted in full in Cox (ed.), *Seven Gothic Dramas*, p. 222.
64. Genest, *Some Account of the English Stage*, vol. 7, pp. 332–3.
65. Lewis, preface to *The Castle Spectre*, in Cox (ed.), *Seven Gothic Dramas*, p. 223.
66. *Ibid.*, pp. 221–2.

67. Lewis, *The Castle Spectre*, Cumberland, Act 1, scene 2.
68. J. Fawcett, *Obi, or, Three-finger'd Jack!*, Duncombe, vol. 59/60. According to Genest, *Some Account of the English Stage*, its fourth performance was on 5 July 1800 at the Haymarket; it was acted thirty-nine times. He described it as having 'considerable merit for the sort of thing' (vol. 7, p. 487). See also the preface to *Obi* and the reproduction of the Duncombe version in Cox (ed.), *Slavery, Abolition and Emancipation, Volume 5, Drama*, pp. 201–19. Julia Swindells in *Glorious Causes: the grand theatre of political change, 1789–1833* (Oxford: Oxford University Press, 2001), pp. 55–60, uses the later dialogue version by W. H. Murray as her source for discussion of the play. Quotations here are taken from Duncombe.
69. Benjamin A. Moseley, *A Treatise on Sugar, with Miscellaneous Medical Observations* (London: G. G. and J. Robinson, 1799).
70. See 'Introduction' to Cox (ed.), *Slavery, Abolition and Emancipation, Volume 5, Drama*, pp. xxi–xxiii.
71. See Alan Richardson, 'Romantic voodoo: Obeah and British culture, 1797–1807', *Studies in Romanticism* 32 (1993), pp. 3–28.
72. *Ibid.*, pp. 7–9. See, more generally, Cedric Robinson, *Black Marxism: the making of the black radical tradition* (Chapel Hill: University of North Carolina Press, 2000).
73. Fawcett, *Obi*, Act 1, scene 1.
74. *Ibid.*
75. *Ibid.*, Act 2, scene 7.
76. *Ibid.*, Act 2, scene 9.
77. *Ibid.*
78. See Davis and Emeljanow, *Reflecting the Audience*. The Surrey was much more successful than the Coburg in attracting a wider, cross-class audience and broadening its repertoire. Both were south of the Thames but the Coburg was not so easy of access and was in a worse district.
79. 'Actors of the present day, no. 3 Mr. O. Smith', in *The Stage or Theatrical Inquisitor* 1:4 (September 1828), pp. 107–116.
80. L. Stephen and S. Lee (eds.), *Dictionary of National Biography* (Oxford: Oxford University Press, 1921–22), vol. 18, p. 516. Smith also played in *Tuckitomba* at Covent Garden, which seems to contain similar ingredients to *Obi*, being set in 'a region to which the imagination would never voluntarily take wing – the West Indies . . . its persons were overseers, slaves and an Obi sorceress'. *New Monthly Magazine* 24 (1 May 1828), p. 198. The role of Jack was also played by T. P. Cooke.
81. Isaac Bickerstaffe, *The Padlock* (London: W. Lowndes, S. Bladon and W. Nicoll, 1789). Also in Cox (ed.), *Slavery, Abolition and Emancipation, Volume 5, Drama*.
82. Peter A. Tasch, *The Dramatic Cobbler: the life and works of Isaac Bickerstaff* (*sic*) (Lewisburg: Bucknell University Press, 1971), p. 158.
83. Bickerstaffe, *The Padlock*, 1789, Act 1, scene 3.
84. *Ibid.*, Act 2, scene 1.
85. *Ibid.*, Act 1, scene 3.

86. *Ibid.*

87. Bickerstaffe, *The Padlock*, Act 2, scene 1.

88. Cox (ed.), *Slavery, Abolition and Emancipation, Volume 5, Drama*, p. 74.

89. Sypher, *Guinea's Captive Kings*, p. 235. See also the discussion in Oldfield, *Popular Politics and British Anti-slavery*, pp. 29–31.

90. William Macready, *The Irishman in London; or, the Happy African* (London: T. N. Longman, 1793).

91. *Ibid.*, Act 1, scene 2.

92. *Ibid.*, Act 2, scene 1.

93. *Ibid.*

94. Henry Bate [H. B. Dudley], *The Blackamoor Wash'd White* (1776) Larpent Collection, British Library microfiche F253/403 (1–3). Catalogued in Larpent under Dudley.

95. Genest, *Some Account of the English Stage*, vol. 6, p. 488. See also Sypher, *Guinea's Captive Kings*, pp. 239–40.

96. Bate, *The Blackamoor Wash'd White*, Act 2, scene 1.

97. Frederick Reynolds, *Laugh When You Can*, Dicks, no. 266. First performed at Covent Garden, 8 December 1798. For Baker, Reed and Jones, *Biographia Dramatica* (1812), vol. 2, p. 364, 'it does not bring all its advantages with it into the closet'.

98. Reynolds, *Laugh When You Can*, Act 1, scene 1.

99. *Ibid.*

100. *Ibid.*, Act 1, scene 2.

101. Adam Lively, *Masks: blackness, race and the imagination* (London: Chatto and Windus, 1998), ch. 2.

102. See Asa Briggs, *The Age of Improvement, 1783–1867* (London: Longman, 1991), pp. 66–74, and Davis, *The Problem of Slavery in the Age of Revolution*, ch. 1.

103. Davis, *The Problem of Slavery in Western Culture*, p. 481.

104. George Colman, *Inkle and Yarico* . . . with remarks by Mrs Inchbald (London: Longman et al., 1816).

105. See Sypher, *Guinea's Captive Kings*, pp. 124ff.

106. *Ibid.*, p. 127.

107. Wheeler has argued that, in the mid-eighteenth century, Native Americans occupied a somewhat indeterminate position in racial discourse, sometimes approximating more closely to Africans, at other times much less so. See *The Complexion of Race*, ch. 3, especially pp. 169–73.

108. George Colman, *Inkle and Yarico*, in Barry Sutcliffe (ed.), *Plays by George Colman the Younger and Thomas Morton* (Cambridge: Cambridge University Press, 1983), Act 1, scene 3.

109. *Ibid.*, Act 3, scene 3.

110. *Ibid.*, Act 3, scene 1.

111. Lively, *Masks*, p. 59.

112. Colman, *Inkle and Yarico*, presented by Straydogs at Battersea Arts Centre, 18–22 August 1998, with music by Samuel Arnold. Directed by Simon Godwin.

113. Colman, *Inkle and Yarico*, Act 2, scene 1.
114. *Ibid.*, Act 3, scene 3.
115. 'Introduction' by J. W. Lake to *The Dramatic Works of George Colman the Younger* ... (Paris: Malepeyre, 1823), vol. 1, p. xi.

CHAPTER 2

1. The story of theatrical regulation and censorship is far too complex to be examined here. The most notable landmark is the Licensing Act of 1737 which inaugurated the Lord Chamberlain's powers of censorship; subsequent legislation decreed that nonpatent theatres both in Westminster and beyond should operate under a system of annual licences for the different genres they specialised in. The 1843 Theatre Regulation Act finally abolished the distinction between legitimate and illegitimate drama and major and minor theatres. See Jane Moody, *Illegitimate Theatre in London, 1770–1840* (Cambridge: Cambridge University Press, 2000).
2. Using Genest's records of performances, plus information gleaned *ad hoc*, I have found records of *The Castle Spectre*, for example, being performed every year up until 1820; *The Revenge* almost every year until 1820 and occasionally thereafter; *Obi* was frequently revived, in 1805, 1818 and 1828 at the patent theatres, and was being performed at the Surrey in 1812 and at the Coburg in 1819; *Laugh When You Can* was in Ira Aldridge's repertoire in the late 1820s and early 1830s. See Genest, *Some Account of the English Stage*. According to Dodds, '*Oroonoko* was played at Drury Lane as late as 1829, and ... in the hundred and thirty-odd years ... since its first night seldom a season passed in which it was not performed at least once' (Dodds, *Thomas Southerne, Dramatist*, p. 158). However, Jordan and Love state that after its revival by Kean in 1817 it subsequently only 'lingered on throughout the nineteenth century' (Jordan and Love (eds.), *The Works of Thomas Southerne*. vol. 1, p. 92).
3. Blackburn, *Overthrow of Colonial Slavery*, p. 155.
4. David Hume, footnote to his essay 'National and moral characters' (1753/4 edition), quoted in Jordan, *White Over Black*, pp. 253–4; Henry Kames, *Sketches of the History of Man* (Edinburgh: W. Creech, 1774), vol. 1; Edward Long's *The History of Jamaica* ... (London: T. Lowndes, 1774), was one of the most virulent and lastingly influential pro-slavery tracts. See, for example, Blackburn, *Overthrow of Colonial Slavery*, pp. 154–6; and Lorimer, *Colour, Class and the Victorians*, pp. 131–4.
5. George Colman, *The Africans; or, War, Love and Duty*, Cumberland, vol. 43. Also available in Cox (ed.), *Slavery, Abolition and Emancipation, Volume 5, Drama*. Quotations are taken direct from Cumberland.
6. *Ibid.*, Act 1, scene 1.
7. Colman, *The Africans*, Act 3, scene 1. Foulah is another name for the Fulani, who early on embraced Islam and whose empire, according to Basil Davidson,

was organised on very similar lines to western feudalism (*The African Slave Trade*, pp. 31–2).

8. *Ibid.*, Act 1, scene 3.
9. *Ibid.*
10. See Jordan, *White Over Black*, pp. 174–5.
11. Colman, *The Africans*, Act 3, scene 3.
12. *Ibid.*, Act 3, scene 2.
13. *Ibid.*, Act 1, scene 1.
14. *Ibid.*, Act 2, scene 4.
15. *Ibid.*, Act 1, scene 2.
16. *Ibid.*, Act 1, scene 2.
17. *Ibid.*, Act 2, scene 4.
18. *Ibid.*
19. Genest, *Some Account of the Stage in England*, vol. 9, p. 569.
20. *Ibid.* See also Jeremy Bagster-Collins, *George Colman the Younger, 1762–1836* (New York: King's Crown Press, 1946), pp. 205–9.
21. D. G., 'Remarks', in Colman, *The Africans*, p. 6.
22. 'Memoir of Mr. Young', *Mirror of the Stage, or New Dramatic Censor* 1:8 (18 November 1822), p. 114.
23. *The Times* (30 July 1808), quoted in Bagster-Collins, *George Colman the Younger*, p. 208.
24. 'Didascalia', *Literary Panorama* 4 (1808), cols. 1134–6.
25. D. G., 'Remarks', in Colman, *The Africans*, p. 6.
26. [William Hazlitt], *The Examiner* 474 (26 January 1817), p. 56. Reprinted in *The Complete Works of William Hazlitt in twenty-one volumes*, ed. P. P. Howe (London: J. M. Dent, 1930), vol. 18, p. 215.
27. *Ibid.*, p. 216.
28. *Ibid.*
29. *Ibid.*, pp. 216–17.
30. *Ibid.*, p. 217.
31. Elsewhere, reviewing Kean's performance as Zanga, Hazlitt remarks that the 'dark, treacherous, fierce, and remorseless character to the Moor ... is more in conformity to our prejudices, as well as to historical truth'. See *The Examiner* (28 May 1815); reprinted in Hazlitt, *The Complete Works*, vol. 5, p. 227.
32. Genest, *Some Account of the Stage in England*, vol. 8, p. 588.
33. *Oroonoko, a tragedy* by Thomas Southern [*sic*], *The Acting Drama* (London: Mayhew, Isaac and Mayhew, 1834); *Oroonoko: a tragedy in five acts* by Thomas Southern ... with remarks by Mrs Inchbald (London: Longman, Hurst, Rees and Orme, [1806]); also Cumberland, vol. 25/6. R. Cumberland's *The British Drama ... containing Oroonoko* (London, C. Cooke, 1817), vol. 11, contains the full text, but more for its interest as Southerne's original creation than out of a wish to see it performed in full. For the purposes of comparison here, I have used the 1834 edition.
34. Southern, *Oroonoko, The Acting Drama*, Act 3, scene 4.
35. *Ibid.*, Act 4, scene 2; see also Southerne, *Oroonoko*, ed. Novak and Rodes.

36. Southerne, *Oroonoko*, ed. Novak and Rodes, Act 4, scene 2.
37. Thomas Morton, *The Slave: a musical drama in three acts* (London: John Miller, 1816).
38. See Sutcliffe (ed.), *Plays by George Colman ... and Thomas Morton*.
39. D. G., 'Remarks', in Thomas Morton, *The Slave: an opera in three acts*, Cumberland, vol. 22, p. 6. Also as *The Slave: a musical drama in three acts* (London: John Miller, 1818); and in Cox (ed.), *Slavery, Abolition and Emancipation, Volume 5, Drama*. Quotations are from the 1818 edition.
40. Genest, *Some Account of the Stage in England*, vol. 8, p. 625.
41. *Ibid.*, p. 603.
42. See D. Mullin, *Victorian Plays: a record of significant productions on the London stage, 1837–1901* (New York: Greenwood, 1987).
43. According to Cox (ed.), *Slavery, Abolition and Emancipation, Volume 5, Drama*, this refers to the rebellion of 1807 which involved the attempt to establish Maroon communities in the jungles of Surinam. The revolt was crushed, and captured rebels were hanged, decapitated and their bodies burnt. See 'Introduction', p. xx.
44. Morton, *The Slave*, 1818 edition, Act 1, scene 1.
45. *Ibid.*
46. *Ibid.*
47. *Ibid.*, Act 1, scene 2.
48. *Ibid.*
49. *Ibid.*
50. *Ibid.*, Act 1, scene 3.
51. *Ibid.*, Act 2, scene 1.
52. *Ibid.*, Act 3, scene 3.
53. *Ibid.*, Act 3, scene 4.
54. *Ibid.*
55. *Ibid.*, Act 3, scene 5.
56. D. G., 'Remarks', in Morton, *The Slave*, Cumberland, [p. 5].
57. Douglas Jerrold, *Descart, the French Buccaneer*, Coburg theatre, 8 September 1828, Dicks, no. 258.
58. *Ibid.*, Act 1, scene 1.
59. *Ibid.*, Act 1, scene 1.
60. *Ibid.*, Act 2, scene 2.
61. *Ibid.*
62. *Ibid.*, Act 1, scene 1.
63. C. P. Thompson, *Jack Robinson and his Monkey*, Surrey theatre, 20 August 1829, Duncombe, no. 27; Lacy, no. 31.
64. *Ibid.*, Duncombe, Act 1, scene 5.
65. *Ibid.*, Act 2, scene 1.
66. *Ibid.*
67. The West African squadron, set up to patrol some 3,000 miles of the coast of West Africa, consisted of two to seven vessels. Despite the fact that by the 1830s most nations had declared slavetrading illegal, the trade continued

apace, with most captives destined for Brazil or Cuba. The numbers directly liberated by naval patrols were comparatively small – Christopher Lloyd estimates around 1,000 'annually before 1825 and about 3,000 annually for the next ten years'. See Christopher Lloyd, *The Navy and the Slave Trade: the suppression of the African slave trade in the nineteenth century* (London: Longmans, Green and Co., 1949), p. 61. Philip Curtin's estimates, however, indicate that the naval blockade '*was* effective in diverting about 8 per cent of the trade, perhaps in keeping the trade from going even higher'. See Philip D. Curtin, *The Atlantic Slave Trade: a census* (Madison: University of Wisconsin Press, 1959), p. 269. Losses of men on the naval patrols were high, especially from epidemic disease. And it was dangerous work. Slaving was highly lucrative and slave vessels were fast and well equipped. See W. E. F. Ward, *The Royal Navy and the Slavers: the suppression of the African slave trade* (London: George Allen and Unwin, 1969).

68. J. T. Haines, *My Poll and my Partner Joe*, Surrey theatre, 31 August 1835 Lacy, vol. 71, no. 1058. In 1835 some 6,899 slaves were liberated alive and twelve slave vessels captured; in 1836 the totals were 5,748 and fifty-three, respectively (Lloyd, *The Navy and the Slave Trade*, p. 275).

69. Haines, *My Poll and my Partner Joe*, Act 1, scene 3.

70. *Ibid.*, Act 2, scene 1.

71. *Ibid.*, Act 1, scene 3.

72. *Ibid.*

73. *Ibid.*, Act 2, scene 2.

74. *Ibid.*

75. *Ibid.*

76. *Ibid.*

77. *Ibid.*

78. Lloyd, *The Navy and the Slave Trade*, pp. 36–8, 32. J. M. W. Turner's painting *Slave Ship*, with its terrible image of slaves thrown overboard to the sharks, was exhibited in 1840.

79. Haines, *My Poll and my Partner Joe*, Act 2, scene 2.

80. *Ibid.*

81. *Ibid.*

82. *Ibid.*, Act 2, scenes 3 and 4.

83. 'Actors of the present day, no. 5, Mr. Macready' in *The Stage; or Theatrical Inquisitor* 6 (December 1828), p. 178.

CHAPTER 3

1. According to James Walvin, the domestic slaves of West Indian planters who were brought to England in their master's retinue retained their enslaved status; others had the status of indentured labourers whose conditions were indistinguishable from slavery. See Walvin, *Black and White*, pp. 191–2. For a different perspective, see Drescher, *Capitalism and Antislavery*.

2. See Vincent Harding, *There is a River: the black struggle for freedom in America* (New York: Vintage Books, 1983), pp. 117–21.

3. See Herbert Marshall and Mildred Stock, *Ira Aldridge: the Negro tragedian* (London: Rockliff, 1958; rpt. Washington, DC: Howard University Press, 1993, with introduction by Errol Hill), chapter 4. (Marshall and Stock also make available much Russian language material that would otherwise have been inaccessible.)

4. See Errol Hill, *Shakespeare in Sable: a history of black Shakespearean actors* (Amherst: University of Massachusetts Press, 1984), pp. 11ff., and Marshall and Stock, *Ira Aldridge*.

5. It was largely owing to the late Edward Scobie, a black historian and close friend of Aldridge's youngest daughter, Amanda (who died in 1956), that what English language records there are survive. He was instrumental in making these available to Aldridge's best-known biographers, Marshall and Stock. Scobie's own work was never finally completed for publication. I am indebted to Jan Carew, Professor Emeritus of Northwestern University, a close friend of Scobie, who generously sent me copies of some of the latter's papers, including Cyril Bruyn Andrews's manuscript, 'Victorian Ebony: the diaries, letters and criticisms of Ira Aldridge'; as I am also to Bernth Lindfors, Professor Emeritus of the University of Texas, Austin, who subsequently sent me a wealth of material, including Owen Mortimer's *Speak of Me as I Am: the story of Ira Aldridge* (Wangaratta, Australia: The Author, 1995) and the *Memoir and Theatrical Career of Ira Aldridge: the African Roscius* (London: Onwhyn, [1848]). Most recently, Professor Lindfors has uncovered evidence that Aldridge's first performance in England was not at the Coburg as stated by Marshall and Stock but at the Royalty (Bernth Lindfors, 'Ira Aldridge's London debut', *Theatre Notebook* 60:1 (2006)).

6. See R. M. Sillard, *Barry Sullivan and His Contemporaries: a histrionic record* (London: T. Fisher Unwin, 1901). Sullivan had performed before Daniel O'Connell, '[t]he Great Liberator', under his 'special patronage' and 'By command', as one playbill put it (Sillard, vol. 2, pp. 74, 135).

7. See Blackburn, *The Overthrow of Colonial Slavery*, ch. 11, and Catherine Hall, *Civilising Subjects: metropole and colony in the English imagination, 1830–1867* (Cambridge: Polity, 2002), pp. 107–9.

8. Announcement in *The Times* (10 October 1825), quoted in Marshall and Stock, *Ira Aldridge*, p. 53.

9. Reproduced in Marshall and Stock, *Ira Aldridge*, facing p. 41.

10. From a mention of an earlier performance, also at the Coburg, in *The Mirror of the Stage, or New Dramatic Censor* 1:12 (13 January 1823), p. 191. A razee is a warship, or ship of the line, cut down in height by the removal of its upper decks.

11. 'The Coburg Theatre', *The Times* (11 October 1825), p. 2, col. 5.

12. See Marshall and Stock, *Ira Aldridge*, p. 43.

13. 'The Coburg Theatre', *The Times* (11 October 1825), p. 2, col. 5. 'Baker-knee'd' means knock-kneed. I have been unable to discover who the reviewer

was – according to *The History of The Times: the Thunderer in the making, 1785–1841* (London: The Times, 1935), it might possibly have been Thomas Talfourd, who joined *The Times* in 1813 and remained 'at least ten years, at the end of which period he was . . . engaged in writing theatrical notices' (p. 425). Frustratingly, it does not indicate who succeeded him as dramatic reviewer.

14. One such crossing sweeper achieved it. Billy Waters, who played the fiddle on the streets as well as keeping a crossing, was made into a character in W. T. Moncrieff's 1821 play *Tom and Jerry*. Portrayed as leading rather a high life, he died in the workhouse in utter poverty, supposedly lamenting that, after *Tom and Jerry*, he was assumed to be well off and in consequence made nothing for his efforts. See the preface to W. T. Moncrieff, *Tom and Jerry; or, Life in London*, Lacy, vol. 88.

15. Quoted in Marshall and Stock, *Ira Aldridge*, p. 63.

16. *A Brief Memoir, and Theatrical Career of Ira Aldridge, the African Tragedian* (London: Henry Pownceby, n.d.), p. 5. This is a shortened version of the anonymous *Memoir and Theatrical Career of Ira Aldridge*.

17. Edward Scobie, *Black Britannia: a history of blacks in Britain* (London: Pall Mall Press, 1972), p. 131. Bernth Lindfors, in an article which uncovers previously unknown information about Aldridge's private life, including an action against him for 'criminal conversation' with the wife of another actor, holds that sexual-racial jealousy of him was a significant factor in his being largely kept off the London stage throughout his career. See Lindfors, '"Nothing extenuate, nor set down aught in malice": new biographical information on Ira Aldridge', *African American Review* 28:3 (1994), pp. 457–72.

18. See Blackburn, *The Overthrow of Colonial Slavery*, p. 450. See also James Walvin, 'The rise of British popular sentiment for abolition, 1787–1832', in Christine Bolt and Seymour Drescher (eds.), *Anti-Slavery, Religion and Reform: essays in memory of Roger Anstey* (London: Dawson, 1980), pp. 149–62.

19. See Lowell Joseph Ragatz, *The Fall of the Planter Class in the British Caribbean, 1763–1833: a study in social and economic history* (New York and London: Century, for American Historical Association, 1928), pp. 427–9.

20. *Ibid.*, p. 429. Of course, this is not evidence of the campaign that Scobie alleges, but that he was a close friend of Aldridge's youngest daughter, to whom, one imagines, stories of Aldridge's early career and certainly his personal documents came down, makes such a claim feasible.

21. 'The Surrey', *Douglas Jerrold's Weekly Newspaper* (25 March 1848), p. 407, col. 2.

22. 'The Surrey', *Era* (26 March 1848), p. 11, col. 4.

23. 'Surrey Theatre', *Morning Post* (21 March 1848), p. 6, col. 5. The 'millions' referred to were the £20 million paid in compensation to slaveowners on abolition for the loss of their 'property'.

24. Almost every comment on his performances, even when dismissive of his ability as a tragic actor, approves his comic powers – but then, it was acceptable for a black to be laughable. 'One of the critics says – "He failed a little in tragedy, but he is excellent in *Mungo*"', *John Bull* (14 April 1833), p. 118, col. 3;

'He ... performed *Mungo* ... with so much humour ... it is doubtful whether his *forte* be not rather comedy than tragedy', *Douglas Jerrold's Weekly Newspaper* (25 March 1848), p. 407, col. 2; 'His Mungo, in the 'Padlock' ... was one of the most successful and irresistibly ludicrous performances it has been our fortune to see', 'Norwich', *Era* (9 January 1848), p. 12, col. 4.

25. 'It is novel to see one who has been obtaining much applause in pourtraying [*sic*] passion in its most poetic shape, descend to the broad farce of mock drunkenness ... it is only a man of natural genius who can do both so as to be commended for the faithfulness of his mimicry', 'The Surrey', *Era* (26 March 1848), p. 11, col. 4; 'It is something rare in these days to shudder at an actor, and be carried away by the natural force of his well-feigned passion ... and then to give way to his drollery as he laps out his capacious tongue, and whimsically proceeds to "clean" Colchester oysters by opening them and eating their contents', 'Bath', *Era* (14 February 1847), p. 10, col. 3.

26. See Marshall and Stock, *Ira Aldridge*, pp. 87–8, 90–5, and Mortimer, *Speak of Me as I Am*, especially pp. 83–4.

27. See Marshall and Stock, *Ira Aldridge*, pp. 287–8, and Hill, *Shakespeare in Sable*, p. 20. Andrews's 'Victorian Ebony' also contains a transcript of a letter from the British Consul at Odessa, dated 2 February 1866, which describes Aldridge's 'reading of the character of the semi-Oriental Jew of the middle ages ... [as] a masterpiece of art'.

28. Quoted by Bernth Lindfors, from an unpublished translation, by Herbert Marshall, of S. Durylin, *Ira Aldridge* (Moscow–Leningrad: State Publishing House, 1940) in Lindfors's '"Mislike me not for my complexion ...": Ira Aldridge in white face', *African American Review* 33:2 (1999), p. 352.

29. See Marshall and Stock, *Ira Aldridge*, pp. 94–5, 177.

30. Lindfors, '"Mislike me not for my complexion"', p. 350.

31. Marshall and Stock, *Ira Aldridge*, p. 65.

32. Quoted *ibid.*, p. 148, from *Northern Whig* (Belfast) (1 May 1838).

33. *Ibid.*, p. 150.

34. *Memoir and Theatrical Career of Ira Aldridge*, p. 12.

35. See Blackburn, *The Overthrow of Colonial Slavery*, ch. 7, especially pp. 273–4, 290. Aldridge was the son of a freeman but even freemen were known to be kidnapped into slavery – whatever their official status.

36. See Nicholas Evans, 'Ira Aldridge: Shakespeare and minstrelsy', *American Theatre Quarterly* (September 2002), pp. 165–87, and Bernth Lindfors, 'The signifying flunkey: Ira Aldridge as Mungo', *The Literary Griot* 5:2 (Fall 1993), pp. 1–11.

37. 'Surrey', *Illustrated London News* 12:310 (1 April 1848), p. 218.

38. Marshall and Stock, *Ira Aldridge*, p. 89.

39. See *ibid.* and also Laurence Hutton, *Curiosities of the American Stage* (London: Osgood, McIlvaine and Co., 1891), p. 96 and facing plate.

40. W. H. Murrey [Murray], *Obi; or, Three-fingered Jack*, Dicks, no. 478, Act 1, scene 1.

41. *Ibid.*
42. *Ibid.*, Act 1, scene 3.
43. *Ibid.*, Act 2, scene 4.
44. *Ibid.*, Act 2, scene 6.
45. *Theatrical Journal* 18:908 (6 May 1857), p. 138.
46. There is substantial literature on anti-Irish racism, referenced in Hazel Waters, 'The Great Famine and the rise of anti-Irish racism', *Race & Class* 37:1 (1995), pp. 95–108.
47. *Belfast Daily Mercury* (13 December 1856) (emphasis added). I am indebted to Bernth Lindfors for information on these performances.
48. Leman T. Rede, *The Road to the Stage* ... (London: J. Onwhyn, 1836), p. 34.
49. See Marvin Rosenberg's *The Masks of Othello* (Berkeley: University of California Press, 1961), for its exposition of the stage history of *Othello*.
50. William Winter, *Shakespeare on the Stage* (New York: Moffat, Yard and Company, 1911), p. 247.
51. William Hazlitt, 'Mr Booth's Iago', in *The Complete Works of William Hazlitt*, vol. 5, p. 357.
52. From *Blackwood's*, quoted in Rosenberg, *Masks of Othello*, p. 62.
53. Quoted most fully in Arthur Colby Sprague, *Shakespearean Players and Performances* (London: A & C Black, 1954), p. 84.
54. Interestingly, John Coleman, who writes about Aldridge in his *Fifty Years of an Actor's Life* (London: Hutchinson, 1904) claims that, when he played Iago to Aldridge's Othello in Bristol, 'The Roscius, who was as dark as ebony, toned his sable hue down to a copper tint; on the other hand, I was black as burnt cork and Indian ink could make me' (p. 402). According to Marshall and Stock, Aldridge's skin colour was naturally copper. Elsewhere, Coleman disparages Aldridge as 'an elderly, obese, woolly-headed Ethiopian' (p. 92) and quotes another actor's description of him as 'a hideous old buck-nigger' (p. 404).
55. Winter, *Shakespeare on the Stage*, p. 252.
56. Sprague, 'Foreword', *Shakespearean Players*.
57. Quoted in Rosenberg, *Masks of Othello*, p. 195.
58. See Joyce Green Macdonald, 'Acting black: *Othello*, *Othello* burlesques and the performance of blackness', *Theatre Journal* 46 (1994), pp. 133–46.
59. Rosenberg, *Masks of Othello*, pp. 29ff.
60. 'A Critique on the Performance of Othello by F. W. Keene Aldridge, the African Roscius' by the author of 'The talents of Edmund Kean delineated' ... (Scarborough: John Cole, 1831).
61. Marshall and Stock, *Ira Aldridge*, p. 103.
62. *Figaro in London* 42 (22 September 1832), p. 168.
63. The early numbers of *Figaro* were largely written by Gilbert Abbot à Beckett alone (the journal was a joint venture with Henry Mayhew. See J. L. Bradley (ed.), *Henry Mayhew: selections from 'London Labour and the London Poor'* (London: Oxford University Press, 1965), pp. xiv–xv). It is also possible that à Beckett might have seen Aldridge while on circuit.

64. See the 'Introduction' to Stanley Wells, *Nineteenth-Century Shakespeare Burlesques* (London: Diploma Press, 1977), vol. 2, p. xi, for a brief discussion of Westmacott. Maurice Dowling's highly successful 1834 burlesque of *Othello*, which had a successful run at the Strand in 1836, is too distant in time and makes no allusion that could be understood as referring to Aldridge; it appears, rather, to cash in on the minstrelsy vogue (reproduced in *ibid.*, pp. 1–43). Dowling's scurrilous and boisterous attack on black capability was premiered in Liverpool, home of the most ardent support for the slave trade, in 1834, when emancipation came into force.

65. *Figaro in London* 70 (6 April 1833), p. 56.

66. In later issues the Garrick was often on the receiving end of *Figaro*'s venom for, allegedly, being the haunt of Jews. See, for example, 'Wit at the Garrick' 233 (May 1836), p. 83.

67. *Figaro in London* 71 (13 April 1833), p. 60.

68. *Figaro in London* 73 (27 April 1833), p. 64.

69. *Figaro in London* 74 (4 May 1833), p. 72.

70. *Figaro in London* 76 and 77 (18 and 25 May 1833), pp. 80 and 84 respectively. Quotations from some of the *Figaro* articles are given by Marshall and Stock (*Ira Aldridge*, pp. 137–8); however, they are unaware of their origin, which is as given in the preceding references.

71. 'Theatricals', *John Bull* (14 April 1833), p. 118, col. 3.

72. 'Covent-Garden Theatre', *The Times* (11 April 1833), p. 3, col. 3.

73. 'Covent Garden', *Athenaeum* 285 (13 April 1833), pp. 235–6. The allegation that Aldridge had been a servant – or in some cases, slave – to one or other of the Wallacks was frequently made. Aldridge had met both brothers in New York; according to his *Memoir*, he brought with him to England a letter of recommendation from Henry Wallack and, according to McCune Smith, he was engaged as a personal attendant to James Wallack on the passage to England (Marshall and Stock, *Ira Aldridge*, pp. 45–6). A slightly different version of the story, which describes a rupture between Aldridge and James Wallack, is given by Aldridge's friend, J. J. Sheahan, writing in *Notes and Queries*, fourth series, 10 (17 August 1872), p. 133.

74. Sheahan, *Notes and Queries*, p. 133.

75. 'The African actor', *Spectator* 250 (13 April 1833), p. 328.

76. 'Theatres', *Morning Post* (11 April 1833), p. [3], col. 4.

77. Quoted in Marshall and Stock, *Ira Aldridge*, pp. 123–4 and 123, respectively.

78. *Memoir and Theatrical Career of Ira Aldridge*, p. 17.

79. 'Lyceum', *Athenaeum* 1605 (31 July 1858), p. 144, cols. 1–2; *The Times* (26 July 1858), p. 9, cols. 2–3.

80. Quoted in full in Marshall and Stock, *Ira Aldridge*, pp. 229–31. The critic G. H. Lewes looked askance at the continental enthusiasm for Aldridge. Writing as 'Vivian' in *The Leader* (5 February 1853), he commented, 'An English troop of unnamed unnameable actors has been playing in various parts of Germany, and Mr. Ira Aldridge, the African, has been the Othello of the troop. Most of you know pretty well what sort of actor *he* is thought to be

in England; nevertheless, he has been received with immense applause, and the papers pronounce him a first-rate Shakespearean actor!' Lewes was equating the overenthusiastic reception of a German actor (Emil Devrient) playing a season in London with that accorded Aldridge. Reprinted in J. Forster and G. H. Lewes, *Dramatic Essays* (London: 1896). I am indebted to Michael Slater for this reference.

81. Jack Gratus, *The Great White Lie: slavery, emancipation and changing racial attitudes* (London: Hutchinson, 1973), pp. 189–90.
82. *Ibid.*, p. 190.
83. I. V. Bridgeman, *The Black Doctor*, Victoria theatre, 13 November 1846, Lacy, no. 331; Ira Aldridge, *The Black Doctor*, City of London theatre, July 1841, Dicks, no. 460. According to Marshall and Stock, *Ira Aldridge*, pp. 155–6, the latter date is an error; the French original was not produced until July 1846, and the author is in fact Thomas Archer. It would make a fascinating subject of study to examine the interrelationship of French colonialism and revolutionary thinking with French dramas dealing with white/black relationships. Many of these, of course, made their way on to the English stage.
84. Bridgeman, *The Black Doctor*, [p. vi]; *The Black Doctor*, attributed to Aldridge, p. 2.
85. *The Black Doctor*, attributed to Aldridge, Act 1, scene 2.
86. *Ibid.*
87. *Ibid.*, Act 1, scene 4.
88. *Ibid.*, Act 2, scene 1.
89. *Ibid.*
90. See the *Era* (14 February 1847), p. 10, col. 3; (2 January 1848), p. 12, col. 4; (9 January 1848), p. 12, col. 4; (16 January 1848), p. 12, col. 2; (2 April 1848), p. 12, col. 1.
91. 'Surrey', *The Satirist or, The True Censor of the Times* (26 March 1848), p. 102, col. 2.
92. *Theatrical Journal* 13:647 (31 March 1852), p. 99, col. 2.
93. Quoted in Andrews, 'Victorian Ebony', p. 87.
94. *Notes and Queries*, fourth series, 10 (9 November 1872), p. 373.
95. 'Britannia Saloon', *Theatrical Journal* 13:641 (24 March 1852), p. 91, col. 2.
96. See Maurice Harney, *Titus Andronicus* (London: Harvester Wheatsheaf, 1990), p. xiv, and A. C. Dessau, *Titus Andronicus* (Manchester: Manchester University Press, 1989), pp. 7–11.
97. *Notes and Queries*, fourth series, 9 (25 May 1872), p. 423.
98. *Notes and Queries*, fourth series, 10 (17 August 1872), p. 132.
99. *Notes and Queries*, fourth series, 10 (9 November 1872), p. 373.
100. Andrews, 'Victorian Ebony', pp. 91–2. The letter is signed C. A. Somervil – whether this is a misreading of Somerset's handwriting or a typing error, I do not know.
101. 'The theatre – "Titus Andronicus"', *Brighton Herald* (6 October 1860), p. [2], col. 6.
102. 'Britannia', *Era* (26 April 1857), p. 10, col. 2.

103. 'Covent-Garden Theatre', *Morning Post* (11 April 1833), p. [3], col. 4.
104. 'Covent-Garden Theatre', *The Times* (11 April 1833), p. 3, col. 3.
105. *Spectator* 250 (13 April 1833), p. 328, and *Athenaeum* 285 (13 April 1833), p. 236.
106. 'Surrey', *The Satirist, or The True Censor of the Times* (2 April 1848), p. 110, col. 2.
107. 'Surrey', *Era* (2 April 1848), p. 12, col. 1.
108. 'The African Roscius', *Era* (22 March 1846), p. 6, col. 3. At times, the reviewer's enthusiasm does run away with him. Considering Aldridge in other parts (Gambia, Rolla), he declares him 'the greatest wonder we have ever seen, even upon the stage'.
109. 'Provincial theatricals, Devonport', *Era* (20 December 1846), p. 10, col. 4.
110. 'Lyceum', *Athenaeum* 1605 (31 July 1858), p. 144, cols. 1–2. His last Desdemona, Madge Kendal, comments in her memoirs on the play that Aldridge would make on the contrast between her white hand and his black one. See Kendal, *Dame Madge Kendal by Herself* (London: John Murray, 1933), p. 87.
111. Photocopy of Aldridge's letter, dated 2 November 1858, from Scobie's papers, in my possession.
112. 'Theatres and Entertainments', *The Times* (26 July 1858), p. 9, col. 2.
113. 'Britannia', *Era* (26 April 1857), p. 10, col. 2.
114. Kendal, *Dame Madge Kendal by Herself*, p. 87.
115. 'Haymarket', *Athenaeum* 1974 (26 August 1865), p. 285, cols. 2–3.
116. Theatre Museum production file for *Othello*, Theatre Royal Haymarket (21 August 1865).
117. Rosenberg, *Masks of Othello*, p. 102. William Winter, whose taste was for the more 'poetic' interpretation was not impressed, though he acknowledged Salvini's greatness as an actor. Frustratingly, Rosenberg does not give dates for Salvini's performances; Winter gives his first performance in America as 16 September 1873 (*Shakespeare on the Stage*, p. 287).
118. Quoted in Rosenberg, *Masks of Othello*, p. 113, from E. T. Mason, *The Othello of Tommaso Salvini* (New York: 1890).
119. Quoted from the *Negro Times* (16 October 1922), in Andrews, 'Victorian Ebony', p. 70. There is also a briefer account in William Wells Brown, *The Black Man: his antecedents, his genius and his achievements* (Boston: James Redpath, 1863), pp. 118–19. Wells Brown claims that this performance was given at the Haymarket – but his book was published two years before that last London performance. The *Othello* that Wells Brown saw must, I think, have been the 1858 one at the Lyceum, in which Stuart did play Iago, and which was obviously an 'occasion' of the sort described by Wells Brown.
120. 'The late Ira Aldridge', *Era* (25 August 1867), p. 10, col. 4.

CHAPTER 4

1. See Blackburn, *The Overthrow of Colonial Slavery*, pp. 287–90. One fascinating sidelight on the war is offered by W. Jeffrey Bolster in *Black Jacks:*

African American seamen in the age of sail (Cambridge, MA: Harvard University Press, 1997). He writes about the self-regulating community, some 1,000 strong, of African American prisoners of war held in Dartmoor whose activities included theatrical performances (pp. 100–30).

2. See, for example, the extracts from *The Clockmaker; or, the sayings and doings of Samuel Slick of Slickville*, *Athenaeum* 558 (7 August 1838), pp. 471–2.

3. See Nils Erik Enkvist, 'Caricatures of Americans on the English stage prior to 1870', *Societas Scientiarum Fennica Commentationes Humanarum Litterarum* 18:1 (1951), pp. 27–47. See also Walter Blair, 'Charles Mathews and his "A Trip to America"', *Prospects* 2 (1976), pp. 1–24.

4. 'English Opera House', *The Times* (26 March 1824), p. 3, col. 4.

5. [Charles Mathews], *The Life and Correspondence of Charles Mathews ... by Mrs Mathews*. Abridged and condensed by Edmund Yates (London: Routledge, Warne and Routledge, 1860), pp. 284, 289.

6. Sam Dennison, *Scandalize my Name: black imagery in American popular music* (New York: Garland Publishing, 1982), pp. 511–12.

7. [Charles Mathews], *The London Mathews, containing an account of this celebrated comedian's trip to America ...* (London: Hodgson, n.d.), p. 10.

8. [Charles Mathews], *Sketches of Mr. Mathews' celebrated trip to America ...* (London: J. Limbird, 1825), p. 9.

9. 'English Opera House', *The Times* (26 March 1824), p. 3, col. 4.

10. *The Mirror of the Stage* 16 (29 March 1824), p. 62.

11. Quoted from a playbill by Enkvist, 'Caricatures of Americans', p. 45.

12. W. T. Moncrieff, *Monsieur Mallét (or, My Daughter's Letter)*, Dicks, no. 936, Act 1, scene 2. Oroonoko's one-man show closes the first Act.

13. 'Adelphi Theatre', *The Times* (23 January 1829), p. 2, col. 5.

14. See R. C. Toll, *Blacking Up: the minstrel show in nineteenth-century America* (New York: Oxford University Press, 1974), ch. 1; Eric Lott, *Love and Theft: blackface minstrelsy and the American working class* (New York: Oxford University Press, 1993); Marian Hannah Winter, 'Juba and American minstrelsy', in A. Bean, J. V. Hatch and B. Macnamara (eds.), *Inside the Minstrel Mask: readings in nineteenth-century blackface minstrelsy* (Hanover and London: Wesleyan University Press, 1996), pp. 223–41; Saidiya V. Hartman, *Scenes of Subjection: terror, slavery, and self-making in nineteenth-century America* (Oxford: Oxford University Press, 1997) and W. T. Lhamon, *Raising Cain: blackface performance from Jim Crow to hip hop* (Cambridge, MA: Harvard University Press, 1998); Ralph Ellison, in 'Change the joke and slip the yoke', in his *Shadow and Act* (New York: Vintage, 1995; first publ. 1958), pp. 45–59, takes issue with the concept of the blackface minstrel as the archetypal 'trickster' figure.

15. See Harding, *There is a River*, pp. 63–72.

16. *Ibid.*, p. 81.

17. *Ibid.*, pp. 94–103. See also Joanne Grant (ed.), *Black Protest: history, documents and analyses, 1619 to the present* (New York: Fawcett, 1968), pp. 53–9.

18. See, for example, Toll, *Blacking Up*; Eileen Southern, *The Music of Black Americans: a history* (New York: W. W. Norton, 1983), pp. 88–95; C. B. Holmberg and G. D. Schneider, 'Daniel Decatur Emmett's stump sermons: genuine Afro-American culture, language and rhetoric in the Negro minstrel show', *Journal of Popular Culture* 19:4 (spring 1986), pp. 27–38; Lott, *Love and Theft*; Peter Fryer, 'The discovery and "appropriation" of African music and dance', *Race & Class* 39:3 (January–March 1998), pp. 1–20; and Lhamon, *Raising Cain*, especially ch. 1.

19. See, in particular, Lhamon, *Raising Cain*; see also Lott, *Love and Theft*, and Dale Cockrell, *Demons of Disorder: early blackface minstrels and their world* (Cambridge: Cambridge University Press, 1997).

20. Alexander Saxton, *The Rise and Fall of the White Republic: class politics and mass culture in nineteenth-century America* (London: Verso, 1990), ch. 7, 'Blackface minstrelsy', pp. 165–6.

21. See Walvin, *Black and White*, pp. 189–90.

22. See, for example, James H. Dormon, 'The strange career of Jim Crow Rice', *Journal of Social History* 3:2 (1970), pp. 109–22. Brief contemporary accounts are given in F. C. Wemyss, *Wemyss' Chronology of the American Stage from 1752 to 1852* (New York: Wm. Taylor and Co., 1852), p. 122, and the same author's *Theatrical Biography* (Glasgow: R. Griffin, 1848), pp. 178–9. All the texts on blackface performance cited contain an account of Rice's story.

23. See, for example, Hutton, *Curiosities of the American Stage*, p. 117.

24. Quoted in Eric Lott, 'Blackface and blackness: the minstrel show in American culture', in Bean, Hatch and Macnamara (eds.), *Inside the Minstrel Mask*, p. 7.

25. See Lhamon, *Raising Cain*, pp. 180–5, p. 180.

26. See Marshall Stearns and Jean Stearns, *Jazz Dance: the story of American vernacular dance* (New York: Macmillan, 1968), pp. 39–42.

27. Dennison, *Scandalize My Name*, p. 50. Dennison does not subscribe to the view that Rice's act represented any genuine attempt at African-derived dance.

28. Charles Mackay, *Through the Long Day: memorials of a literary life during half a century* (London: W. H. Allen, 1887), vol. 1, p. 133.

29. 'John Benjamin Dunn, the English Jim Crow' in *Actors by Daylight or Pencilings in the Pit* 42 (15 December 1838), p. 331.

30. See *Figaro in London* 250 (17 September 1836), p. 156.

31. *Figaro in London* 249 (10 September 1836), p. 151–2.

32. 'Music and the drama', *Athenaeum* 584 (5 January 1839), p. 15, col. 2.

33. *The Idler and Breakfast Table Companion* 48/9 (10 February 1838).

34. See J. Suddaby, 'A theatrical evening in 1838: "Jim Crow", "Mr. Ferguson", and "Pickwickians"', *Dickensian* 7:7 (July 1909), pp. 172–8. I am indebted to Michael Slater for this reference.

35. See review of *The Origin of Jim Crow*, *Athenaeum* 503 (17 June 1837), p. 440; *Actors by Gaslight; or, 'Boz' in the Boxes* 35 (15 December 1838), p. 278 for one of the many political references; John Briggs, *The History of Jim Crow* (London: Smallfield and Son, 1839); *The Humorous Adventures of Jump Jim Crow* (Glasgow, n.d.); Enkvist, 'Caricatures of Americans'; and Michael Pickering,

'White skin, black masks: "Nigger" minstrelsy in Victorian England', in J. S. Bratton (ed.), *Music Hall Performance and Style* (Milton Keynes: Open University Press, 1986), pp. 70–91.

36. Dormon, 'The strange career of Jim Crow Rice', p. 113, quoting from *Spirit of the Times* (6 May 1837).
37. See Peter Fryer, *Staying Power: the history of black people in Britain* (London: Pluto, 1984), pp. 81–8, 231–2.
38. Hans Nathan, *Dan Emmett and the Rise of Early Negro Minstrelsy* (Norman: University of Oklahoma Press, 1962), p. 70, quoted in Marshall and Stearns, *Jazz Dance*, p. 41.
39. Marshall and Stearns, *Jazz Dance*, p. 41.
40. Quoted in Malcolm Morley, 'Jim Crow and Boz's Juba', *Dickensian* 47:297 (December 1950), p. 32.
41. 'Our Miscellany', *Actors by Daylight or Pencilings in the Pit* 1 (3 March 1838), p. 7.
42. Briggs, preface, *History of Jim Crow*.
43. *Ibid.*, p. 176.
44. *Ibid.*, p. 182 (emphasis added).
45. *Athenaeum* 640 (1 February 1840), p. 94, col. 3.
46. *Natchez Free Trader* (8 April 1836), quoted in Dormon, 'The strange career of Jim Crow Rice', p. 121.
47. 'Surrey', *Athenaeum* 458 (6 August 1836), p. 556, col. 1 (emphasis added).
48. *Figaro in London* 258 (12 November 1836), p. 188.
49. For this history, see, for example, George F. Rehin, 'Harlequin Jim Crow: continuity and convergence in blackface clowning', *Journal of Popular Culture* 9:3 (1975), pp. 682–701; J. S. Bratton, 'English Ethiopians: British audiences and black-face acts, 1835–1865', *Yearbook of English Studies* 11 (1981), pp. 127–42; Rehin, 'Blackface street minstrels in Victorian London and its resorts: popular culture and its racial connotations as revealed in polite opinion', *Journal of Popular Culture* 15:1 (1981), pp. 19–38; Michael Pickering, 'White skin, black masks: "Nigger" minstrelsy in Victorian England'; and Pickering 'Mock blacks and racial mockery: the "nigger" minstrel and British imperialism', in J. S. Bratton et al., *Acts of Supremacy: the British empire and the stage* (Manchester: Manchester University Press, 1991), pp. 179–236. See also D. Lorimer, 'Bibles, banjoes and bones: images of the Negro in the popular culture of Victorian England', in B. M. Gough (ed.), *In Search of the Visible Past: history lectures at Wilfrid Laurier University, 1973–4* (Waterloo, Ontario: Wilfrid Laurier University Press, 1975), pp. 31–50.
50. [T. D. Rice], *Bone Squash: a burletta in one act*, BL Addl. Mss. 42953 ff. 313–9, Act 1, scene 1, leaf 314; also often referred to as *Bone Squash Diabolo*. W. T. Lhamon has collated the various texts, both English and American, of a number of Jim Crow plays, including this one, in his *Jump Jim Crow: lost plays, lyrics and street prose of the first Atlantic popular culture* (Cambridge, MA: Harvard University Press, 2003). However, I have confined myself to the

mss. versions extant in the BL, since these would have formed the core of Rice's English performances.

51. *Ibid.*
52. *Ibid.*, Act 1, scene 2, leaf 315.
53. 'Surrey Theatre', *The Times* (13 September 1836), p. 2, col. 4.
54. *Ibid.*
55. T. Parry, *The Peacock and the Crow: a farce in two acts*, BL Addl. Mss. 42940 ff. 371–97. Also in Lhamon, *Jump Jim Crow*. *Figaro in London* 271 (11 February 1837), p. 24, reported of this that 'it is almost unprecedented in foolery and poverty both of language and incident . . . the audience was bent on wreaking summary vengeance on the author's head, and hooted the thing off'.
56. T. D. Rice, *The Virginia Mummy: a farce in one act*, BL Addl. Mss. 42940 ff. 822–867, incomplete. Also in Lhamon, *Jump Jim Crow*.
57. See the review in the *Athenaeum* 293 (8 June 1833), p. 364, col. 3. According to the summary given of the plot, a lover who is thrown out of his beloved's house by her antiquarian father plans to get back in by disguising himself as a merchant from India, with a mummy for sale. The title of the farce is not given.
58. *The Virginia Mummy*, Act 1, scene 3, leaves 836–8.
59. Lhamon, *Raising Cain*, p. 172.
60. Dormon, 'The strange career of Jim Crow Rice', pp. 117–18.
61. W. L. Rede, *Life in America – the flight – the pursuit – the voyage*, BL Addl. Mss. 42939 ff. 444–79, probably based on his 1825 *The Flight to America*.
62. *Ibid.*, Act 2, scene 1, leaf 457 verso.
63. *Ibid.*, Act 3, scene 2, leaf 471 verso.
64. *Ibid.*, Act 3, scene 2, leaf 472.
65. Shane White, *Stories of Freedom in Black New York* (Cambridge, MA: Harvard University Press, 2002), pp. 200–1. The parades were held on 5 July to avoid clashes with whites celebrating 4 July – the date of final manumission in New York was 4 July 1827.
66. Rede, *Life in America*, Act 3, scene the last, leaf 479.
67. *Ibid.*, Act 3, scene the last, leaf 478.
68. *Ibid.*, Act 3, scene 3.
69. 'Adelphi', *Actors by Daylight or Pencilings in the Pit* 2:44 ([December 1838]), p. 21.
70. *Jim Crow's Vagaries, or Black Flights of Fancy: containing a choice collection of Nigger melodies . . .* (London: Orlando Hodgson, [1860]), p. 13.
71. Lhamon, *Raising Cain*, p. 205.
72. W. H. Oxberry and J. Gann, *Mr. Midshipman Easy!*, Surrey theatre, 26 September 1836, Duncombe, vol. 29/30.
73. Frederick Marryat, *Mr Midshipman Easy* (London: Everyman, 1970, first publ. 1836). Marryat was one of the travel writers who later published his American experiences, finding much to disparage in the new nation. His book was critically reviewed in the *Athenaeum* 636:4 (January 1840), p. 9.
74. Oxberry and Gann, *Midshipman Easy*, Act 1, scene 3.
75. *Ibid.*

76. *Figaro in London* 252 (1 October 1836), p. 164. Marryat, a half-pay captain, was 'a coxcomb' in *Figaro*'s view.
77. *Actors by Daylight or Pencilings in the Pit* 2:45 (5 January 1839), p. 26.
78. Sillard, *Barry Sullivan and his Contemporaries*, p. 44.
79. T. P. Taylor, *Jim Crow in His New Place*, BL Addl. Mss. 42950 ff. 593–602b. Also in Lhamon, *Jump Jim Crow.*
80. See *Actors by Daylight or Pencilings in the Pit* 1:41 (8 December 1838), p. 327; also nos. 42 (p. 334); 43 (p. 342); 46 (p. 55). In the issue for 2 February 1839 (49) it was announced that 'Jim Crow Rice is about to quit London for the provinces; he intends to return to America in the Autumn' (p. 101). See also *Athenaeum* 584 (5 January 1839), p. 15. Pickering, 'White skin, black masks', p. 74, states that after Rice came to England in 1836, he made only one more visit, in 1842. An absence during some of 1838, however, may have been the period when Harper and Dunn both attempted to step into Rice's shoes, though neither was reckoned as good.
81. Harper appeared as Jim Crow in *The Nigger What Sweeps the Crossings*, Royal Victoria Theatre, December 1838 (poster, University of Bristol Theatre Collection) and again in Cork in 1841 and, no doubt, on many occasions in between. See Sillard, *Barry Sullivan and his Contemporaries*, pp. 86–7.
82. 'Douglass's rebuke of a local actor named Bateman for performing "Jim Crow ... apes of the negro" seemed unwarranted to the editor [of the *Limerick Reporter*], who thought Bateman a "clever actor".' See *The Frederick Douglass Papers, series one, Speeches, Debates and Interviews, Volume 1, 1841–6*, ed. J. W. Blassingame (New Haven: Yale University Press, 1979), pp. 76–7.
83. *Actors by Daylight or Pencilings in the Pit* 31 (29 September 1838), p. 246.
84. 'If Mr. Dunn were a foreigner how clever he would be, but being *only* an Englishman, his merit is not appreciated by his countrymen' ('Garrick', *Figaro in London* 362 (19 November 1838), p. 191)).
85. E. Fitzball, *The Negro of Wapping or, the boat builder's hovel*, Garrick theatre, 16 April 1838, Duncombe, vol. 29/30.
86. *Ibid.*, Act 1, scene 1.
87. *Ibid.*
88. *Ibid.*, Act 2, scene 3.
89. *Ibid.*
90. 'Garrick', *Actors by Daylight or Pencilings in the Pit* 1 (21 April 1838), p. 63.
91. Lorimer, 'Bibles, banjoes and bones', p. 41.
92. *Ibid.*, p. 44.
93. *North Star* (27 October 1848). Quoted in Lott, 'Blackface and blackness', p. 3. Lott goes on to argue that white audiences were not nearly so derisive of African American culture as Douglass suggests, an argument taken even further by Lhamon in *Raising Cain*. Douglass, however, was in the social milieu of the time and was a fighter for black freedom with intimate knowledge of the inscape of nineteenth-century racism. It is not unknown, in this country in the twenty-first century, for racist attitudes to coexist with consumption, in one way or another, of minority culture.

94. Philip Foner, *Frederick Douglass: a biography* (New York: Citadel Press, 1964), pp. 343–4.
95. R. J. M. Blackett, *Building an Antislavery Wall: black Americans in the Atlantic abolitionist movement, 1830–1860* (Ithaca: Cornell University Press, 1989, first publ. 1983), p. 160.
96. 'Uncle Sam's peculiarities. American niggers. – Hudson River steam-boat dialogues', *Bentley's Miscellany* 6 (1839), p. 262.
97. *Ibid.*, p. 264.
98. *Ibid.*, p. 263.
99. *Ibid.*
100. *Ibid.*, p. 266.
101. *Ibid.*, pp. 267, 268, 269.
102. *Ibid.*, p. 265.
103. *Ibid.*, p. 271.

CHAPTER 5

1. Edward Stirling, *Yankee Notes for English Circulation*, Duncombe, vol. 46. See also Morley, 'Jim Crow and Boz's Juba', pp. 28–32.
2. Stirling, *Yankee Notes*, Act 1, scene 3.
3. *Ibid.*, Act 1, scene 1.
4. *Ibid.*
5. *Ibid.*
6. *Ibid.*, Act 1, scene 2.
7. *Ibid.*
8. *Ibid.*
9. 'The Adelphi', *The Times* (27 December 1842), p. 5, col. d.
10. Harry Reynolds, *Minstrel Memories: the story of burnt cork minstrelsy in Great Britain from 1836 to 1927* (London: Alston Rivers, 1928), p. 83.
11. The phrase is Philip Allingham's, in 'The roots of Dickens's *Christmas Books* and plays in early nineteenth-century melodrama and pantomime', www.victorianweb.org/authors/dickens/pva.pav56.html.
12. See, for example, William J. Mahar, 'Black English in early blackface minstrelsy: a new interpretation of the sources of minstrel show dialect', *American Quarterly* 37:2 (1985), pp. 260–85, and Holmberg and Schneider, 'Daniel Decatur Emmett's stump sermons'.
13. Toll, *Blacking Up*, p. 36.
14. Mackay, *Through the Long Day*, vol. 1, pp. 133–4.
15. Quoted from Coleman in Broadbent, *Annals of the Liverpool Stage*, p. 159. Fanny Kemble, unlikely as it might seem, had been married to an American slaveowner. In her *Journal of a Residence on a Georgia Plantation in 1838–1839*, she recalled: 'I have seen Jim Crow – the veritable James: all the contortions, and springs, and flings, and kicks, and capers you [her correspondent] have been beguiled into accepting as indicative of him are spurious, faint, feeble,

impotent – in a word, pale Northern reproductions of the ineffable black conception. It is impossible for words to describe the things these people did with their bodies, and, above all, with their faces' (*Journal of a Residence on a Georgia Plantation in 1838–1839*, ed. John A. Scott (New York: A. A. Knopf, 1961, first publ. 1863), p. 131.)

16. *The Wood Demon; or One O'Clock*, BL Addl. Mss. 43003 ff. 576–616, Act 1, scene 1, leaf 586. This light-hearted pastiche – one of the musicians declares, 'I'm not a black, but an unhappy wight' – contains one of the few contemporary references I have come across in popular theatre to the Irish Famine, which was then reaching its peak. Some fairies are displaying in 'dissolving views' portents of the hero's destiny, one of which, most improbably, is a 'caricature representation of the aphis vastator or potatoe blight'. When the view changes to the Erl King attacking the hero, 'The aphis turns into a phiz, you know.' It is a surreal moment (Act 2, scene 1, leaf 591). According to *Era*, which praised it highly, it was written by Albert Smith and Charles Kenny: 'one of the best written burlesques we have ever witnessed' ('Lyceum', *Era* (9 May 1847), p. 11, col. 2.)

17. Toll, *Blacking Up*, p. 38, quoting from *Spirit of the Times* (16 October 1847).

18. See Bratton, 'English Ethiopians', p. 128, and Lorimer, *Colour, Class and the Victorians*, pp. 86–7.

19. *Douglas Jerrold's Weekly Newspaper* (23 January 1847), p. 93, col.1. They are all opera singers; Lablache should be Lablanche.

20. G. D. Pitt, *Toussaint L'Ouverture or the Black Spartacus*, 1846, BL Addl. Mss. 42995 ff. 225–53. Only Act 1 is still extant. The 'plot' does have a tenuous connection with reality, in that Toussaint, born a slave but subsequently granted his freedom, did allow the plantation manager who had freed him to escape. See Hochschild, *Bury the Chains*, pp. 257–8.

21. A. L. V. Campbell, *More Ethiopians!! or 'Jenny Lind' in New York*, 1847, BL Addl. Mss. 43003 ff. 727–59.

22. Preface to *ibid*, leaf 729.

23. *Ibid.*, Act 1, scene 1, leaf 735.

24. *Ibid.*, leaves 735–6. Some punctuation added in this and subsequent quotations.

25. *Ibid.*, leaf 737.

26. *Ibid.*, leaves 738–9.

27. *Ibid.*, Act 1, scene 2, leaves 747, 749, 750.

28. See, for example, Pickering, 'Mock blacks and racial mockery'.

29. Campbell, *More Ethiopians*, Act 1, scene 2, leaf 758.

30. *Somebody's in the House with Dinah, or the invitation to the Nigger Ball*, BL Addl. Mss. 43004 ff. 367–394.

31. *Ibid.*, Act 1, scene 1, leaves 368, 369.

32. Both quotations from *ibid.*, leaves 372, 373.

33. *Ibid.*, Act 1, scene 1, leaf 393. (There appear to be no scene divisions.)

34. Bratton, 'British heroism and the structure of melodrama', p. 54.

35. Edward Stirling, *The Cabin Boy*, French, no. 559, Act 2, scene 1.
36. *Ibid.*
37. G. D. Pitt, *The Black Bayaderes, or the Rival Serenaders*, BL Addl Mss. 43003 ff. 380–428.
38. *Ibid.*, Act 1, scene 2, leaf 392.
39. *Ibid.*, Act 1, scene 3, leaf 401 verso. The reference is to the potato blight and to the volatile social and economic situation.
40. *Ibid.*, Act 1, scene 1, leaves 382–3.
41. *Ibid.*, leaves 383, 382 verso.
42. *Ibid.*, leaf 387.
43. Davis and Emeljanow, *Reflecting the Audience*, p. 194.
44. *Ibid.*, p. 195.
45. According to Asa Briggs, the gradual economic revival after 1842, than which 'there was no gloomier year in the whole nineteenth century', was broken by a 'further financial crisis in 1847' marked by 'acute distress. In 1847 and 1848 . . . social conflict became articulate and acute' (Briggs, *The Age of Improvement*, pp. 295–6).
46. George Wilson, *The Male and Female Serenaders, or Native Talent's Best*, BL Addl. Mss. 43003 ff. 644–664.
47. Edward Stirling, *The Buffalo Girls, or, the Female Serenaders*, Surrey theatre, 17 April 1847, Duncombe, vol. 59, Act 1, scene 1.
48. *Ibid.*
49. *Ibid.*
50. Mackay, *Through the Long Day*, p. 134.
51. See Lorimer, *Colour, Class and the Victorians*, p. 87.
52. Gilbert Abbot à Beckett, *The Quizziology of the British Drama* (London: Punch, 1846), pp. 14–15.
53. G. W. Moore [The Christy Minstrel], *'Bones' his Anecdotes and Goaks* (*sic*) (London: C. H. Clarke, [1870]), pp. 4–7.
54. Lorimer, *Colour, Class and the Victorians*, p. 88.
55. 'St. James's Theatre', *The Man in the Moon* 3 (1847), p. 182. I am indebted to Michael Slater for this reference.
56. See Marshall and Stock, *Ira Aldridge*, p. 170.
57. Robert Knox, preface, *The Races of Men: a philosophical enquiry into the influence of race over the destinies of nations* (London: Henry Renshaw, 1862, first publ. 1850), [p. v].
58. See especially Philip D. Curtin, *The Image of Africa: British ideas and action, 1780–1850* (Madison: University of Wisconsin Press, 1964), pp. 377–81. See also Lorimer, *Colour, Class and the Victorians*, pp. 136–7, and Hall, *Civilising Subjects*, pp. 48–9.
59. Long, *History of Jamaica*, quoted in Curtin, *Image of Africa*, p. 43. In Curtin's view, 'Long's greatest importance was in giving an "empirical" and "scientific" base that would lead on to pseudo-scientific racism . . . [the *History of Jamaica*] was used again and again for three-quarters of a century by British and

Continental polygenists of scientific repute, and it provided a set of ready made arguments for any publicist who wanted to prove the "fact" of African inferiority' (p. 45).

60. Thomas Carlyle, 'Occasional discourse on the Nigger question', first published in *Fraser's Magazine* (December 1849); *Latter-Day Pamphlets* (London, 1853), pp. 3, 8, 16.

61. See Patricia Hollis, 'Anti-slavery and British working-class radicalism in the years of reform', in Bolt and Drescher (eds.), *Anti-slavery, Religion and Reform*, pp. 294–315. Although this deals specifically with the reform years, and with opposition to abolitionism on the grounds that the lot of the English working class was worse than that of slaves, it does demonstrate how frequently the analogy was made, especially in Chartist literature. See also Lorimer, *Colour, Class and the Victorians*, ch. 5, which covers the early 1850s. Bridging the gap is Blackett, *Building an Antislavery Wall* – see, for example, pp. 19–24. Davis, in *The Problem of Slavery in the Age of Revolution*, quotes from Engels, *The Condition of the Working Class in England in 1844* (1845), which he describes as one of the 'greatest of anti-slavery tracts', pp. 467–8.

62. See William Wells Brown, *Sketches of Places and People Abroad* (Boston: John P. Jewett, 1855), p. 313; Lorimer, *Colour, Class and the Victorians*; and Blackett, *Building an Antislavery Wall*; pp. 48–9.

63. See Blackett, *Building an Antislavery Wall*, pp. 17–23.

64. See Williams, *Capitalism and Slavery*, pp. 150–3, and Hall, *Civilising Subjects*, pp. 202–3, 353.

65. See Hall, *Civilising Subjects*, chs. 2 and 3.

66. *Ibid.*, p. 353.

67. Stepan, *The Idea of Race in Science*, p. 41. In Knox's own words, 'the great question of the day, the question of race, has been touched on by ponderous quarterlies and sprightly weeklies, some admitting most of my views as already proven, others qualifying them in a variety of ways' (Knox, *The Races of Men*, p. 77.)

68. See Curtin, *Image of Africa*, ch. 15.

69. See *ibid.*, p. 368. See also Lorimer, *Colour, Class and the Victorians*, p. 137. Curtin argues that Knox's importance for the development of scientific racism has been underrated (*Image of Africa*, pp. 377–81).

CHAPTER 6

1. See Marshall and Stock, *Ira Aldridge*, pp. 29–30.
2. See, for example, Dormon, 'The strange career of Jim Crow Rice', p. 112.
3. Curtin, *Image of Africa*, p. 327.
4. See Hall, *Civilising Subjects*, pp. 72–9, and Jordan, *White Over Black*, pp. 174–7.
5. *Figaro in London* 208 (28 November 1835), p. 197.

6. Is the odd name meant to suggest that Mahone is some kind of piratical Arab slaver? But there are no other indications to this effect, and usually such characterisations are quite unambiguous.
7. E. Fitzball, *The Koeuba; or, the Pirate Vessel*, Cumberland, vol. 12.
8. 'Remarks', in *ibid.*, p. 6.
9. *Ibid.*, Act 2, scene 1.
10. *Ibid.*, Act 2, scene 5.
11. *Ibid.*, Act 1, scene 3.
12. *Ibid.*, Act 2, scene 1.
13. *Ibid.*
14. *Ibid.*, Act 2, scene 2.
15. See George M. Fredrickson, *The Black Image in the White Mind: the debate on Afro-American character and destiny, 1817–1914* (New York: Harper and Row, 1971), pp. 74–82, and John G. Mencke, *Mulattoes and Race Mixture: American attitudes and images, 1865–1918* (Ann Arbor: UMI Research Press, 1979), ch. 2, especially pp. 50–1.
16. From extracts taken from Knox's *The Races of Men*, in Philip D. Curtin (ed.), *Imperialism* (London: Macmillan, 1971), pp. 12–22, 21. In a supplementary section, 'An enquiry into the laws of human hybridité', published in the 1862 edition of his work, Knox elaborated his ideas: 'By the cross of a white man with a mulatto woman of no very deep die, dark blood has been observed to hold its ground . . . for a hundred and fifty years . . . with time the hybrid breed will gradually lose its peculiar moral and physical nature . . . some of the offspring reverting to one species, others to the other' (p. 491).
17. Curtin, *Image of Africa*, p. 374; see also Lorimer, *Colour, Class and the Victorians*, p. 135.
18. Curtin, *Image of Africa*, pp. 366–7.
19. *Ibid.*, pp. 375–6.
20. *Ibid.*, pp. 381–2.
21. *Ibid.*, p. 381.
22. See Lorimer, *Colour, Class and the Victorians*, pp. 139–44.
23. See Hall, *Civilising Subjects*, pp. 74–8.
24. See Booth, *Theatre in the Victorian Age*, p. 143.
25. B. N. Webster, *The Quadroon Slave*, licensed 26 October 1841, BL Addl. Mss. 42960 ff. 326–414. According to the *Athenaeum*, it was produced at the Haymarket 'for the sake of a new part for Mdlle Celeste; though she does not appear to advantage, and it has no other claims to notice' (732 (6 November 1841), p. 860, col. 3). A very similar, but much later, title is listed by Allardyce Nicoll: *The Quadroon; or, the Slave Bride*, performed at the Victoria in October 1857. See *A History of English Drama, 1660–1900* (Cambridge: Cambridge University Press, 1955–9), vol. 5. This does not seem to be extant, so there is no way of comparing the two.
26. Webster, *The Quadroon Slave*, Act 2, scene 1, leaf 399.
27. *Ibid.*, Act 1, scene 1, leaf 345.
28. *Ibid.*, Act 1, scene 1, leaf 346.

29. *Ibid.*, Act 1, scene 1, leaves 346–7.
30. *Ibid.*, Act 1, Scene 1, leaf 350.
31. Winthrop Jordan, in *White Over Black*, describes the 'pattern of miscegenation' in the West Indies: 'White women . . . did not sleep with Negro men, let alone marry them. Nor did white men actually marry Negroes or mulattoes: as one usually temperate planter [Bryan Edwards] declared, "The very idea is shocking." Yet white men commonly, almost customarily, took Negro women to bed with little pretense at concealing the fact. Colored mistresses were kept openly . . . Negro concubinage was an integral part of island life, tightly interwoven into the social fabric' (p. 140). Fernando Henriques, in *Children of Caliban: miscegenation* (London: Secker and Warburg, 1974) quotes an account of Jamaican life from the early 1820s: 'Every unmarried White man, and of every class, has his Black or his Brown mistress with whom he lives openly . . . the man who lives in open adultery – that is, who keeps his Black or Brown mistress in the very face of his wife and family, and of the community – has generally as much outward respect shewn him . . . as if he had been guilty of no breach of decency, or dereliction of moral duty' (p. 100, from John Stewart, *An Account of Jamaica and its Inhabitants* (London, 1823), pp. 173–4).
32. See Jennifer DeVere Brody, *Impossible Purities: blackness, femininity and Victorian culture* (Durham: Duke University Press, 1998), especially ch. 1. This sometimes inaccurate and overwritten book nonetheless contains some thought-provoking insights into what is implied by the figure of, in Brody's formulation, 'the mulattaroon'.
33. Henry Hughes, *Treatise on Sociology, theoretical and practical* (Philadelphia: Lippincott, Crambo and Co., 1854), p. 31.
34. Webster, *The Quadroon Slave*, Act 2, scene 1, leaf 394 (emphasis added).
35. *Ibid.*, Act 2, scene 1, leaves 392–3.
36. *Ibid.*, Act 2, scene 1, leaf 413.
37. Stirling, *The Cabin Boy*. For the French origin of the play, see the review in *The Times* (10 March 1846), p. 6, col. 6. The salient scenes and dialogue were also lifted by J. Courtney, under the title *The Ship Boy; or, the White Slave of Guadeloupe*, 1847, BL Addl. Mss. 43003 ff. 337–53b.
38. Stirling, *The Cabin Boy*, Act 1, scene 1.
39. 'Madame Celeste [is] seen in the boat rowing lustily through the surge, and finally disappearing through the back of the stage' (*The Times* (10 March 1846), p. 6, col. 6).
40. Stirling, *The Cabin Boy*, Act 2, scene 1.
41. *Ibid.*
42. *Ibid.*
43. *Ibid.*
44. *Ibid.*
45. 'Adelphi', *Era* (15 March 1846), pp. 5–6, col.1.
46. Captain Williams, *The Woman of Colour*, licensed 22 October 1853, BL Addl. Mss. 52943E, Act 1, scene 1, leaf 6.
47. *Ibid.*, Act 2, scene 1, leaf 24.

48. That is, 'against amalgamation' – the cant term for interracial mixing and miscegenation. Williams, *The Woman of Colour*, Act 3, scene 1, leaf 44 verso.

49. *Ibid.*, Act 1, scene 1, leaf 8 verso. All Americans are the same: the man of business and slavedriver Peabody is appalled at the thought of marrying a woman with even 'half a quarter of a drop of black blood in her veins – with the breadth of a hair of colour, round the root of her thumb nail' (*ibid.*, Act 2, scene 1, leaf 20 verso).

50. Williams, *The Woman of Colour*, Act 2, scene 2, leaf 35 verso.

51. 'Surrey', *Era* (20 November 1853), p. 10, cols. 1–2.

52. Williams, *The Woman of Colour*, Act 3, scene 1, leaves 42–3.

53. The first law against miscegenation was passed in 1661, in Maryland. By 1914, according to Clinton Cox, 'twenty-nine states had statutes making miscegenation an offence punishable by imprisonment for periods ranging from thirty days in Delaware to ten years in Florida, Mississippi and North Carolina'. See Clinton Cox, 'From Columbus to Hitler and back again', *Race & Class* 43:3 (2002), p. 44.

54. Indeed, William Makepeace Thackeray, in *Vanity Fair* (1848), had satirised the attempt of the cash-poor Osborne family to marry son George off against his will to an ugly but rich and well-meaning black heiress from the West Indies.

55. Dion Boucicault, *The Octoroon; or, Life in Louisiana*, in Peter Thomson (ed.), *Plays by Dion Boucicault* (Cambridge: Cambridge University Press, 1984), Act 2, scene 1, p. 147.

56. Thomson (ed.), *Plays by Dion Boucicault*, p. 9. See also the discussion of the play in Brody, *Impossible Purities*, pp. 46–58.

57. [Charles William] Shirley Brooks, *The Creole; or, Love's Fetters*, Lyceum theatre, 8 April 1847, Lacy [1850], Dicks, no. 1009. Quotations are taken from Lacy.

58. Preface to *ibid.*, p. 3.

59. *Ibid.*, Act 1, scene 1.

60. *Ibid.*, Act 1, scene 2.

61. *Ibid.*, Act 2, scene 1.

62. *Ibid.*, Act 2, scene 3.

63. *Ibid.*

64. *Ibid.*, Act 3, scene 3.

65. *Ibid.*, Act 3, scene 4.

66. *Ibid.*

67. A further racial twist to this equation is quoted by Brody. In the words of the race scientist Josiah Nott, 'when a Negro man married a white woman, the offspring partook more largely of the Negro type than when the reverse connection had effect'. See Josiah Nott, *An Essay on the Natural History of Mankind, viewed in connection with Negro Slavery* (Mobile: Dade, Thompson, 1851), cited by Brody, *Impossible Purities*, p. 54.

68. 'Lyceum', *Era* (11 April 1847), p. 10, col. 3. *The Times* was rather less enthusiastic, believing that the piece 'was somewhat too slight for three acts',

but that the plot was constructed 'with a degree of ingenuity which shows a great advance in dramatic art on the part of the author' ('Lyceum theatre' (9 April 1847), p. 4, col. 6).

69. See *Era* (18 April 1847), p. 11, col. 2; (25 April 1847), p. 11, cols. 1–2; (2 May 1847) p. 11, col. 1; (16 May 1847), p. 11, col. 3. *The Wood Demon* (see ch. 5) began its run at the Lyceum in early May, 1847 ('Lyceum', *Era* (9 May 1847), p. 11, col. 2).

70. Charles O'Bryan, *Lugarto the Mulatto*, Lacy, vol. 31, no. 460. (1850 was also the year of publication of Knox's *Races of Men*.)

71. 'Surrey', *Era* (26 May 1850), p. 12, col. 3.

72. O'Bryan, *Lugarto*, Act 1, scene 1.

73. John Van Evrie, *White Supremacy and Negro Subordination: or, Negroes a subordinate race, and (so-called) slavery its normal condition* (New York: Van Evrie, Horton and Co., 1868), pp. 148, 162, 164, 167, cited in Mencke, *Mulattoes and Race Mixture*, pp. 101–2. *White Supremacy* was first published as a pamphlet in 1853.

74. Knox, *The Races of Men*, in Curtin (ed.), *Imperialism*, pp. 12–22, 21.

75. O'Bryan, *Lugarto*, Act 1, scene 1.

76. Both quotations from 'Surrey', *Era* (26 May 1850), p. 12, col. 3.

77. Tom Robertson, *The Half Caste; or, the Poisoned Pearl*, Lacy, vol. 97, no. 241.

78. *Ibid.*, Act 3, scene 1.

79. *Ibid.*

80. *Ibid.*

81. 'Surrey', *Era* (26 May 1850), p. 12, col. 3.

82. C. H. Hazlewood, *The Staff of Diamonds*, French, no. 104.

83. See Lloyd, *The Navy and the Slave Trade*, chs. 16–18, and Howard Temperley, *British Anti-Slavery, 1833–1870* (London: Longman, 1972), especially chs. 9 and 12. Although the Brazilian government made importing slaves illegal in 1850, so numbers dropped sharply after that, Curtin notes that the 1860s were 'the last important decade of the trade' and that it 'exceeded the rate for any period before the seventeenth century' (Curtin, *The Atlantic Slave Trade*, p. 269). C. H. Hazlewood's *Ashore and Afloat* (French, no. 106), performed at the Surrey in 1864, deals with the latter trade, with its second act taken up with a naval anti-slavery action against Algiers. But the objects of the exercise, the African slaves, have completely disappeared from the scene. Unlike *My Poll and my Partner Joe*, played at the Surrey more than twenty-five years earlier, there is no shipboard liberation of captives, no African presence at all – yet another way in which the African has been cut from the narrative of slavery.

84. Inikori, *Africans and the Industrial Revolution*, pp. 378–9.

85. Hazlewood, *The Staff of Diamonds*, Act I, scene 1.

86. *Ibid.*

87. *Ibid.*

88. *Ibid.*

89. *Ibid.*

90. *Ibid.*

91. *Ibid.*
92. *Ibid.*, Act 2, scene 3.
93. *Ibid.*, Act 1, scene 1.
94. *Ibid.*
95. *Ibid.*, Act 2, scene 6.
96. *Ibid.*
97. *Ibid.*, Act 1, scene 1.

CHAPTER 7

1. See Blackett, *Building an Antislavery Wall*; Audrey A. Fisch, '"Negrophilism" and British nationalism: the spectacle of the black American abolitionist', *Victorian Review* 19:2 (Winter 1993), pp. 20–47 and '"Repetitious accounts so piteous and harrowing": the ideological work of American slave narratives in England', *Journal of Victorian Culture* 1:1 (1996), pp. 16–34.
2. See Blackett, *Building an Antislavery Wall*, for a detailed and informative account of the activities of black abolitionists in Britain.
3. *New York Express*, quoted in *The Anti-Slavery Standard* (1 July 1847), cited in Fisch, '"Negrophilism", p. 20.
4. See, for example, Temperley, *British Anti-Slavery*, and David Turley, *The Culture of English Anti-Slavery, 1780–1860* (London: Routledge, 1991).
5. See Lorimer, *Colour, Class and the Victorians*, ch. 4, and Hall, *Civilising Subjects*, chs. 2 and 3.
6. Harriet Beecher Stowe, *Uncle Tom's Cabin*, ed. Jean Fagan Yellin (Oxford: Oxford University Press, 1998). *Uncle Tom's Cabin* was initially serialised in *The National Era*, June 1851–April 1852, and published in two volumes in March 1852. The first, pirated editions appeared in England in July 1852.
7. See Harry Birdoff, *The World's Greatest Hit – Uncle Tom's Cabin* (New York: S. F. Vanni, 1947), ch. 7, 'Of the Tomitudes abroad', pp. 144–65.
8. E. Fitzball, *Thirty-five Years of a Dramatic Author's Life*, 2 vols. (London: T. C. Newby, 1859), vol. 2, pp. 260–1.
9. *Uncle Tom's Cabin: a hippodrama in two acts*, Astley's, 22 November 1852, BL Addl. Mss. 52935 ff.
10. 'City of London Theatre', *Era* (16 January 1853), p. 10, col. 3.
11. G. D. Pitt, *Uncle Tom's Cabin: a nigger drama*, Royal Pavilion theatre, 9 October 1852, BL Addl. Mss. 52935I. This manuscript has obviously been bound out of sequence and inserted into it is a second act, in a completely different hand, clearly from a different play.
12. Jane Tompkins, 'Sentimental power: *Uncle Tom's Cabin* and the politics of literary history', in Tompkins, *Sensational Designs: the cultural work of American fiction, 1790–1960* (Oxford: Oxford University Press, 1985), pp. 124, 135.
13. Stowe's preface, *Uncle Tom's Cabin*, p. 3.
14. The history of dramatic censorship is long and complex, as is the development of what was felt fit to be portrayed on stage and what was not. The 1843

Theatre Regulation Act gave absolute discretionary powers to the Lord Chamberlain to forbid the performance of any play judged contrary to the preservation of good morals, decorum or the public peace. According to Michael Booth, 'In these areas [religion and politics] the Examiner of Plays had to be vigilant, and many a passage containing an alleged or actual political or religious allusion was struck out of an otherwise acceptable script' (Booth, *Theatre in the Victorian Age*, p. 146).

15. Attributed to Abraham Lincoln, Stowe, *Uncle Tom's Cabin*, back cover.
16. Mark Lemon and Tom Taylor, *Slave Life; or, Uncle Tom's Cabin*, Adelphi theatre, 29 November 1852, Webster, vol. 17, no. 191.
17. Taylor was the author of the highly popular *Ticket of Leave Man*, noted for its realistic depiction of criminality (there is a film version of this, starring Todd Slaughter); Mark Lemon is best known as the editor of *Punch*.
18. 'The Theatres', *Spectator* 1275 (4 December 1852), pp. 1159–60.
19. *Ibid.*
20. *Uncle Tom's Cabin; or, the Negro Slave*, Standard theatre, 8 September 1852, BL Addl. Mss. 52934C. (Note the use of the less pejorative 'Negro' in the title.)
21. 'Standard Theatre', *Era* (19 September 1852), p. 12, col. 3.
22. See Lorimer, *Colour, Class and the Victorians*, ch. 4.
23. *Uncle Tom's Cabin; or, the Negro slave*, 52934C, Act 1, scene 1, leaves 14–15.
24. *Ibid.*, leaves 16–17 (punctuation added).
25. Eliza Vincent, *Uncle Tom's Cabin; or, the Fugitive Slave!*, Victoria theatre, 15 September 1852, BL Addl. Mss. 52934F.
26. *Ibid.*, Act 1, scene 3, leaf 7.
27. *Ibid.*, Act 2, scene 1, leaf 13, verso.
28. E. Fitzball, *Uncle Tom's Cabin*, Olympic theatre, 20 September 1852, BL Addl. Mss. 52934G.
29. *Ibid.*, Act 1, scene 3, leaves 22–3.
30. *Ibid.*, Act 1, scene 3, leaves 25–6.
31. 'Provincial Theatricals', *Era* (14 November, 1852), p. 11, col. 4.
32. Fitzball, *Uncle Tom's Cabin*, 52934G, Act 1, scene 3, leaf 22.
33. *Ibid.*, Act 1, scene 3, leaf 23.
34. *Ibid.*, Act 2, scene the last, leaf 73. 'Forgotten' could also be transcribed as 'forgott me'.
35. 'The theatres', *Spectator* 1275 (4 December 1852), pp. 1159–60.
36. 'Adelphi', *Era* (5 December 1852), p. 10, col. 4.
37. *Uncle Tom's Cabin; or, the Negro Slave*, 52934C, Act 1, scene 1, leaf 1 (punctuation added in this and subsequent quotations).
38. *Ibid.*, leaf 23.
39. *Ibid.*, leaf 25.
40. '[W]hat the world sees as the curse of racial inferiority and cultural deprivation, *Uncle Tom's Cabin* views as the blessing of racial superiority and earthly trial. This Christian transvaluation enables Stowe to include the racist stereotypes of plantation fiction in her novel' (Yellin, 'Introduction' to Stowe, *Uncle Tom's Cabin*, p. xix).

41. Vincent, *Uncle Tom's Cabin; or, the Fugitive Slave!*, 52934F, Act 1, scene 4, leaf 7, verso.

42. G. H. George, *A Colour'd Commotion: an Ethiopian extravaganza*, BL Addl. Mss. 52934E.

43. Pitt, *Uncle Tom's Cabin*, 52935I.

44. *Ibid.*, Act 1, scene 1, leaf 4.

45. Fitzball, *Uncle Tom's Cabin*, 52934G, Act 1, scene 4, leaf 35, verso.

46. See Birdoff, *The World's Greatest Hit*, pp. 152–3, and the discussion by Judith Williams, 'Uncle Tom's women', in H. J. Elam and D. Krasner (eds.), *African American Performance and Theater History: a critical reader* (Oxford: Oxford University Press, 2001), pp. 19–39.

47. 'The theatres', *Spectator* 1275 (4 December 1852), p. 1160.

48. 'Adelphi', *Era* (5 December 1852), p. 10, col. 4.

49. Richard Shepherd and William Creswick, *Uncle Tom's Cabin*, Surrey theatre, 27 October 1852, BL Addl. Mss. 52934K, Act 1, scene 3.

50. G. L. Aiken, *Uncle Tom's Cabin; or, life among the lowly* (New York, French, 1868, no. 217); Birdoff, *The World's Greatest Hit*, p. 5. There is an enormous literature on Tom dramas in America, but it is beyond my scope here.

51. Lemon and Taylor, *Slave Life*, Act 1, scene 4.

52. Vincent, *Uncle Tom; or, the Fugitive Slave!*, 52934F, Act 1, scene 1, leaf 5.

53. Fitzball, *Uncle Tom's Cabin*, 52934G, Act 1, scene 2, leaf 17.

54. *Uncle Tom's Cabin; or, the Negro Slave*, 52934C, Act 1, scene 1, leaf 9 (punctuation added).

55. It is interesting to note that the version which most stresses George's desire for liberty (by Shepherd and Creswick for the Surrey) is also the one which makes him the half-brother of the white plantation owner, St Clair. This encounter, in turn, fits in with one of the themes of domestic melodrama – the reuniting of sundered family elements.

56. Fitzball, *Uncle Tom's Cabin*, 52934G, Act 1, scene 1, leaf 7.

57. *Ibid.*, Act 1, scene 1, leaves 7–8.

58. 'Surrey', *Era* (7 November 1852), p. 10, col. 2.

59. 'Surrey', *Illustrated London News* 588 (6 November 1852), p. 382, cols. 1–2.

60. Shepherd and Creswick, *Uncle Tom's Cabin*, 52934K, Act 2, scene 2, leaf 17, verso.

61. *Ibid.*, leaf 18, verso.

62. *Ibid.*, leaf 18.

63. *Ibid.*, Act 3, scene 3, leaves 34, verso and 35.

64. *Ibid.*, Act 3, scene 4, leaf 35, verso.

65. *Ibid.*, Act 3, scene 5.

66. Lemon and Taylor, *Slave Life*, Act 3, scene 3.

67. *Ibid.*, Act 1, scene 2.

68. *Ibid.*, Act 1, scene 4.

69. 'Olympic', *Illustrated London News* (30 October 1852), pp. 354–5, cols. 3, 1.

70. 'Adelphi', *Era* (5 December 1852), p. 10, col. 4.

71. 'Sadler's Wells', *Era* (2 January 1853), p. 11, col. 1.

72. *Illustrated London News* (26 February 1853), p. 166. See also H. P. Bolton, *Dickens Dramatized* (London: Mansell, 1987), p. 33. According to Fitzball himself, 'The crowd to witness the representation of "Uncle Tom's Cabin" at [Drury Lane] was so immense, that many accidents occurred from the pressure outside. In the theatre not a word was heard, from those who could not obtain seats stamping the rogues march, and kicking up the most appalling noises in the galleries' (*Thirty-five Years of a Dramatic Author's Life*, p. 261).

73. 'Drury Lane', *Era* (2 January 1853), p. 10, col. 1.

74. *Uncle Tom and Lucy Neal; or, Harlequin Liberty and Slavery*, Pavilion theatre, 24 December 1852, BL Addl. Mss. 52936Z.

75. 'Pavilion', *Era* (2 January 1853) p. 11, col. 3.

76. *Uncle Tom and Lucy Neal*, 52936Z, Act 1, scene 3.

77. *Ibid.*, Act 1, scene 2, leaf 4.

78. J. R. Planché, *Mr. Buckstone's Ascent of Mount Parnassus*, Haymarket theatre, 28 March 1853, Lacy, vol. 10, Act 1, scene 1, p. 21.

79. 'Haymarket', *Era* (3 April 1853), p. 10, col. 1.

80. Planché, *Mr. Buckstone's Ascent*, Act 1, scene 1, p. 22.

81. 'Strand', *Era* (24 October 1852), p. 10, col. 4.

82. *Ibid.*

83. All quotations in this paragraph are taken from 'Lyceum', *Era* (21 November 1852), p. 6, col. 1.

84. 'Contemporary literature of America', *Westminster Review* (January 1853), p. 298.

85. In America, of course, it was a different story. Birdoff, in *The World's Greatest Hit*, has detailed with panache and at some length the ways in which 'Uncle Tom' was the continuing staple of a genuine American folk theatre.

86. Harriet Beecher Stowe, *Dred: a tale of the Great Dismal Swamp*, ed. and intro. Judie Newman (Halifax: Ryburn, 1992, first publ. 1856), p. 13.

87. Announcements in the *Era* of, respectively, 19 October; 2 November; 21 September; 9 November 1856; all p. 1. According to Birdoff, in *The World's Greatest Hit* (p. 161), Astley's produced an equestrian version of *Dred* in December 1856.

88. According to Newman, 'On 25th August, 1856, almost coincidentally with the publication of *Dred*, the Governor of South Carolina received a report that "a very secure retreat for runaway Negroes" existed in a large swamp in the state, where escaped slaves had for years settled ... A group of slaveholders attacked them and were beaten off' (Newman, 'Introduction' to Stowe, *Dred*, p. 23).

89. *Ibid.*, p. 22.

90. *Dred: a tale of the Great Dismal Swamp*, Surrey theatre, 14 October 1856, BL Addl. Mss. 52961N. According to the *Era* ('Surrey' (26 October 1856), p. 11, col. 2), the author of the piece was F. Phillips.

91. 'Surrey Theatre', *The Times* (22 October 1856), p. 7, col. 5.

92. *Dred: a tale of the Great Dismal Swamp*, 52961N, Act 1, scene 5, leaf 24.

93. 'Surrey', *Era* (26 October 1856), p. 11, col. 2.
94. 'Surrey Theatre', *The Times* (22 October 1856), p. 7, col. 5.
95. 'Surrey', *Era* (26 October 1856), p. 11, col. 2.
96. *Ibid.* Dred was played here by Creswick, whose *Uncle Tom* play, co-authored with Shepherd, was one of the most vehement in condemning slavery.
97. *Ibid.*
98. *Dred: a tale of the Great Dismal Swamp*, 52961N, Act 2, scene 1, leaf 26.
99. 'Surrey', *Era* (26 October 1856), p. 11, col. 2.
100. Both passages from *Dred: a tale of the Great Dismal Swamp*, 52961N, Act 1, scene 3, leaves 12 and 13.
101. 'Surrey', *Era* (26 October 1856), p. 11, col. 2.
102. 'Surrey Theatre', *The Times* (22 October 1856), p. 7, col. 5.
103. W. E. Suter, *Dred: a tale of the Dismal Swamp*, Lacy, vol. 57, no. 848, Act 1, scene 1.
104. *Ibid.*
105. *Ibid.*, Act 1, scene 4.
106. *Ibid.*
107. *Ibid.*, Act 2, scene the last.
108. *Ibid.*
109. *Ibid.*, p. iii.
110. *Ibid.*, Act 2, scene 2.
111. *Ibid.*, Act 1, scene 1.
112. J. Johnson Towers, *Dred: a tale of the Great Dismal Swamp*, Victoria theatre, 22 September 1856, BL Addl. Mss. 52962G, Act 1, scene 2, leaf 20.
113. The same revelation, that Tom Gordon is of mixed race, appears to come in the Britannia's version, though this ends with a fight of the slaves against Tom in which he is shot. 'Britannia, Hoxton', *Era* (5 October 1856), p. 11, col. 1.
114. Towers, *Dred*, 52962G, Act 2, scene 9.

AFTERWORD

1. See, for example, V. G. Kiernan, *The Lords of Human Kind: European attitudes to the outside world in the imperial age* (London: Weidenfeld and Nicolson, 1969), pp. 46–8.
2. For a brief but valuable indication of the way attitudes towards Indian culture changed, see G. G. Joseph, 'Cognitive encounters in the age of imperialism', *Race & Class* 35: 3 (1995), pp. 39–56.
3. See Hall, *Civilising Subjects*, in particular pp. 275–6 and 434–41.
4. See Bernard Semmel, *The Governor Eyre Controversy* (London: Macgibbon and Kee, 1962); Eric Williams, *British Historians and the West Indies* (London: Deutsch, 1966), chs. 7 and 8; Bolt, *Victorian Attitudes to Race*, ch. 3; and Lorimer, *Colour, Class and the Victorians*, ch. 9. Williams quotes extensively from contemporary comment.
5. Stepan, *The Idea of Race in Science*, p. xix.

6. See, for example, John M. MacKenzie (ed.), *Imperialism and Popular Culture* (Manchester: Manchester University Press, 1986).
7. Harding, *There is a River*, p. 95.
8. 'Lyceum', *Era* (16 November 1856), p. 10, cols. 1–2.
9. 'Surrey', *Era* (14 September 1856), p. 11, cols. 1–2.
10. *Era*, respectively, (14 September 1856), p. 11, col. 4; (21 September 1856), p. 12, col. 2 ('Jersey'); (5 October 1856), p. 12, col. 1.

Bibliography

PRIMARY MATERIAL — PLAYS

Plays are listed under author where known, collections under editor. Details are fuller for some titles than others in the same series because of differences in binding processes. The convention is followed of identifying nineteenth-century published plays by series publisher and number.

Aiken, G. L., *Uncle Tom's Cabin; or, life among the lowly*, French, 1868, no. 217

Aldridge, Ira, *The Black Doctor*, Dicks, no. 460

Bate, Henry [H. B. Dudley], *The Blackamoor Wash'd White* (1776) Larpent Collection, BL microfiche F253/403 (1–3). Catalogued in Larpent under Dudley

Behn, Aphra, *Abdelazer, or the Moor's Revenge*, reprinted in Janet Todd (ed.), *The Works of Aphra Behn, Volume 5, The Plays, 1671–1677* (London: Pickering and Chatto, 1996)

Bellamy, Thomas, *The Benevolent Planters* (London: Debrett, 1789)

Bickerstaffe, Isaac, *The Padlock* (London: W. Lowndes, S. Bladon and W. Nicoll, 1789)

Boucicault, Dion, *The Octoroon; or, Life in Louisiana*, in Thomson (ed.), *Plays by Dion Boucicault*

Bridgeman, I. V., *The Black Doctor*, Lacy, no. 331

Brooks, [Charles William] Shirley, *The Creole; or, Love's Fetters*, Lacy; Dicks, 1009

Campbell, A. L. V., *More Ethiopians!! or 'Jenny Lind' in New York*, 1847, BL Addl. Mss. 43003 ff. 727–759

Colman, George, the Younger, *The Africans; or, War, Love and Duty*, Cumberland, vol. 43

Colman, George, the Younger, *Inkle and Yarico* . . . with remarks by Mrs Inchbald (London: Longman et al., 1816)

Courtney, J., *The Ship Boy; or, the White Slave of Guadeloupe*, BL Addl. Mss. 43003 ff. 337–353b

Cox, Jeffrey N., (ed.), *Seven Gothic Dramas, 1789–1825* (Athens: Ohio University Press, 1992)

Cox, Jeffrey N., (ed.), *Slavery, Abolition and Emancipation: writings in the British romantic period, Volume 5, Drama* (London: Pickering and Chatto, 1999)

Dred: a tale of the Great Dismal Swamp, BL Addl. Mss. 52961N

Fawcett, J., *Obi, or, Three-finger'd Jack!*, Duncombe, vol. 59/60

Ferriar, John, *The Prince of Angola, a tragedy, altered from the play of Oroonoko and adapted to the circumstances of the present time* (Manchester: J. Harrop, 1788)

Fitzball, E., *The Koeuba; or, the Pirate Vessel*, Cumberland, vol. 12

Fitzball, E., *The Negro of Wapping or, the boat builder's hovel*, Duncombe, vol. 29/30

Fitzball, E., *Uncle Tom's Cabin*, BL Addl. Mss. 52934G

George, G. H., *A Colour'd Commotion: an Ethiopian extravaganza*, BL Addl. Mss. 52934E

Haines, J. T., *My Poll and my Partner Joe*, Lacy, no. 1058

Hazlewood, C. H., *Ashore and Afloat*, French, no. 106

Hazlewood, C. H., *The Staff of Diamonds*, French, no. 104

Jerrold, Douglas, *Descart, the French Buccaneer*, Dicks, no. 258

Jordan, R., and Love, H. (eds.), *The Works of Thomas Southerne, Volume 2* (Oxford: Clarendon, 1988)

Lake, J. W. (ed.), *The Dramatic Works of George Colman the Younger* ... (Paris: Malepeyre, 1823)

Lemon, Mark, and Taylor, Tom, *Slave Life; or, Uncle Tom's Cabin*, Webster, vol. 17, no. 191

Lewis, M. G., *The Castle Spectre*, Dicks, no. 35; Cumberland, vol. 15; also in Cox (ed.), *Seven Gothic Dramas*

Lhamon, W. T., *Jump Jim Crow: lost plays, lyrics and street prose of the first Atlantic popular culture* (Cambridge, MA: Harvard University Press, 2003)

Macready, William, *The Irishman in London; or, the Happy African* (London: T. N. Longman, 1793)

Moncrieff, W. T., *Monsieur Mallét (or, My Daughter's Letter)*, Dicks, no. 936

Moncrieff, W. T., *Tom and Jerry; or, Life in London*, Lacy, vol. 88; Cumberland, vol. 33; Richardson's New Minor Drama, 1828; Dicks, no. 82

Morton, Thomas, *The Slave, or the Mother and her Child: a musical drama in three acts* (London: John Miller, 1816); Cumberland, vol. 22

Murrey [Murray], W. H., *Obi; or, Three-fingered Jack*, Dicks, no. 478

O'Bryan, Charles, *Lugarto the Mulatto*, Lacy, vol. 31, no. 460

Oxberry, W. H., and Gann, J. G., *Mr. Midshipman Easy!*, Duncombe, vol. 29–30

Parry, T., *The Peacock and the Crow: a farce in two acts*, BL Addl. Mss. 42940 ff. 371–97

Pitt, G. D., *The Black Bayaderes, or the Rival Serenaders*, BL Addl. Mss. 43003 ff. 380–428

Pitt, G. D., *Toussaint L'Ouverture or the Black Spartacus*, BL Addl. Mss. 42995 ff. 225–53

Pitt, G. D., *Uncle Tom's Cabin: a nigger drama*, BL Addl. Mss. 52935I

Planché, J. R., *Mr Buckstone's Ascent of Mount Parnassus*, Lacy, vol. 10

Rede, W. L., *Life in America – the flight – the pursuit – the voyage*, BL Addl. Mss. 42939 ff. 444–79

Reynolds, Frederick, *Laugh When You Can*, Dicks, no. 266

[Rice, T. D.], *Bone Squash: a burletta in one act*, BL Addl. Mss. 42953 ff. 313–19

Rice, T. D., *The Virginia Mummy: a farce in one act*, BL Addl. Mss. 42940 ff. 822–67, incomplete

Robertson, Tom, *The Half Caste; or, the Poisoned Pearl*, Lacy, vol. 97, no. 241

Shakespeare, William, *Othello*, Arden edition, ed. M. R. Ridley (London: Methuen, repr. 1985)

Shakespeare, William, *Titus Andronicus*, Arden edition, ed. Jonathan Bate (London: Routledge, 1995)

Shepherd, Richard, and Creswick, William, *Uncle Tom's Cabin*, BL Addl. Mss. 52934K

Somebody's in the House with Dinah or the invitation to the Nigger Ball, BL Addl. Mss. 43004 ff. 367–94

Southern (*sic*), Thomas, *Oroonoko, a tragedy*, *The Acting Drama* (London: Mayhew, Isaac and Mayhew, 1834); *Oroonoko: a tragedy in five acts . . .* with remarks by Mrs Inchbald (London: Longman, Hurst, Rees and Orme, [1806]); R. Cumberland's *The British Drama . . . containing Oroonoko* (London: C. Cooke, 1817), vol. II; *Oroonoko . . . with remarks by D. G.*, Cumberland, vol. 25/6

Southerne, Thomas, *Oroonoko*, ed. M. E. Novak and D. S. Rodes (London: Edward Arnold, 1977; also in Jordan and Love (eds.), *Works of Thomas Southerne*

Stirling, Edward, *The Buffalo Girls, or, the Female Serenaders*, Duncombe, vol. 59

Stirling, Edward, *The Cabin Boy*, Lacy, vol. 104; French, no. 559

Stirling, Edward, *Yankee Notes for English Circulation*, Duncombe, vol. 46

Sutcliffe, Barry (ed.), *Plays by George Colman the Younger and Thomas Morton* (Cambridge: Cambridge University Press, 1983)

Suter, W. E., *Dred: a tale of the Dismal Swamp*, Lacy, vol. 57, no. 848

Taylor, T. P., *Jim Crow in His New Place*, BL Addl. Mss. 42950 ff. 593–602b

Thompson, C. P., *Jack Robinson and his Monkey*, Duncombe, no. 27; Lacy, no. 31

Thomson, Peter (ed.), *Plays by Dion Boucicault* (Cambridge: Cambridge University Press, 1984)

Towers, J. Johnson, *Dred: a tale of the Great Dismal Swamp*, BL Addl. Mss. 52962G

Uncle Tom and Lucy Neal; or, Harlequin Liberty and Slavery, BL Addl. Mss. 52936Z

Uncle Tom's Cabin: a hippodrama in two acts, BL Addl. Mss. 52935FF

Uncle Tom's Cabin; or, the Negro Slave, BL Addl. Mss. 52934C

Vincent, Eliza, *Uncle Tom's Cabin; or, the Fugitive Slave!*, BL Addl. Mss. 52934F

Webster, B. N., *The Quadroon Slave*, BL Addl. Mss. 42960 ff. 326–414

Wells, Stanley, *Nineteenth-Century Shakespeare Burlesques, Volume 2, Maurice Dowling (1834) to Charles Beckington (1847)* (London: Diploma Press, 1977)

Captain Williams, *The Woman of Colour*, BL Addl. Mss. 52943E

Wilson, George, *The Male and Female Serenaders, or Native Talent's Best*, BL Addl. Mss. 43003 ff. 644–664

The Wood Demon; or One O'Clock, BL Addl. Mss. 43003 ff. 576–616

Young, Edward, *The Revenge: a tragedy* (London: J. Rivington and Sons, 1776). Also included in Mrs Inchbald's *British Theatre* (London: Longman Hurst, 1806), vol. 4, and *The Acting Drama: containing all the popular plays standard and modern*, revised by J. P. Kemble (London: Mayhew, Isaac and Mayhew, 1834), among others.

PRIMARY MATERIAL – BACKGROUND

à Beckett, Gilbert Abbot, *The Quizziology of the British Drama* (London: Punch, 1846)

Baker, D. E., *Biographia Dramatica or, a Companion to the Playhouse* (London: Rivingtons, 1782)

Baker, D. E., Reed, Isaac, and Jones, Stephen, *Biographia Dramatica, or a Companion to the Playhouse* ... (London: Longman Hurst, 1812), 3 vols.

Behn, Aphra, *Oroonoko, or the Royal Slave* in *Oroonoko and Other Writings* (Oxford: Oxford University Press, 1994, first publ. 1688)

Bradley, J. L. (ed.), *Henry Mayhew: selections from 'London Labour and the London Poor'* (London: Oxford University Press, 1965)

A Brief Memoir, and Theatrical Career of Ira Aldridge, the African Tragedian (London: Henry Pownceby, n.d.)

Briggs, John, *The History of Jim Crow* (London: Smallfield and Son, 1839)

Brown, William Wells, *The Black Man: his antecedents, his genius and his achievements* (Boston: James Redpath, 1863)

Brown, William Wells, *Sketches of Places and People Abroad* (Boston: John P. Jewett, 1855)

Carlyle, Thomas, 'Occasional discourse on the Nigger question', first published in *Fraser's Magazine* as 'Occasional discourse on the Negro question' (December 1849); *Latter-Day Pamphlets* (London: 1853)

Coleman, John, *Fifty Years of an Actor's Life* (London: Hutchinson, 1904)

Colman, George, the Younger, *Random Records* (London: Henry Colburn and Richard Bentley, 1830), 2 vols.

'Contemporary literature of America', *Westminster Review* (January 1853), 287–302

'A Critique on the Performance of Othello by F. W. Keene Aldridge, the African Roscius' by the author of 'The talents of Edmund Kean delineated' ... (Scarborough: John Cole, 1831)

Douglass, Frederick, *The Frederick Douglass Papers, series one, Speeches, Debates and Interviews, Volume 1, 1841–6*, ed. J. W. Blassingame (New Haven and London: Yale University Press, 1979)

Fitzball, E., *Thirty-five Years of a Dramatic Author's Life* (London: T. C. Newby, 1859), 2 vols.

Genest, John, *Some Account of the English Stage from the Restoration in 1660 to 1830* (Bath: Carrington, 1832), 10 vols.

Hazlitt, William, *The Complete Works of William Hazlitt in Twenty-one Volumes*, ed. P. Howe, *Volume 5, Lectures on the English Poets and A View of the English Stage*; *Volume 18, Art and Dramatic Criticism* (London: J. M. Dent, 1930)

Hughes, Henry, *Treatise on Sociology, theoretical and practical* (Philadelphia: Lippincott, Crambo and Co., 1854)

The Humorous Adventures of Jump Jim Crow (Glasgow, n.d.)

Hutton, Laurence, *Curiosities of the American Stage* (London: Osgood, McIlvaine and Co., 1891)

Jim Crow's Vagaries, or Black Flights of Fancy: containing a choice collection of Nigger melodies . . . (London: Orlando Hodgson, [1860])

Kames, Henry, *Sketches of the History of Man* (Edinburgh: W. Creech, 1774)

Kemble, Fanny, *Journal of a Residence on a Georgia Plantation in 1838–1839*, ed. John A. Scott (New York: A. A. Knopf, 1961, first publ. 1863)

Kendal, Madge, *Dame Madge Kendal by Herself* (London: John Murray, 1933)

Knox, Robert, *The Races of Men: a philosophical enquiry into the influence of race over the destinies of nations* (London: Henry Renshaw, 1862, first publ. 1850)

Mackay, Charles, *Through the Long Day: memorials of a literary life during half a century* (London: W. H. Allen, 1887)

Marryat, Frederick, *Mr Midshipman Easy* (London: Everyman, 1970, first publ. 1836)

[Mathews, Charles], *The Life and Correspondence of Charles Mathews . . .* by Mrs Mathews. Abridged and condensed by Edmund Yates (London: Routledge, Warne and Routledge, 1860)

[Mathews, Charles], *The London Mathews, containing an account of this celebrated comedian's trip to America . . .* (London: Hodgson, n.d.)

[Mathews, Charles], *Sketches of Mr. Mathews' celebrated trip to America . . .* (London: J. Limbird, 1825)

Memoir and Theatrical Career of Ira Aldridge: the African Roscius (London: J. Onwhyn, [1848])

Moore, G. W. [The Christy Minstrel], *'Bones' his Anecdotes and Goaks* (*sic*) (London: C. H. Clarke, [1870])

Moseley, Benjamin A., *A Treatise on Sugar, with Miscellaneous Medical Observations* (London: G. G. and J. Robinson, 1799)

Oulton, W. C., *A History of the Theatres of London . . . in three volumes* (London: Chapple, Simpkin and Marshall, 1818)

Rede, Leman T., *The Road to the Stage . . .* (London: J. Onwhyn, 1836)

Reynolds, Harry, *Minstrel Memories: the story of burnt cork minstrelsy in Great Britain from 1836 to 1927* (London: Alston Rivers, 1928)

Sheahan, J. J., *Notes and Queries*, fourth series, 10 (17 August 1872), 133

Smith, Richard John [O], *A Collection of Materiel* [*sic*] *Towards an History of the English Stage* (London: The Author [1825]), 25 vols.

Stowe, Harriet Beecher, *Dred: a tale of the Great Dismal Swamp*, ed. and intro. Judie Newman (Halifax: Ryburn, 1992, first publ. 1856)

Stowe, Harriet Beecher, *Uncle Tom's Cabin*, ed. Jean Fagan Yellin (Oxford: Oxford University Press, 1998, first publ. 1852)

'Uncle Sam's peculiarities. American niggers. – Hudson River steam-boat dialogues, *Bentley's Miscellany* 6 (1839), pp. 262–71
Wemyss, F. C., *Wemyss' Chronology of the American Stage from 1752 to 1852* (New York: Wm. Taylor and Co., 1852)
Wemyss, F. C., *Theatrical Biography* (Glasgow: R. Griffin, 1848)

JOURNALS

Actors by Daylight or Pencilings in the Pit
Actors by Gaslight; or, 'Boz' in the Boxes
Athenaeum
Douglas Jerrold's Weekly Newspaper
The Drama or Theatrical Pocket Magazine
Era
The Examiner
Figaro in London
The Idler and Breakfast Table Companion
John Bull
Literary Panorama
London Magazine and Monthly Critical and Dramatic Review
The Mirror of the Stage, or New Dramatic Censor
New Monthly Magazine
Notes and Queries
Oxberry's Dramatic Biography and Histrionic Anecdotes
The Satirist or, The True Censor of the Times
The Stage; or Theatrical Inquisitor
Theatrical Journal

SECONDARY MATERIAL – BOOKS

Andrews, Cyril Bruyn, 'Victorian Ebony: the diaries, letters and criticisms of Ira Aldridge' (unpublished ms.)
Anstey, Roger, and Hair, P. E. H. (eds.), *Liverpool: the African Slave Trade and Abolition: essays to illustrate current knowledge and research* (Liverpool: Historic Society of Lancashire and Cheshire, occasional series, vol. 2, 1989)
Bagster-Collins, Jeremy, *George Colman the Younger, 1762–1836* (New York: King's Crown Press, 1946)
Barthelemy, A. G., *Black Face, Maligned Race: the representation of blacks in English drama from Shakespeare to Southerne* (Baton Rouge and London: Louisiana State University Press, 1987)
Bean, A., Hatch, J. V., and Macnamara, B. (eds.), *Inside the Minstrel Mask: readings in nineteenth-century blackface minstrelsy* (Hanover and London: Wesleyan University Press, 1996)

Birdoff, Harry, *The World's Greatest Hit – Uncle Tom's Cabin* (New York: S. F. Vanni, 1947)

Blackburn, Robin, *The Overthrow of Colonial Slavery, 1776–1848* (London: Verso, 1988)

Blackett, R. J. M., *Building an Antislavery Wall: black Americans in the Atlantic abolitionist movement, 1830–1860* (Ithaca: Cornell University Press, 1989, first publ. 1983)

Bolster, W. Jeffrey, *Black Jacks: African American seamen in the age of sail* (Cambridge, MA: Harvard University Press, 1997)

Bolt, Christine, *Victorian Attitudes to Race* (London: Routledge, 1971)

Bolt, Christine, and Drescher, Seymour (eds.) *Anti-Slavery, Religion and Reform: essays in honour of Roger Anstey* (London: Dawson, 1980)

Bolton, H. P., *Dickens Dramatized* (London: Mansell, 1987)

Booth, Michael, *English Melodrama* (London: Herbert Jenkins, 1965)

Booth, Michael, *Theatre in the Victorian Age* (Cambridge: Cambridge University Press, 1991)

Bratton, J. S. (ed.), *Music Hall Performance and Style* (Milton Keynes: Open University Press, 1986)

Bratton, J. S. et al., *Acts of Supremacy: the British empire and the stage* (Manchester: Manchester University Press, 1991)

Briggs, Asa, *The Age of Improvement, 1783–1867* (London: Longman, 1991)

Broadbent, R. J., *Annals of the Liverpool Stage from the Earliest Period to the Present Time* (Liverpool: Edward Howell, 1908)

Brody, Jennifer DeVere, *Impossible Purities: blackness, femininity and Victorian culture* (Durham and London: Duke University Press, 1998)

Brooks, Peter, *The Melodramatic Imagination: Balzac, Henry James, melodrama, and the mode of excess* (New Haven: Yale University Press, 1995, first publ. 1976)

Cockrell, Dale, *Demons of Disorder: early blackface minstrels and their world* (Cambridge: Cambridge University Press, 1997)

Craton, Michael, *Testing the Chains: resistance to slavery in the British West Indies* (Ithaca: Cornell University Press, 1982)

Curtin, Philip D., *The Atlantic Slave Trade: a census* (Madison: University of Wisconsin Press, 1959)

Curtin, Philip D., *The Image of Africa: British ideas and action, 1750–1850* (Madison: University of Wisconsin Press, 1964)

Curtin, Philip D. (ed.), *Imperialism* (London: Macmillan, 1971)

Davidson, Basil, *The African Slave Trade* (Boston: Little Brown, 1980)

Davis, David Brion, *The Problem of Slavery in the Age of Revolution, 1770–1823* (Oxford: Oxford University Press, 1999, first publ. 1975)

Davis, David Brion, *The Problem of Slavery in Western Culture* (Oxford: Oxford University Press, 1988, first publ. 1967)

Davis, Jim, and Emeljanow, Victor, *Reflecting the Audience: London theatregoing, 1840–1880* (Hatfield: University of Hertfordshire Press, 2001)

Dennison, Sam, *Scandalize my Name: Black imagery in American popular music* (New York: Garland Publishing, 1982)

Dessau, Alan C., *Titus Andronicus* (Manchester: Manchester University Press, 1989)

Disher, Maurice Willson, *Blood and Thunder* (London: Frederick Muller, 1949)

Dodds, J. W., *Thomas Southerne, Dramatist* (New Haven and London: Humphrey Milford, 1933)

Donohue, Joseph (ed.), *The Cambridge History of the British Theatre, Volume 2, 1660–1895* (Cambridge: Cambridge University Press, 2004)

Donohue, Joseph, *Theatre in the Age of Kean* (Oxford: Blackwell, 1975)

Drescher, Seymour, *Capitalism and Antislavery: British mobilization in comparative perspective* (Basingstoke: Macmillan, 1986)

Foner, Philip, *Frederick Douglass: a biography* (New York: Citadel Press, 1964)

Fredrickson, George M., *The Black Image in the White Mind: the debate on Afro-American character and destiny, 1817–1914* (New York: Harper and Row, 1971)

Fryer, Peter, *Staying Power: the history of black people in Britain* (London: Pluto, 1984)

Gerzina, Gretchen, *Black England: life before emancipation* (London: John Murray, 1995)

Grant, Joanne (ed.), *Black Protest: history, documents and analyses, 1619 to the present* (New York: Fawcett, 1968)

Gratus, Jack, *The Great White Lie: slavery, emancipation and changing racial attitudes* (London: Hutchinson, 1973)

Hall, Catherine, *Civilising Subjects: metropole and colony in the English imagination, 1830–1867* (Cambridge: Polity, 2002)

Harding, Vincent, *There is a River: the black struggle for freedom in America* (New York: Vintage Books, 1983)

Harney, Maurice, *Titus Andronicus* (London: Harvester Wheatsheaf, 1990)

Hartman, Saidiya V., *Scenes of Subjection: terror, slavery, and self-making in nineteenth-century America* (Oxford: Oxford University Press, 1997)

Hays, M., and Nikolopolou, A. (eds.), *Melodrama: the cultural emergence of a genre* (London: Macmillan, 1998)

Henriques, Fernando, *Children of Caliban: miscegenation* (London: Secker and Warburg, 1974)

Hill, Errol, *Shakespeare in Sable: a history of black Shakespearean actors* (Amherst: University of Massachusetts Press, 1984)

The History of 'The Times': the Thunderer in the making, 1785–1841 (London: The Times, 1935)

Hochschild, Adam, *Bury the Chains: the British struggle to abolish slavery* (Basingstoke: Macmillan, 2005)

Howell, R. C., *The Royal Navy and the Slave Trade* (London: Croom Helm, 1987)

Inikori, Joseph, *Africans and the Industrial Revolution in England: a study in international trade and economic development* (Cambridge: Cambridge University Press, 2002)

Jackson, Russell (ed.), *Victorian Theatre* (London: A. & C. Black, 1989)

Jordan, Winthrop, *White Over Black: American attitudes toward the Negro, 1550–1812* (Baltimore: Penguin, 1969)

Kiernan, V. G., *The Lords of Human Kind: European attitudes to the outside world in the imperial age* (London: Weidenfeld and Nicolson, 1969)

Knight, William G., *A Major London 'Minor': the Surrey theatre, 1805–1865* (London: Society for Theatre Research, 1997)

Lhamon, W. T., *Raising Cain: blackface performance from Jim Crow to hip hop* (Cambridge, MA: Harvard University Press, 1998)

Lively, Adam, *Masks: blackness, race and the imagination* (London: Chatto and Windus, 1998)

Lloyd, Christopher, *The Navy and the Slave Trade: the suppression of the African slave trade in the nineteenth century* (London: Longmans, Green and Co., 1949)

Lorimer, Douglas, *Colour, Class and the Victorians: English attitudes to the Negro in the mid-nineteenth century* (Leicester: Leicester University Press, 1978)

Lott, Eric, *Love and Theft: blackface minstrelsy and the American working class* (New York: Oxford University Press, 1993)

MacKenzie, John M. (ed.), *Imperialism and Popular Culture* (Manchester: Manchester University Press, 1986)

Marshall, Herbert, and Stock, Mildred, *Ira Aldridge: the Negro tragedian* (London: Rockliff, 1958; rpt. Washington, DC: Howard University Press, 1993, with introduction by Errol Hill)

Martin, Waldo E., Jr, *The Mind of Frederick Douglass* (Chapel Hill: University of North Carolina Press, 1984)

Mencke, John G., *Mulattoes and Race Mixture: American attitudes and images, 1865–1918* ([Ann Arbor]: UMI Research Press, 1979)

Moody, Jane, *Illegitimate Theatre in London, 1770–1840* (Cambridge: Cambridge University Press, 2000)

Mortimer, Owen, *Speak of Me as I Am: the story of Ira Aldridge* (Wangaratta, Australia: The Author, 1995)

Mullin, D., *Victorian Plays: a record of significant productions on the London stage, 1837–1901* (New York: Greenwood, 1987)

Nicoll, Allardyce, *A History of English Drama, 1660–1900* (Cambridge: Cambridge University Press, 1955–9), vols. 4 and 5

Oldfield, J. R., *Popular Politics and British Anti-Slavery: the mobilisation of public opinion against the slave trade, 1787–1807* (London: Frank Cass, 1998)

Ostendorf, Berndt, *Black Literature in White America* (Brighton: Harvester, 1982)

Ragatz, Lowell Joseph, *The Fall of the Planter Class in the British Caribbean, 1763–1833: a study in social and economic history* (New York and London: Century, for American Historical Association, 1928)

Robinson, Cedric, *Black Marxism: the making of the black radical tradition* (Chapel Hill: University of North Carolina Press, 2000, first publ. 1983)

Rodney, Walter, *How Europe Underdeveloped Africa* (London: Bogle-L'Ouverture, 1972)

Root, R. L., *Thomas Southerne* (Boston: Twayne, 1981)

Rosenberg, Marvin, *The Masks of Othello* (Berkeley: University of California Press, 1961)

Saxton, Alexander, *The Rise and Fall of the White Republic: class politics and mass culture in nineteenth-century America* (London: Verso, 1990)

Schama, Simon, *Rough Crossings: Britain, the slaves and the American Revolution* (London: BBC Books, 2005)

Scobie, Edward, *Black Britannia: a history of blacks in Britain* (London: Pall Mall Press, 1972)

Semmel, Bernard, *The Governor Eyre Controversy* (London: Macgibbon and Kee, 1962)

Shyllon, F. O., *Black People in Britain, 1555–1833* (London: Oxford University Press for Institute of Race Relations, 1977)

Sillard, R. M., *Barry Sullivan and his Contemporaries: a histrionic record* (London: T. Fisher Unwin, 1901)

Sivanandan, A., *Communities of Resistance: writings on black struggles for socialism* (London: Verso, 1990)

Southern, Eileen, *The Music of Black Americans: a history* (New York: W. W. Norton, 1983)

Sprague, Arthur Colby, *Shakespearean Players and Performances* (London: A. & C. Black, 1954)

Stearns, Marshall, and Stearns, Jean, *Jazz Dance: the story of American vernacular dance* (New York: Macmillan, 1968)

Stepan, Nancy, *The Idea of Race in Science: Great Britain, 1800–1960* (London: Macmillan, 1982)

Stephen, L., and Lee, S. (eds), *Dictionary of National Biography* (Oxford: Oxford University Press, 1921–22)

Swindells, Julia, *Glorious Causes: the grand theatre of political change, 1789–1833* (Oxford: Oxford University Press, 2001)

Sypher, Wylie, *Guinea's Captive Kings: British anti-slavery literature of the XVIIIth century* (New York: Octagon Books, 1969, first publ. 1942)

Tasch, Peter A., *The Dramatic Cobbler: the life and works of Isaac Bickerstaff* (Lewisburg: Bucknell University Press, 1971)

Temperley, Howard, *British Anti-Slavery, 1833–1870* (London: Longman, 1972)

Toll, R. C., *Blacking Up: the minstrel show in nineteenth-century America* (New York: Oxford University Press, 1974)

Turley, David, *The Culture of English Anti-Slavery, 1780–1860* (London: Routledge, 1991)

Walvin, James, *Black and White: the Negro and English society 1555–1945* (London: Allen Lane, 1973)

Ward, W. E. F., *The Royal Navy and the Slavers: the suppression of the African slave trade* (London: George Allen and Unwin, 1969)

Wheeler, Roxann, *The Complexion of Race: categories of difference in eighteenth-century British culture* (Philadelphia: University of Pennsylvania Press, 2000)

White, Shane, *Stories of Freedom in Black New York* (Cambridge, MA: Harvard University Press, 2002)

Williams, Eric, *British Historians and the West Indies* (London: Deutsch, 1966)

Williams, Eric, *Capitalism and Slavery* (London: Deutsch, 1964)

Winter, William, *Shakespeare on the Stage* (New York: Moffat, Yard and Company, 1911)

Wiseman, S. J., *Aphra Behn* (Plymouth: Northcote, 1996)

SECONDARY MATERIAL – ARTICLES AND CHAPTERS

Blair, Walter, 'Charles Mathews and his "A Trip to America"', *Prospects* 2 (1976), pp. 1–24

Booth, Michael R., 'East End and West End: class and audience in Victorian London', *Theatre Research International* 2:2 (1977), pp. 98–103

Bratton, J. S., 'British heroism and the structure of melodrama', in Bratton et al., *Acts of Supremacy*, pp. 18–61

Bratton, J. S., 'English Ethiopians: British audiences and black-face acts, 1835–1865', *Yearbook of English Studies* 11 (1981), pp. 127–42

Carew, Jan, 'The end of Moorish enlightenment and the beginning of the Columbian era', *Race & Class* 33:3 (1992), pp. 3–16

Carlisle, Carol Jones, 'The nineteenth-century actors *versus* the closet critics of Shakespeare', *Studies in Philology* 51:4 (October 1954), pp. 599–625

Cowhig, Ruth, 'Actors, black and tawny, in the role of Othello – and their critics', *Theatre Research International* 4:2 (1979), pp. 133–46

Cox, Clinton, 'From Columbus to Hitler and back again', *Race & Class* 43:3 (2002), pp. 39–49

Davidson, Basil, 'Columbus: the bones and blood of racism', *Race & Class* 33:3 (1992), pp. 17–26

Donohue, Joseph, 'The theatre from 1800–1895', in Donohue (ed.) *Cambridge History of the British Theatre*

Dormon, James H., 'The strange career of Jim Crow Rice', *Journal of Social History* 3:2 (1970), pp. 109–22

Eaton, Walter Prichard, 'Dramatic evolution and popular theatre: playhouse roots of our drama', *American Scholar* 4:2 (1935), pp. 148–59

Ellison, Ralph, 'Change the joke and slip the yoke', in Ellison, *Shadow and Act* (New York: Vintage, 1995, first publ. 1958), pp. 45–59

Enkvist, Nils Erik, 'Caricatures of Americans on the English stage prior to 1870', *Societas Scientiarum Fennica Commentationes Humanarum Litterarum* 18:1 (1951), pp. 1–168

Evans, Nicholas, 'Ira Aldridge, Shakespeare and minstrelsy', *American Theatre Quarterly* (September 2002), pp. 165–87

Fisch, Audrey A., ' "Exhibiting Uncle Tom in some shape or other": the commodification and reception of *Uncle Tom's Cabin* in England', *Nineteenth Century Contexts* 17:2 (1993), pp. 145–58

Fisch, Audrey A., ' "Negrophilism" and British nationalism: the spectacle of the black American abolitionist', *Victorian Review* 19:2 (1993), pp. 20–47

Fisch, Audrey, ' "Repetitious accounts so piteous and harrowing": the ideological work of American slave narratives in England', *Journal of Victorian Culture* 1:1 (1996), pp. 16–34

Fryer, Peter, 'The discovery and "appropriation" of African music and dance', *Race & Class* 39:3 (1998), pp. 1–20

Hatch, James V., 'Here comes everybody: scholarship and black theatre history', in Thomas Postlethwaite and Bruce A. McConachie (eds.), *Interpreting the Theatrical Past: essays in the historiography of performance* (Iowa: University of Iowa Press, 1989), pp. 148–65

Hollis, Patricia, 'Anti-slavery and British working-class radicalism in the years of reform', in Bolt and Drescher (eds.), *Anti-slavery, Religion and Reform*, pp. 294–315

Holmberg, C. B., and Schneider, G. D., 'Daniel Decatur Emmett's stump sermons: genuine Afro-American culture, language and rhetoric in the Negro minstrel show', *Journal of Popular Culture* 19:4 (1986), pp. 27–38

Joseph, G. G., 'Cognitive encounters in the age of imperialism', *Race & Class* 35:3 (1995), pp. 39–56

Lindfors, Bernth, 'Ira Aldridge's London debut', *Theatre Notebook* 60:1 (2006)

Lindfors, Bernth, ' "Mislike me not for my complexion . . .": Ira Aldridge in white face', *African American Review* 33:2 (1999), pp. 347–54

Lindfors, Bernth, ' "Nothing extenuate, nor set down aught in malice"; new biographical information on Ira Aldridge', *African American Review* 28:3 (1994), pp. 457–72

Lindfors, Bernth, 'The signifying flunkey: Ira Aldridge as Mungo', *The Literary Griot* 5:2 (Fall 1993), pp. 1–11

Lorimer, D., 'Bibles, banjoes and bones: images of the Negro in the popular culture of Victorian England', in B. M. Gough (ed.), *In Search of the Visible Past: history lectures at Wilfrid Laurier University, 1973–4* (Waterloo, Ontario: Wilfrid Laurier University Press, 1975), pp. 31–50

Lott, Eric, 'Blackface and blackness: the minstrel show in American culture', in Bean, Hatch and Macnamara (eds.), *Inside the Minstrel Mask*, pp. 3–32

MacDonald, Joyce Green, 'Acting black: *Othello*, *Othello* burlesques and the performance of blackness', *Theatre Journal* 46 (1994), pp. 231–49

Mahar, William J., 'Black English in early blackface minstrelsy: a new interpretation of the sources of minstrel show dialect', *American Quarterly* 37:2 (1985), pp. 260–85

Morley, Malcolm, 'Jim Crow and Boz's Juba', *Dickensian* 47:297 (December 1950), pp. 28–32

Pickering, Michael, 'Mock blacks and racial mockery: the "nigger" minstrel and British imperialism', in Bratton et al., *Acts of Supremacy*, pp. 179–236

Pickering, Michael, 'White skin, black masks: "Nigger" minstrelsy in Victorian England', in Bratton (ed.), *Music Hall Performance and Style*, pp. 70–91

Rehin, George F., 'Blackface street minstrels in Victorian London and its resorts: popular culture and its racial connotations as revealed in polite opinion', *Journal of Popular Culture* 15:1 (1981), pp. 19–38

Rehin, George F., 'Harlequin Jim Crow: continuity and convergence in blackface clowning', *Journal of Popular Culture* 9:3 (1975), pp. 682–701

Richardson, Alan, 'Romantic voodoo: Obeah and British culture, 1797–1807', *Studies in Romanticism* 32 (1993), pp. 3–28

Senelick, Laurence. 'Traces of *Othello* in *Oliver Twist*', *Dickensian* 70:373 (May 1974), pp. 97–102

Siemon, James R., '"Nay, that's not next": *Othello*, V.ii in performance, 1760–1900', *Shakespeare Quarterly* 37 (1986), pp. 38–51

Sivanandan, A., 'Challenging racism: strategies for the 1980s', in Sivanandan, *Communities of Resistance*, pp. 63–76

Suddaby, J., 'A theatrical evening in 1838: "Jim Crow", "Mr. Ferguson", and "Pickwickians"', *Dickensian* 7:7 (July 1909), pp. 172–8

Tompkins, Jane, 'Sentimental power: *Uncle Tom's Cabin* and the politics of literary history', in Tompkins, *Sensational Designs: the cultural work of American fiction 1790–1960* (Oxford: Oxford University Press, 1985), pp. 122–46

Walvin, James, 'The rise of British popular sentiment for abolition 1787–1832', in Bolt and Drescher (eds.), *Anti-Slavery, Religion and Reform*, pp. 149–162

Waters, Hazel, 'The Great Famine and the rise of anti-Irish racism', *Race & Class* 37:1 (1995), pp. 95–108

Williams, Judith, 'Uncle Tom's women', in H. J. Elam and D. Krasner (eds.), *African American Performance and Theater History: a critical reader* (Oxford: Oxford University Press, 2001), pp. 19–39

Winter, Marian Hannah, 'Juba and American minstrelsy', in Bean, Hatch and Macnamara (eds.), *Inside the Minstrel Mask*, pp. 224–41

Index

LaVergne, TN USA
15 December 2009
167006LV00003B/55/P